HIGH SOCIETY

The English Social Élite, 1880–1914

HIGH SOCIETY

The English Social Élite, 1880–1914

PAMELA HORN

ALAN SUTTON

First published in the United Kingdom in 1992 by
Alan Sutton Publishing Limited
Phoenix Mill · Far Thrupp · Stroud · Gloucestershire

First published in the United States of America in 1993 by
Alan Sutton Publishing Inc · Wolfeboro Falls · NH 03896–0848

British Library Cataloguing in Publication Data

Horn, Pamela
High Society: The English Social Élite, 1880–1914
I. Title
942.108108621

ISBN 0-7509-0039-3

Library of Congress Cataloging in Publication Data applied for

Typeset in 10/13 Imprint.
Typesetting and origination by
Alan Sutton Publishing Limited.
Printed in Great Britain by
The Bath Press, Avon.

Contents

The members of the house-party, though surely spoilt by the surfeits of entertainment that life had always offered them showed no disposition to be bored by each other's familiar company, and no inclination to vary the programme which they must have followed on innumerable Sunday afternoons since they first emerged from the narrowness of school or schoolroom, to take their place in a world where pleasure fell like a ripened peach for the outstretching of a hand. . . . A large proportion of their conversation seemed to consist in asking one another what they had thought of such-and-such an entertainment, and whether they were going to such-and-such an other.

Vita Sackville-West, *The Edwardians* (1960 edn.), 11–12.

Acknowledgements

I should like to thank all those who have helped me with the preparation of this book by providing information and illustrations, or who have assisted in other ways. In particular, my thanks are due to the Earl of Pembroke, Lord Egremont, Sir Edmund Fairfax-Lucy, Bart., the Hon. Mrs Crispin Gascoigne and Robin Dower and the Trustees of the Trevelyan Family Papers for their kind co-operation in allowing me to consult, and quote from, family papers in which they hold the copyright. I am also grateful to the National Trust and Luton Museum and Art Gallery for permitting me to use photographs in which they hold the copyright.

As always, I have received much efficient assistance from staff at the various libraries and record offices at which I have worked and I am indebted to them. These include the Bodleian Library, Oxford, the British Library, the Newspaper Library, Colindale, the Public Record Office, the House of Lords Record Office, the India Office Library, the Welsh Folk Museum, National Museum of Wales (particularly Mr A. Lloyd Hughes), the Stadtarchiv, Bad Ems (particularly Herr Sarholz), the Greater London Library and Record Office, the Libraries of the Universities of Newcastle and Reading, and various county record offices in which I have researched. Among these are the offices for Northamptonshire, Oxfordshire, Suffolk (at both Ipswich and Bury St Edmunds), West Sussex (where Mrs P. Gill, County Archivist, kindly made arrangements for me to consult the Petworth House Archives), and Wiltshire.

Finally, my thanks are due, as ever, to my husband who has not merely accompanied me on a number of research 'expeditions', but has helped and advised in countless other ways. Without his assistance this book would not have been written.

PAMELA HORN, July 1992

CHAPTER ONE

The London Season and its Role

> . . . the ingoings and outgoings of Society, its sayings and doings and misdoings, are the theme of the journalist and novelist, the essayist and biographer; and . . . of the popular preacher. Everything connected with it seems to be unconsciously magnified . . . in the eyes of the British Public. The benevolence of a prince or a duke, for instance, seems much nobler than that of a mere merchant. . . . Contrariwise, the vices of Society loom much larger than those of ordinary folk.

HUGH E.M. STUTFIELD, *The Sovranty (sic) of Society* (1909), 16.

To contemporaries as well as to many later commentators, High Society during the late Victorian and Edwardian years was notorious for its exuberance, its ostentation and its pleasure-seeking. 'Every kind of extravagance became the fashion,' wrote Lady Airlie of the reign of Edward VII. 'Money was the passport to society. Almost anyone who had enough of it could procure, sooner or later, an invitation to the splendid Court Balls at Windsor and the evening receptions at Buckingham Palace.'[1] Lady St Helier agreed. In comparing life in the early 1900s with that half a century before she was struck by the relatively modest outlays on luxurious display in the 1860s:

> I well remember the quite angry protest which was made about a ball given in Carlton House Terrace, where £1,000 was rumoured to have been spent on the floral decorations for the night, this being considered a terribly reckless and unjustifiable act of extravagance. That sum, and double, is often spent nowadays in a single night on one entertainment; and the luxury of dinners and extravagant menus make the expenditure of those days seem a mere bagatelle. Plovers' eggs at 2s. 6d. apiece, forced strawberries, early asparagus, *petits poussins*, and the various dishes which are now considered almost a necessity by anyone aspiring to give a good dinner, were then unheard of; and though a longer and more varied menu was presented, still the cost was nothing in comparison with what it now is.[2]

To the young George Cornwallis-West, indeed, there was no period in recent history, other than perhaps that immediately preceding the French Revolution, in which wealth

1

King Edward VII and Queen Alexandra driving in Hyde Park, *c*. 1902. (The author)

and conspicuous consumption were so blantantly displayed as in the Edwardian years. 'Not . . . the death duties brought in . . . a few years previously, or Mr Lloyd George's rabid anti-wealth speeches at Limehouse and elsewhere, [in 1909] acted as a deterrent to extravagance.'[3]

With the increasing pervasiveness of plutocratic values, even presentation at Court, the symbol of an upper-class girl's entry into adult society, lost much of its earlier prestige. In 1841, nine out of ten of the women presented had been from titled and landed families. Fifty years later, for the first time, the proportion was under half.[4] As *Etiquette for Ladies and Gentlemen* acidly pointed out, although presentation was still 'the hall-mark demanded of those who aspire to fashionable life', it no longer possessed distinction: 'nearly every one with any pretensions to wealth or position contrives to get an entrance to her Majesty's Drawing-room.'[5]

Yet the old values were not altogether abandoned by Society's leaders and the influence of the Court remained paramount. 'State Balls at Buckingham Palace, Royal entertainments and Royal attendance at certain functions gave a stamp of authority' to the entire social round, concluded one critic.[6] Certainly Sir Edward Hamilton, writing in the summer of 1887, considered there was 'hardly a Ball now with any pretentions (sic) to smartness' which was not attended by the Prince of Wales and at which he remained 'till a very late hour. . . . His capacity for amusing himself is extraordinary; for he is able to get on with hardly any sleep. Some 4 or 5 hours appear to suffice for him. This morning he was on Parade at 10 o'clock punctually for the trooping of the colours in celebration of the Queen's Birthday.'[7] (See also Appendix B).

Lady Brooke, the future Countess of
Warwick, in the 1880s. (Frances Countess
of Warwick, *Life's Ebb and Flow*, 1929)

To Lady Brooke (later the Countess of Warwick), the London world of the 1880s in which she played such an active part was divided into two distinct strands:

> There was a group around the retired and ultra-exclusive Court of Queen Victoria's widowhood, and another group of the young and gay around the Prince and Princess of Wales. This was 'the Marlborough House set.' . . . My own position in my early married days was the somewhat onerous, if privileged one, of having a foot in both the Court and the Marlborough House groups. But, as might be expected, my interests were with youth and gaiety from the start.[8]

Even that generalization, however, over-simplifies the true position, since there were many fashionable late Victorians and Edwardians who did not fit into either of these categories. Among them were the forty or fifty members of a select coterie which emerged in the 1880s and was labelled 'the Souls' by contemporaries. They prided themselves on their wide intellectual interests, their love of art and literature, their wit, and the discretion with which their sexual liaisons were conducted – in sharp contrast to the more blatant promiscuity of the Prince of Wales's circle. At the height of the London Season 'the Souls' held weekly readings and lectures, and often disconcerted dinner

Queen Victoria in the 1880s. (Frances
Countess of Warwick, *Life's Ebb and
Flow*, 1929)

partners by discussing 'faith and freedom with the soup'. They also evolved their own
esoteric jargon in communicating with one another and were endlessly involved in a
narcissistic analysis of their emotions.[9] Yet, for a time, they exerted considerable social
influence. As the Countess of Warwick admitted: 'I think they sent us all back to reading
more than we otherwise should have done, and this was an excellent thing for us.'[10]

In the moral sphere also, despite some decline in standards compared to the middle of
the nineteenth century, those upper-class women who too obviously flouted convention
were punished for it by being excluded from Court circles, although the peccadilloes of
their menfolk earned no such penalty. As the society magazine, *The Queen*, warned in
the early 1900s, it was unthinkable for a woman to have an open affair with anyone if she
wished to retain her standing and respectability. 'Women should strenuously and fiercely
cling to the conventions and not overstep them,' it declared firmly. ' . . . To take only the
commonsense view . . . the strongest woman will find herself utterly alone, while the
partner of her indiscretion still has the entrée to his friends and a place in society, forever
denied to her.' As Consuelo Vanderbilt, who married the 9th Duke of Marlborough in
1895, later declared, it was not adultery but cheating at cards which led to a man being
ostracized.[11]

The erosion of moral standards was nonetheless sufficiently obvious to alarm some members of the old-established aristocracy and gentry. Lady Dorothy Nevill, for one, bewailed the fact that compared to her youth in the 1840s and 1850s, the 'forces of mammon' had taken over 'the influence which rank and long lineage once enjoyed':

> Birth to-day is of small account, whilst wealth wields an unquestioned sway . . . The conquest of the West End by the City has brought about a complete change of tone, for whereas in former days little was heard of stocks and shares, money-making . . . has become an ordinary subject of conversation . . . [and] a large part of so-called society – women as much as men – spend their time eagerly watching for what they hope may prove to be a good thing.[12]

She referred sourly to the 'successful speculator, who, by some lucky coup, suddenly finds himself welcome in houses where formerly he would scarcely have been allowed in the servants' hall'.[13] Other aspects of social relations had been affected adversely, too: 'It is, I think, a good deal owing to the preponderance of the commercial element in Society that conversation has sunk to its present dull level of conventional chatter.'[14]

The peerage was likewise influenced by the growing spirit of commercialism and industrialization during the last years of Queen Victoria's reign. Between 1885 and 1914 men with a business background represented, on average, nearly a third of all the new peers created. In the previous half century they had accounted for about one-tenth.[15] Although a number owed their elevation to their political activities rather than their economic role, a growing number did not. Already by 1905 the *Saturday Review* was protesting against 'this policy of adulterating the peerage with mere wealth', and the Liberal Governments between 1906 and 1914 reinforced the trend. 'The list of government supporters [in the House of Lords] for the final reading of the 1911 Parliament Bill looked more like the *Directory of Directors* . . . than a roll-call of the traditional titled élite,' comments David Cannadine drily.[16]

Among those newly ennobled were men engaged in undertakings which ranged from railways, armaments and machinery to metallurgy, chemicals, shipping, textiles, mining, brewing, and building, to say nothing of those involved in traditional banking and mercantile enterprises. By 1900 the Yorkshire coal and iron family of Pease boasted three peerages, and the leading banking family, the Barings, no less than four.[17] At the end of the nineteenth century around a quarter of all leading bankers in the City of London could claim an aristocratic father-in-law, and the Barings alone were linked by marriage to such leading families as those of the Marquis of Bath, Earl Spencer, Earl Grey and Lord Suffield.[18]

On a less elevated level there were also baronetcies for many of the newly-rich gold and diamond magnates from South Africa, despite widespread reservations concerning their vulgarity and love of ostentatious display. The first to be so honoured was the immensely rich Julius Wernher, who received his title shortly after contributing generously to one of King Edward VII's favourite charities. When Sir Julius died in 1912 he was reputed to be the wealthiest man 'ever recorded by Somerset House'.[19]

Lady Tweedsmuir, looking back on her youth in the early 1900s, was struck by the way society at that time was 'expanding and becoming more moneyed . . . a less rural standard was creeping in'.[20] But some critics were more forthright. 'There might just as well have been a Goddess of Gold erected for overt worship – the impression of worship in thought, feeling and action could hardly have been stronger', wrote the social commentator, Beatrice Webb, in 1906, after dining at Bath House, Piccadilly, with the Wernhers and a number of fellow financiers and friends; 'wealth – wealth – wealth – was screamed aloud wherever one turned.'[21]

This trend was aggravated by the fact that a growing number of established landed families, seeing their estate incomes eroded by agricultural depression, were forced to withdraw from the London scene in order to economize. At Savernake the 5th Marquess of Ailesbury succeeded in 1894 to a seriously neglected estate burdened by 'terrible jointures' payable to the dowagers and with a much reduced rent roll. He immediately resolved to lead the modest life of a country gentleman and made no attempt to pursue an aristocratic round in London.[22] Another sufferer was the 2nd Earl of Verulam, who died in 1895. He reduced the time he spent in London for the Season from four or five months to two, and during that time lived in houses rented for the purpose at a relatively modest 30 guineas a week.[23]

Even grandees like Earl Spencer were forced to cut back. Not only did he sell the famous Althorp library in 1892 to Mrs Rylands, widow of a Manchester millionaire, but he began to let Spencer House in London. In the autumn of 1895, he and his wife also embarked on a world tour. 'Rents are very bad and tenants calling out for further help,' he wrote to a friend from Althorp. 'It will be a relief to shut up shop here for six months.'[24]

It was, indeed, indicative of the changing balance of economic power within the nation that whereas up to about 1880 over half of all the millionaires in Britain had been landowners, after that date businessmen and financiers held the leading position.

Yet despite these developments, the overall character of London's 'High Society' at the turn of the century had changed far less than critics suggested. The old nobility remained dominant in both numbers and social standing if not always in wealth, while the influence of the *nouveaux riches*, although growing, was still comparatively modest. The vast majority of those at the peak of the social pyramid were related by blood or marriage, 'and the most glittering prizes were in the hands of those people who lived for part of the year in large London houses, and for the rest in even larger houses on their country estates' – just as they had always done.[25] This mutual familiarity was reflected in their practice of using nicknames for one another. That applied even to the Prince of Wales's own family. Each of his five children had a nickname, with the elder son, Prince Eddy, known as 'Collars-and-Cuffs' because of his efforts to disguise his long neck and long arms by wearing a high, stiff collar and wide cuffs. His brother, the future King George V, was known as 'Sprat', and the three princesses, Louise, Victoria and Maud, as Toots, Gawks and Snipey, respectively: '. . . you must notice that Toots is practising her steps for the tiresome court ball, that Gawks is going to bed instead like Cinderella, and that Snipey is trying to console herself with a song,' wrote eighteen-year-old Princess Louise to her father's private secretary, Francis Knollys, on one occasion.[26]

In 1900, the *Saturday Review* joined in the debate, arguing that if by 'Society' was meant those who led similar lives and had 'directly or indirectly some social acquaintance with one another, and [were] in the habit of meeting in the same house or at the same

THE DUCHESS OF WELLINGTON'S GARDEN PARTY AT APSLEY HOUSE

Last Wednesday, after a lapse of more than a quarter of a century, the famous reception-rooms at Apsley House were once more thrown open, the occasion being a garden party given by the Duchess of Wellington. With the exception of gatherings to witness the Jubilee processions in 1887 and 1897 it was the first important social function held at Apsley House since the fancy-dress ball given by Elizabeth Duchess of Wellington, who was Mistress of the Robes in 1875. The scene in the grounds depicted here was drawn for THE TATLER by Mr.F. H. Townsend.

The Duchess of Wellington's Garden Party at Apsley House, London. (*The Tatler*, 17 July, 1901). (British Library Newspaper Library) resorts', then on physical grounds alone membership of such a group must be limited. Admittedly it had expanded compared to the early nineteenth century, when the élite had probably numbered little more than four hundred people – 'a set rather than a society – an ultra-fashionable clique'. But if the word 'Society' were given the most comprehensive meaning possible, the total at the close of the Victorian era could not be more than six thousand. Even that estimate was:

> excessive to a grotesque degree. If anyone in London, in a position to command Society, was to give a garden party which comprised three thousand guests, though certain distinguished members of Society might be absent from it, it would inevitably contain a considerable contingent of persons who, except in their own estimation, were hardly in Society at all; whilst it would be utterly impossible to give two such parties on the same day, without including an exceedingly large minority, with whom this fashionable majority had socially no connexion.[27]

The influence of 'mere wealth' was exaggerated. 'When people say that money . . . will do anything, they forget that the money in question must be money in very great quantities. A man with fifty thousand a year, or even with twenty thousand, may, if he knows his business, make his way in Society, no matter how obscure his origin; but five or six thousand a year will socially do nothing for anybody, who is not . . . eligible for reasons quite other than his income. Such being the case . . . , it is necessary to remember that new fortunes of twenty thousand a year and upwards are even in these days rare.'[28]

Significantly, when the young American-born Consuelo Duchess of Marlborough married, in 1895, her husband told her there were just two hundred families whose lineage and patronymics and titles she must remember. 'I learned that snobbishness was an enthroned fetish which [spread] its tentacles into every stratum of British national life.'[29] So, although the possession of great wealth might ease the process of assimilation into the upper ranks of society, the scale of the transformation was nowhere as great as disgruntled contemporaries imagined.

Lady Jeune, the future Lady St Helier, who was herself an active member of High Society, likewise emphasized the narrow geographical boundaries within which the social élite lived. In 1902 she wrote:

> If we take the area in London inhabited by what we call Society and measure it roughly by Oxford Street on the north, the House of Commons on the south, Alexandra Gate to the South Kensington Museum on the west, and Regent Street on the east, we easily realise how small a portion of that huge town is comprised in it. Outside that area are streets and squares of large houses inhabited by rich and well-to-do people, who are neither seen nor known by – and never go into what the papers call – Society.[30]

Most of the non-landed super-rich, like the Jewish financier, Sir Ernest Cassel, who was a close friend of the Prince of Wales, and the American, William Waldorf Astor, were well aware of the importance of having a 'good' address and of not living on the 'wrong' side of Hyde Park. Often they used their wealth to rent the town houses of hard-pressed members of the traditional ruling class before going on to purchase their own property. Astor rented Lansdowne House from the Marquess of Lansdowne for a time before buying his own place in St. James's Square, and Cassel moved from Grosvenor Square to Brook House in Park Lane, formerly the residence of Lord Tweedmouth.[31] Barney Barnato, who had risen from an impoverished childhood in the East End of London to become one of the principal South African mining millionaires, rented Spencer House while he built his own mansion in Park Lane. Another of the so-called 'Randlords', Otto Beit, took over the Duke of Richmond's house in Belgrave Square.[32]

Property agents specializing in the sale or rental of town houses to the upper-classes were fully conscious of the value of having the 'right' location. Hence Messrs Wilson Brothers of South Audley Street advised well-to-do clients in March 1871 that they had houses in 'all the fashionable positions of the West End of Town'. A list of properties to be let during the Season – that is between April or May and the end of July – revealed that a fourteen-bedroomed house in Grosvenor Place, with six sitting rooms and 'good' stabling commanded a substantial 800 guineas (the present-day equivalent would be over fifty times as much), while a property in Wilton Crescent, with eleven bedrooms and five sitting rooms, plus stabling, cost 650 guineas. At the lower end of the scale, an eight-bedroomed house in Devonport Street, Gloucester Square was on offer at 8 guineas a week, or around 100 guineas for the whole Season.[33]

Family connections and an appropriate residence were, however, not the only matters which preoccupied those anxious to be counted among society's leaders. Much weight

One of the fashionable centres for High Society to congregate – Rotten Row, Hyde Park, *c.* 1900. (The author)

9

was placed on the observance of precedence and etiquette. In the 1880s Burke's Peerage published a *Book of Precedence* and so important had the question become a decade later that *Etiquette for Ladies and Gentlemen* advised all hostesses to consult Burke or some similar work whenever they were uncertain about the precise status of their guests, so that embarrassing mistakes could be avoided.[34] 'Society,' wrote Hugh Stutfield in 1909, '. . . has a literature all to itself. Books on manners and deportment rain on us like autumn leaves.'[35]

Certainly Consuelo Marlborough remembered spending many hours in making sure that the rules of precedence were strictly adhered to for guests at dinner-parties. This applied not merely to seating arrangements but to the procession in to dinner.

> It was, I think, at my first big [weekend house-party] that I carefully listed in their order of precedence the four earls who were to be our guests, and I believed I had given to each the status due to him. It was therefore a considerable surprise when one of them informed me that on the second evening I had not given him precedence over Lord B. as I should have done.[36]

On another occasion when she was visiting Althorp, the Spencer family seat, she had to sit next to her host at every meal and had as her other neighbour the Brazilian ambassador, so strictly were the rules of precedence obeyed in that household.

Similar sensitivity on the issue of rank was encountered by the Countess of Airlie, when she was a Lady of the Bedchamber to Queen Mary. It was one of her duties to assemble the ladies invited to Windsor Castle for Ascot week in appropriate order, so that when the King and Queen entered the room they could walk down the line and shake hands with everybody before they paired off to go into dinner. 'Sometimes I had difficulty . . . There was always an argument when Winifred, Duchess of Portland, was in the party because she insisted on putting herself at the head, although the Duchess of Roxburghe was actually entitled to this place.'[37]

It was symptomatic of these concerns that in 1905 a special committee was appointed 'to consider and report whether any . . . steps should be taken to safeguard the status of the holders of Baronetcies, and to prevent the assumption of the title of Baronet by persons who have no right thereto'. In its report the committee estimated that perhaps seventy-seven baronetcies (or 5 to 6 per cent of the total) were held by persons who had assumed the rank improperly, possibly because the last legitimate holder had died, leaving only a collateral relation who had assumed the title of 'his own spontaneity', or, in rare cases, because the title had been adopted without 'any colour of right' at all. The committee also discovered that the baronets had a grievance of their own, arising from the fact that in India it was the practice for wives to take rank and precedence according to their husband's official position. 'This . . . makes it possible . . . for the wife of any commoner, who may be in a higher official position than a baronet, although of inferior social rank to him, to take precedence before the baronet's wife,' the committee reported sternly. 'We think it only proper that the title of a baronet should carry with it in India the same privileges as it does in other portions of the Empire, and we recommend that steps be taken . . . to remedy this grievance.'[38]

Socialites, anxious to see and be seen, strolling in Hyde Park on a Sunday, *c*. 1902. (The author)

Despite the shift towards plutocratic values in some circles, therefore, up to 1914 the broad social and political scene was dominated by a relatively few major landed families. This meant that virtually all the leading hostesses, who were so important in upper-class society, came from that background. But they needed certain personal attributes if they were to enjoy long-term success. Chief among these were beauty, charm, and a ready wit, this last being perhaps the most important, since a hostess must be able to 'engage her guests in serious discussion, not merely light-hearted banter, be ready to intervene to forestall a clash between rivals, and keep herself well informed about events as well as personalities'. Hence Lansdowne House became a favourite resort of politicians not merely because of its attractive setting but because Lady Lansdowne possessed a flair for entertaining. The intelligent and ambitious Marchioness of Londonderry used her husband's leading position in the Tory party to make Londonderry House 'the rallying point of all Conservatism', while the Duchess of Buccleuch at Montagu House, received only the 'most exclusive circle in London'. According to the Countess of Warwick, herself no mean social leader, the Duchess regarded the 'unfavoured' as 'all of the outer darkness'.[39] She bitterly disliked the vulgarity and ostentation of the 'smart' set surrounding the Prince of Wales and prided herself on knowing none of them personally. On only one occasion did she entertain a Jew, and then it was as a personal favour to Edward VII.[40]

At the end of the nineteenth century an invitation to Devonshire House was another eagerly sought after mark of recognition among the socially ambitious. This applied particularly to the famous fancy-dress ball given by the Duchess of Devonshire in July 1897, during the celebrations to mark Queen Victoria's Diamond Jubilee. 'For weeks, not to say months, beforehand it seemed the principal topic of conversation,' wrote Lady Randolph Churchill. 'The absorbing question was what characters our friends and ourselves were going to represent . . . The men, oddly enough, were even more excited over their costumes than the women, and many paid fabulous sums for them . . . Every coiffeur in London and Paris was requisitioned.' The society magazine, *Lady's Realm*, considered it 'undoubtedly . . . one of the great fancy-dress balls of the Victorian Era . . . Beside this brilliant ball everything else seemed tame.'[41]

Those wives of great families who did not play their full part in the social round were considered to be neglecting their duty. *The Tatler* in 1910 commented unfavourably on the Duchess of Norfolk because although she entertained 'a few house-parties in the country' she did 'scarcely anything in London'. With such a splendid home as Norfolk House in St. James's Square surely she 'might be good for a ball, a concert, or at any rate some dinners and parties. But no, [she seems] to make no sort of effort to add to the gaieties of London. And then [her] country-house parties are limited to a small and very exclusive set, which is chiefly composed of the Roman Catholic community. None of us are (*sic*) intended to live on a pedestal in these democratic days, not even when we are at the head of the British peerage.[42]

Central to this pleasure-seeking world was of course, the London Season itself. For those involved in politics there was a return to the capital in February in time for the opening of the new Parliamentary session, but for other members of the social élite the Season began in April or May and lasted to late July. After that came 'regular summer migrations to Cowes and the grouse moors and to the country mansion at Christmas'.[43]

The importance of the Season lay in its role in bringing together the country's leading families for social, political, and especially marital contacts. The calculating attitude adopted by some families is well exemplified in letters written by Lady Augustus Hervey and her mother, Mrs Hodnett, to young Frederick Hervey, the future 4th Marquess of Bristol. Lady Augustus, the widow of a younger son of the Hervey family, had very limited finances. Hence she needed to choose her forays into society with care.

> Your Mother is in London again at St. James's Square [wrote Mrs Hodnett to Frederick, on 23 July, 1884]. She left here on Monday to go on Tuesday with a party to dine . . . at a Country House (Highlands) 13 Miles from London . . . to meet the Prince of Wales, Lady Claud Hamilton, Lady Mansfield, Mrs & Miss Chamberlain . . . the Prince invited her also to a supper at the new Club to . . . see some Tableaux . . . She met a small party but of considerable distinction; she has many requests and invites but refuses all but those that may benefit her.[44]

A similar attitude applied the following March, when Lady Augustus announced her intention of bringing out her elder daughter during the coming Season:

> I am going to make a last kick & take Maria to a Drawing-room . . . & take her out *once* or *twice* during the season. Your Auntie Geraldine [the then Marchioness of Bristol] has offered to take her when she (Maria) is invited & I don't care to go – I

London's Social Calendar

Jany.
Theatre and Pantomime Season.
Winter Social Functions.
Charity Dances and Balls.

Feb.
Cruft's Dog Show.
Waterloo Cup (Coursing).
Chelsea Arts Club Fancy Dress Ball.
Badminton Championship Meetings.
Parliament Opens.
Levees and Court Receptions.

March
Oxford and Cambridge Athletic Sports.
Oxford and Cambridge Boat Race
Lincolnshire Handicap.
Grand National Steeplechase, Liverpool.

April
Easter Sacred Concerts at Albert Hall.
Opera Season commences.
Earl's Court Dog Show.
Shakespeare Birthday Festival at Stratford.
St. George's Day Banquet.
2,000 Guineas Stakes at Newmarket.
Brooklands Auto Racing Club Meeting.

May
Royal Academy Opens (about 1st).
London Polo Season commences (about 5th).
Exhibitions at Earl's Court and Shepherd's Bush Open.
The Temple Flower Show.
Kempton Race Meeting — Jubilee Stakes.
Royal Institute of Painters in Water Colour. Annual Exhibition.
Ladies' Golf Championship.
Royal Naval and Military Tournament.
Empire Day (24th).
Amateur Golf Championship.
Meet of the Coaching Club, Hyde Park.
The Derby — Epsom Summer Race Meeting

June
Four-in-hand Club Meet. Hyde Park.
King's Birthday Celebrations (3rd).
Trooping of the Colours. (4th).
Eton "Fourth of June" Celebrations.
Actors' Benevolent Fund Garden Fête.
Richmond Royal Horse Show.
Royal Ascot Race Meeting (about 18th).
Brooklands Auto Racing Club Meeting.
All-England Lawn Tennis Championships. Wimbledon.
International Horse Show at Olympia.
Speech Day at Harrow.
Open Golf Championship.
Royal Society of Portrait Painters Annual Exhibition.
Army Cup (Polo). Hurlingham.
Royal Motor Yacht Club Races
Aldershot Day (Polo). Hurlingham.
Inter-regimental Polo Tournament. Hurlingham.

July
Henley Royal Regatta (1 to 5).
Independence Day (U.S.A.) Banquet (4th).
The National Rose Show.
Oxford and Cambridge Cricket Match. Lord's.
Royal London Yacht Club's Races.
Eton and Harrow Cricket Match at Lord's.
Gentlemen & Players (cricket). Lord's.
Eclipse Stakes at Sandown.
Goodwood Race week commences (about 26th).
King's Coronation Cup Final (Polo). Ranelagh.

Aug.
Cowes Regatta.
Shakespeare Festival. Stratford-on-Avon.
Grouse, Hare and Stag Shooting begins (12th).
Folkestone Lawn Tennis Week.
Dublin Royal Horse Show.

Sept.
Partridge Shooting begins (1st).
The Braemar Gathering. Highland Sports.
The St. Leger Stakes. Doncaster.

Oct.
Pheasant Shooting begins (1st).
Newmarket Race Meeting. (The Cæsarewitch).
Trafalgar Day (21st).
Autumn Session of Parliament Opens
Royal Institute of Oil Painters' Exhibition.
The Cambridgeshire Newmarket Meeting.

Nov.
Motor Show at Olympia.
Lord Mayor's Show and Banquet (9th).
Banquet of American Society in London.

Dec.
Smithfield Club Cattle Show. Agricultural Hall.
Kennel Club Show at Olympia.
Pantomime Season at Theatres begins (26th).
New Year's Eve Festivities at the Savoy Hotel (31st).

London's Social Calendar, *c.* 1914. (Greater London Photograph Library)

Lady Augustus Hervey, the lively mother of the 4th Marquess of Bristol. (The National Trust and Suffolk Record Office, Bury St Edmunds)

think it will be always! It is a desperate undertaking . . . clothes for a girl out costs as much & more than a young man's Education – so I am now on a *desperate speculation*.[45]

In subsequent letters there is a good deal more in a similar vein.

In essence many of the elaborate rituals of the Season had evolved to accommodate the marriage plans of the sons and daughters of the upper classes. It was a process which the author, Marie Corelli, disapprovingly referred to as a business of 'bargain and sale'. 'A marriage is "arranged" as a matter of convenience or social interest; lawyers draft settlements and conclude the sale.' It was this which lay behind the balls, the dinners, the suppers, the parties to Hurlingham and Ascot, and much else besides.[46]

The Season's significance as the annual focus of activity of the fashionable world – and the importance of the royal family at its core – is indicated by the fact that when Queen Victoria died in January 1901, King Edward VII decreed that there should be no mourning after April. Otherwise the Season could not have taken place and this would have disrupted the whole social network.[47] Nonetheless the general tone in 1901 was muted and in July of that year *Lady's Realm* lamented the effect the Queen's death had had on the social round:

> In normal years there is a long vista of gaiety to look back upon: balls and parties have followed each other in quick succession; new stars have risen in the social firmament;

. . . fortunes have been made and lost; some mothers have married their daughters and are looking forward to a well-earned rest, while others have reluctantly come to the conclusion that London is the last place in which a girl is likely to marry; but this season has been practically non-existent. . . . The total absence of all Court functions and the closing of the great London houses, most of which are more or less connected with the Court, have resulted in a season which has been curiously tame and uneventful. There have been a number of small parties and even dances – these last mostly of the 'boy and girl' order; but everything . . . has been kept very much in the minor key.[48]

It was very different from Lady Randolph Churchill's experiences in the 1880s, when the onset of the Season had been considered so important that no 'votary of fashion would willingly miss a week or a day.' Between October and February:

the town was a desert. Religiously, however, on the 1st of May, Belgravia . . . would open the doors of its freshly-painted and flower-bedecked mansions. Dinners, balls, and parties succeeded one another without intermission till the end of July, the only respite being at the Whitsuntide [parliamentary] recess. A few of the racing people might go to Newmarket for a week, but the fashionable world flocked only to the classic races – the Derby, Ascot and Goodwood.[49]

Parties were arranged for Hurlingham to watch the pigeon-shooting or to the Botanical Gardens where fashionable flower-shows were held. But most memorable of all was the gaiety and bustle of Rotten Row. Each day between 12 noon and 2 p.m. – or in later years between 9 a.m. and 11 a.m. – the Park was the place where the fashionable world congregated to ride, drive or walk and converse with friends. It was a brilliant and animated scene, with many of the ladies, clad in close-fitting, braided habits, riding side-saddle on thoroughbred hacks, while the men wore irreproachable frock-coats, pearl-grey trousers, boots and the inevitable tall hat. For two hours a 'smartly-dressed crowd jostled one another walking slowly up and down on each side of the Row', while many of the equestrians were followed at a respectful distance by a groom, 'dressed in livery with a high hat and cockade'.[50]

In the afternoon the stately barouche made its appearance, with high-stepping horses, bewigged coachmen, and powdered footmen in gorgeous livery. . . . The writing of ceremonious notes, the leaving of cards, not to speak of *visites de digestion*, which even young men were supposed to pay, took up most afternoons.[51]

Nor was it only the young who participated in these activities. Even in her seventies Mary Elizabeth Lucy of Charlecote Park, Warwickshire, continued to go up to town for a few weeks during the Season to renew friendships, attend dinner-parties, and enjoy concerts and the theatre, despite her family's cash problems. In 1881, when aged seventy–seven, she remained in London for three weeks during June and July. Over that period she had two luncheon engagements, seven dinner-parties, two visits to the theatre, two attendances at concerts and four at the Opera. There were also two parties, and on 4 July after dining with Lord and Lady O'Neill she accompanied them to a performance of Gilbert and Sullivan's *Patience*: 'It was so the rage that it was almost impossible to get places – some of the airs were pretty but the words are so silly, and the characters are so absurdly foolish . . . that I had hardly *patience* to sit it out,' was her critical conclusion.[52]

About twenty years later it was the kaleidoscopic quality of the whole social scene which was etched on the memory of Cynthia Charteris during her first Season. She remembered the striped awnings, the powdered footmen, the soaring marble staircases of the grand houses she visited. Then there were the tiaras worn by smiling hostesses, 'azaleas in gilt baskets; white waistcoats, violins, . . . names on pasteboard cards, quails in aspic . . . strawberries and cream, tired faces of cloakroom attendants, washed streets in blue dawns, sparrows pecking about the empty pavements'.[53]

For Beatrice Potter, on the other hand, it was the sheer complexity of the fashionable world into which she was propelled that most impressed her. At its heart was a series of overlapping social circles which each represented particular dominant forces within the governing élite:

> There was the Court, representing national tradition and custom; there was the Cabinet and ex-Cabinet, representing political power; there was a mysterious group of millionaire financiers representing money; there was the racing set . . . representing sport. All persons who habitually entertained and who were entertained by the members of any one of these key groups could claim to belong to London Society. These four inner circles crossed and recrossed each other owing to an element of common membership . . . Surrounding and solidifying these four intersecting social circles was . . . the British aristocracy. . . . [T]he new rich of the British Empire and the United States were assimilated by marriage, or by the sale of honours to persons of great riches but with mean minds and mediocre manners, in order to replenish the electoral funds of the 'ins' and 'outs'. . . . Scattered in this pudding-stone of men of rank and men of property were jewels of intellect and character, cultivated diplomatists from all the countries of the world, great lawyers, editors of powerful newspapers, scholarly ecclesiastics . . .; the more 'stylish' of the permanent heads of Government departments, and here and there a star personage from the world of science, literature or art. . . . To this . . . heterogeneous crowd were added from time to time topical 'lions, . . . with strictly temporary tickets of admission for the season of their ephemeral notoriety.[54]

Beatrice, like her fellow débutantes, pursued a pleasurable but feverish round of endless distractions which filled her days and sapped her mental and physical energy. Apart from preparing for the all-important presentation at Court, there were daily rides in Rotten Row, afternoon calls, and innumerable luncheon- and dinner-parties, to say nothing of balls, amateur theatricals, and various 'sham philanthropic excrescences'. In the meantime as 'one form of entertainment was piled on another, the pace became fast and furious . . . I discovered that personal vanity was an "occupational disease" of London Society . . . By the end of the season, indigestion and insomnia had undermined physical health; a distressing mental nausea, taking the form of cynicism about one's own and other people's character, had destroyed all faith in and capacity for steady work.'[55]

Even girls like Margaret Thomas, the future Viscountess Rhondda, who had little interest in the traditional social round, nonetheless considered it their duty to participate in the Season's frivolities. Margaret left St. Leonards, an exclusive girls' boarding school, at the end of the April term and 'came out' the following May. As she wryly remembered, during the next three months she and her mother went to a dance on most nights of the week, interspersed with occasional 'At Homes'. It was her mother's task to act as chaperon:

> I accompanied her to afternoon parties, sometimes small, for talk only; sometimes large, when people played or sang to us; from my point of view the only alleviation at either was the tea-table. But even the supper . . . failed to alleviate the tedium of the dances. Every night my mother and I would have an argument as to what time it was possible to go home – before supper, I implored: but my mother was firm; when one took a girl to a dance it was customary to stay until supper was over, and until supper was over she would stay.[56]

Margaret followed this routine for three successive seasons and only escaped when she went up briefly to Oxford University. On coming down she resolutely refused to resume it. Yet despite her dislike of the whole rigmarole, she accepted uncritically the validity of

Chaperon and débutante sitting out at a ball, *c*. 1900. (The author)

a system which caused a 'particularly affectionate and conscientious mother (who, if left to please herself, would have desired to spend three-quarters of her time either painting . . . or working in her garden . . .) that she could best do her duty by martyrising herself into dragging a bored and not even socially successful daughter through a series of aimless and useless functions'. In retrospect, Margaret realized that the system was based on promoting suitable marriages between members of the social élite, but at the time she was not 'particularly conscious of the connection . . . And I rather doubt whether my mother was . . . Her sole concern was to do for her daughter what had been done for her, and what other mothers did for theirs'.[57] Eventually, when Margaret did marry, her spouse was the son of a minor landed family from her native Wales.

Other débutantes, like Maria Hervey, were soon criticized by ambitious relatives if they did not conform to the standards of behaviour expected of them. When Maria first came out her grandmother reported approvingly that she had been 'called pretty by every one and is a favorite (sic)'. However, she was also somewhat tongue-tied, and this was soon identified by her mother as a reason why she was failing to encourage potential suitors. At one particular ball she had thrown away all her opportunities, Lady Augustus complained, '& had scarce a word or a *smile*' for one partner. 'I was very disappointed for it made her look like a fool to everyone.'[58] In November 1887 Maria finally married Sir Charles Welby, a modest Lincolnshire landowner and minor politician. But this was scarcely the brilliant match her mother was seeking.

Another victim of maternal disapproval was Evelyn Murray, youngest daughter of the Duke of Atholl. In 1890, at the age of twenty-two, she had already experienced problems both with her health and with her relations with her parents, especially her mother. Two years later the Duchess was complaining of her daughter's failure to take advantage of the Season. 'She avoids Balls and goes to Battersea museum almost every day. She does not like riding out in a carriage. When will it end?'[59] Lady Evelyn's preference for reading late at night and visiting museums instead of pursuing a social round which might secure her a suitable husband was unacceptable to her mother. The Duchess consequently laid down terms under which her daughter was to be allowed to remain at her home, Blair Castle:

> I *must* have *respect* and *obedience*. I do not want to stop your Gaelic or any of your amusements if you will do them in moderation and not neglect other duties. . . . [I]f you come home you will quite make up your mind to do *all* I wish in everything including your dress.[60]

When Lady Evelyn refused to accept these conditions the breach between mother and daughter became final. Soon after she went into exile in Belgium, where she remained for the rest of her life, living on the £25 per month allowed her by her father, with an extra £5 to pay for a female companion.[61]

Fortunately most family disputes were resolved more happily than this and many girls had pleasant memories of the Season and its gaieties. Since as Lady Aberdeen tartly observed, it was well understood that 'nobody could . . . come to the front without participating in Society to some degree.'[62]

For the Duchess of Marlborough, viewing matters from a transatlantic perspective, her first Seasons in 1896 and 1897 were marked by a 'brilliant succession of festivities'. She and her husband dined out nearly every night, and there were also innumerable parties, often several taking place on a single evening. Discretion had to be exercised 'in one's acceptances in order to survive the three months' season which ended with the ball at Holland House, the Earl of Ilchester's house in Kensington'. This ball was especially popular, for there was a large and beautiful garden where couples could wander at will. 'Whether it was the moonlight, or the end of the season and the dispersal of London society for the summer, no one knew; but it is certain that many marriages were settled at the Holland House balls.'[63]

During the afternoons there were drives to Ranelagh to watch inter-regimental polo matches, and there were serious days when 'Parliament claimed our attention and we sat behind the grille in the Speaker's Gallery listening to Mr Arthur James Balfour, leader of the Conservative party in the House of Commons, winding up a debate in the elegant and scholarly manner still in practice.' Sometimes the Duchess would sit in the Peeresses' gallery in the House of Lords listening to Lord Rosebery castigating the Conservative government and to the 'dignified but no less caustic defence' of the Prime Minister, the Marquess of Salisbury. These varied London activities were interspersed with regular Saturday to Monday house-parties, when twenty-five or thirty guests, each accompanied by a valet or lady's maid, would assemble at Blenheim Palace, the Marlboroughs' Oxfordshire seat.

For the menfolk, politics, sport, card-playing, and gambling were the major preoc-cupations of the Season, combined with visits to the theatre, and obligatory appearances at dinner-parties, concerts, and balls. Maurice Baring's recollections of the summer of 1896 capture the atmosphere of some of these events:

> I went to the Derby that year and backed Persimmon; to the first performance of Mrs Campbell's *Magda* the same night; I saw Duse at Drury Lane and Sarah Bernhardt at Daly's; I went to Ascot; I went to balls; I stayed at Panshanger; and at Wrest, at the end of the summer, where a constellation of beauty moved in muslin and straw hats and yellow roses on the lawns of gardens designed by Le Nôtre, delicious with ripe peaches on old brick walls, with the smell of verbena, and sweet geranium; and stately with large avenues, artificial lakes and white temples; and we bicycled in the warm night past ghostly cornfields by the light of a large full moon.[64]

In those circles where plutocratic values and conspicuous consumption were gaining a growing sway, however, the Prince of Wales – later Edward VII – and his Marlborough House 'set' were regarded as setting the pattern. Prominent among the Prince's friends were bankers and industrialists, many of them foreign and some of them Jewish; it was he who also welcomed into the 'inner circle' the American heiresses who were marrying into aristocratic families impoverished by the effects of agricultural depression. He found American girls livelier, better educated, and less hampered by etiquette than their English counterparts.[65] But not all of his compatriots agreed with this more open approach, and it is possible to detect a note of xenophobia in the discontent expressed in *Lady's Realm* when it discovered that the four attendant duchesses at his coronation

Playing croquet at Hurlingham, *c.* 1900. (The author)

were to include the American-born Duchess of Marlborough. 'There are twenty-seven dukes,' it observed sourly; 'and although a few are widowers and unmarried, we can produce a fair share of duchesses of British birth, without including [an] American.'[66]

More seriously in the 1880s and 1890s the Prince's raffish lifestyle and his relentless pursuit of pleasure were blamed for undermining moral standards among the social élite. On one occasion a deputation of ladies led by the Duchess of Leeds, the Marchioness of Tavistock, the Marchioness of Bristol and the Countesses of Aberdeen, Zetland, Haddington and Stanhope even approached the Archbishop of Canterbury to ask him to do something about the unsatisfactory conduct of the heir to the throne. According to the Archbishop's son, they wanted his father to stop the moral rot they believed was ruining London.

> Girls newly 'come out' . . . of high tone and upright intentions, were speedily corrupted by it, and what they had been brought up to regard as evil they soon regarded as natural and inevitable; young married women had no standard of morality at all, and the centre of the mischief was the Marlborough House set. They wanted my father to start a sort of moral mission for women of their class. . . . Finally they . . . agreed that my father should talk to the Prince about the harm that was going on 'for he would listen to no one else.'[67]

Such a career as that of the 4th Marquess of Ailesbury exemplified the darker aspects of High Society life in the late nineteenth century. Of the Marquess, who was described as 'a young man of low tastes, bad character and brutal manners', one Prime Minister commented that 'his mind was a dunghill, of which his tongue was the cock.' In May 1884, before he was twenty-one, he married Julia Haseley, better known as the actress Doll Tester, 'late of the refreshment department of the Theatre Royal, Brighton, and more recently, of the chorus at *The Empire* and elsewhere'. In 1887 he was expelled from the Jockey Club for fraud in connection with the running of one of his horses, and in 1892 he went bankrupt. Two years later he died at the house of his agent in Brixton, apparently of heart failure, at the age of thirty, leaving a heavily encumbered estate to be rescued by his successor.[68] For some years the 5th Marquess occupied a small house on the estate and kept the property going largely with the help of a bank overdraft and by letting the shooting rights.[69]

It was the Prince of Wales's role in tolerating, and even apparently condoning, reckless conduct among his friends that concerned many of his subjects when be became King in 1901. The 'reaction from the austerity and rigid moral code of Queen Victoria's Court caused the pendulum to swing in the opposite direction', wrote the Countess of Airlie.[70] The novelist, Henry James, expressed similar concerns. While lamenting the Queen's death, he stressed his anxiety about the effect this would have on the country: 'the Prince of Wales is an arch vulgarian . . . nearly sixty, and, after all he has done besides of the same sort, is carrying on with Mrs George Keppel in a manner of the worst men for the

A reception and stage supper at the Lyceum theatre, London, *c.* 1902. (The author)

dignity of things. His succession, in short, is ugly and makes all for vulgarity and frivolity.'[71]

Mary Curzon, wife of the Viceroy of India, on a six-months' holiday in England in 1901, was equally critical. She reported gloomily to her husband on the mediocrity and triviality of the people whom she was meeting in London. 'Everyone is doing the same old thing – just flirting, and dining, and dawdling.' With the disappearance of Queen Victoria's influence, all reverence had gone out of people's lives.

> There is nobody who stands apart, and up aloft in your heart and mind. 'Edward the Caresser' is only made fun of, and there is a new story of him and Favorita [Mrs Keppel] every day. The whole scandal is public property.[72]

Indeed, according to Lord Balcarres, shortly before the coronation in the summer of 1902 there were cries of 'where's Alice [Mrs Keppel]?' when Edward attended the opera, and the 'box at the Abbey to be filled by his friends is called the "Loose Box".'

Yet despite these comments, the abiding impression of the London social scene during the Edwardian years was not of its decadence and corruption but of the sheer range of activities, entertainments and pleasures which it offered, and the closely integrated social network upon which it depended. 'To . . . appreciate the ramifications of a London Season', wrote Harold Macfarlane in 1909, 'it is necessary to bring together . . . the various methods in which Society occupies the 2,160 hours that, roughly speaking, comprise the period over which the Season extends.' Not only were there courts, levées, state dinners, balls, Royal garden parties, and the like, but many of these functions were themselves subdivided into different categories. The balls, for example, included private and semi-private dances as well as countless charity functions. The list of dinners likewise ranged from regimental banquets, Empire Day celebrations, and political and Derby Day dinners, to those held in private houses or for philanthropic purposes.

> The receptions . . . are divided up into almost as many classes as the dinners, while the *raisons d'être* of the numerous conversaziones are almost bewildering in the range of subjects which should, but rarely do, monopolize the conversation. The opera, the theatres, and concerts galore bring to the coffers of those who provide them some £600,000 in the course of the Season. . . . Sales of work, musical receptions at the Mansion House and elsewhere, picture shows, meetings in aid of charities, Congresses, lectures, May Meetings and Primrose League [i.e. Conservative Party] fixtures, exhibitions, the Horse Show, Military Tournament, cricket, croquet, lawn tennis, and other sporting events, bring together great crowds of people. . . . The Henley Regatta, the Bisley meeting, Ascot, the Fourth of June at Eton, Speech Day at Harrow, ballooning at Hurlingham and Ranelagh, and countless garden parties, of which the Countess of Jersey's series at Osterley Park and Lady Phillimore's at Cam House are among the foremost, are also important items of the Season that assist to . . . occupy the time of those who pursue the giddy round of pleasure.[73]

Small wonder that the young Duchess of Marlborough at the end of her first Season should confess she was so exhausted that on going to the seaside to recuperate she slept for twenty-four hours without waking.[74]

'For these months nobody is ever alone, nobody ever pauses to think; no one ever attempts to understand,' was the critical conclusion of the leading Liberal politician, C.F.G. Masterman; '. . . for the most part, it is talk – talk – talk; talk at luncheon and tea and dinner; talk at huge, undignified crowded receptions, . . . [and] talk at dances and at gatherings, far into the night; with the morning devoted to preparation for further talking in the day to come.' Occasionally elemental matters did intrude, such as marriages and 'those unexpected deaths which refuse to postpone themselves to a more convenient out-of-season'.[75] But for the most part Masterman viewed High Society as an aggregation of clever and agreeable people who were trying 'with a desperate seriousness to make something of a life spared the effort of wage-earning'.

Just how valid these views were on the daily round of the men and women who made up the nation's social élite will emerge in the following chapters. Suffice it here to point out that they were the last generation to experience the comforts and opulence of a glittering world which was to disappear for ever in 1914, with the outbreak of the First World War.

CHAPTER TWO

Daily Round: The Man's World

[Lord Fermor] had set himself to the serious study of the great aristocratic art of doing absolutely nothing. He had two large town houses, but preferred to live in chambers as it was less trouble, and took most of his meals at his club. He paid some attention to the management of his collieries in the Midland counties, excusing himself for this taint of industry on the ground that the one advantage of having coal was that it enabled a gentleman to afford the decency of burning wood on his own hearth. . . . He was a hero to his valet, who bullied him, and a terror to most of his relations, whom he bullied in turn.

OSCAR WILDE, *The Picture of Dorian Gray* in Isobel Murray ed., *The Writings of Oscar Wilde* (1990 edn.), 71.

I n many respects Oscar Wilde's fictional Lord Fermor fitted the popular image of a well-to-do 'man-about-town' at the end of Queen Victoria's reign. Self-confident and self-regarding, with an innate sense of superiority, such men were accustomed to living in the public eye and to enjoying the deference which they considered their due.[1]

At this date it was still possible for an unmarried man to live comfortably in London on an annual income of a thousand pounds. According to George Cornwallis-West, a pleasant bachelor flat in Mayfair could be rented for £150 a year, while the best tailor in Savile Row would make a suit of evening clothes for eleven guineas, and a morning suit for about eight guineas. Dress shirts could be bought for ten and sixpence, and membership of a good club offered both companionship and meals at modest cost.[2] It was partly on this account that the number of clubs virtually doubled between the early 1880s and 1914, by which date there were over two hundred of them in London.[3] It was at the Bachelors' Club, for example, that the young George Curzon entertained about forty of his friends in July 1889, prior to setting off for a 'cure' in Switzerland.[4] And in July 1891, Sir Edward Hamilton selected the short-lived Amphitryon Club, with its excellent cuisine, as the venue for a dinner with Francis Knollys, private secretary to the

Prince of Wales. The food was extremely good '& we sat talking till nearly 11.30'.[5] In this way clubs made it possible for an unattached man 'to continue to operate in the social sphere without maintaining his own establishment'.[6] It also had the side effect of encouraging a later marriage age for men, which was another feature of upper-class Victorian life in the final quarter of the nineteenth century.

W.H. Mallock, the son of a Devon landed family of moderate means, was one bachelor who conformed to this archetypal picture of a male member of the social élite. He spent about three months each year in London for the Season and two months at his home in Devon. His winters were spent abroad, mostly on the Riviera, and the remainder of his time was taken up with country-house visits to friends and relatives in various parts of the United Kingdom. In London his daily routine deviated little. The mornings were spent in writing, responding to invitations to various social events, and attending to other personal matters. Afterwards he strolled in the park with a friend:

> Then, more often than not, came a luncheon at two o'clock, to which many of the guests had been bidden . . . as the result of some chance meeting. A garden-party, such as those which took place at Sion House or at Osterley, would occupy now and again the rest of an afternoon; but the principal business of every twenty-four hours began with a long dinner at a quarter-past eight, or sometimes a quarter to nine. For any young man who took part in the social movement, dinner would be followed by two, or by more "At Homes." Then, when midnight was approaching, began the important balls, of which any such young man would show himself at an equal number, and dance, eat quails, or sit with a suitable companion under palm-trees, as

'A late riser.' A young 'man-about-town' waited on by his valet in bachelor chambers, c. 1900. (The author)

the case might be; whilst vigilant chaperons, oppressed by the weight of their tiaras, would ask each other. 'Who is the young man who is dancing with *my* daughter?'[7]

As a preparation for this adult world most young men would have attended one of the leading public schools, with Eton, Harrow and Winchester especially favoured. At Eton they would be dressed in a distinctive uniform of long trousers, black tailcoat, white tie, waistcoat and a top hat, and would be instructed in the importance of doing their duty and learning to 'play the game'. 'You have learned the contrast between the short space of human life and the infinite breadth of God's commandment . . . You have learned to distinguish between true and false liberty,' declared Edmond Warre, headmaster of Eton from 1884 to 1904, in a final sermon to the boys before relinquishing his post.[8] A similar note was struck by the memorial verses displayed in the porch at Winchester College chapel to commemorate the deaths of thirteen former pupils during the Crimean War of 1854–5:

> Think upon them thou who art passing by to day
> Child of the same family: bought by the same Lord.
> Keep thy foot when thou goest into this house of God
> There watch thine armour and make thyself ready by prayer
> To fight and to die
> The faithful soldier and servant of Christ
> And of thy Country.

However, not all of the boys conformed to these heroic ideals. The young Derrick

Eton boys outside the tuck shop. 'Rowland's', *c.* 1914. (The author)

Wernher and some of his friends became involved in illegal betting transactions while they were at Eton in 1905, thereby causing considerable parental anxiety, and eliciting promises from Derrick to do better in the future. Those promises he signally failed to keep.[9]

The extolling of the virtues of Greek civilization and values also led to a strong undercurrent of homosexuality at many of the schools. At Eton in the 1890s the 'boy loves' of Maurice Brett, younger son of the future 2nd Viscount Esher, were the subject of his father's prurient interest.[10] It was probably with these kinds of relationships in mind that Lady Selborne, whose sons were at Winchester, condemned public schools as 'sinks of iniquity' in one letter to the eldest boy.[11]

After school, for many of these young men came a spell at Oxford or Cambridge Universities or travels around the principal cultural centres of Europe. For those intent on a military career there was attendance at the Royal Military College at Sandhurst or the Royal Military Academy at Woolwich, which together trained the vast bulk of army officers.[12] The naval college at Dartmouth served a similar purpose for those desiring to enter the Royal Navy.

Younger sons, in particular, were expected to pursue an independent career unless the family were unusually wealthy. For them, the army, the navy, the public service or the learned professions were, by tradition, the favourite options. Employment became especially important among families hit by the effects of agricultural depression and

Spectators at an Eton v. Liverpool cricket match in the summer of 1911. (The author)

declining rental income. According to a contemporary, in the early twentieth century there was a greater demand for paid employment among men of good education and social standing than there had ever been before. He quoted one case where among the applicants for the post of companion to a gentleman 'of weak intellect' was a middle-aged baronet – even though the salary was a mere £200 a year with board. In another instance an established sporting club near London received over five hundred applicants when it appealed for a new secretary, preferably a retired army officer.[13]

In the case of the eldest son and heir, attention was turned to teaching him the rudiments of estate management in readiness for the time when he would assume the reins of power. There might also be a spell as a Member of Parliament, so that he could preserve the family's political interests and influence. For the owners of the largest estates this could involve the exercise of formidable power. Welbeck Abbey, seat of the Duke of Portland, was described by one man as 'more like a principality than anything else . . . Within the borders of Welbeck Abbey, His Grace the Duke of Portland, wielded an almost feudal indisputable power'. Similarly, at Eaton in Cheshire the 1st Duke of Westminster in the 1890s employed over three hundred servants (including ground staff). There was a newly-built estate light railway and a private fire brigade equipped with uniforms and appliances by the Duke.[14] He also took a deep personal interest in the running of his estates both in Cheshire and in London, and during his thirty years of ownership spent more than £350,000 on his Cheshire property alone. This included the construction of almost fifty new farm houses and 360 cottages, as well as schools, churches, and village halls. He was equally interested in the demolition of slum property in Chester and its replacement by modern dwellings. According to his biographer, there was not 'any useful local society or organization, church or chapel, hospital or school that was not indebted to the unstinted assistance of the Duke's time and money'.[15]

The owner, or the heir, of such major properties would also mark the special events of his life by communal celebrations. In 1901, the coming-of-age festivities of the 7th Earl Stanhope at Chevening lasted for more than a week. They included a communion service at the parish church, presentations from tenants and friends, two balls (one of them for the servants), a luncheon for the tenants and neighbours, a dinner for employees, and entertainment for the children.[16]

Richard Greville Verney, who succeeded his father as Lord Willoughby de Broke in 1902, was one young aristocrat who followed the traditional path of the social élite. After attending Eton, he went up to New College, Oxford in 1888. There he found the life of an undergraduate a welcome contrast to the regimentation of school. Not only did he have a bedroom and sitting-room of his own, with a man-servant to wait upon him, but if he were so inclined,

> every day could be turned into a half-holiday; to be able to ask almost any number of friends to a party in your rooms; . . . to belong to one or two good clubs; to enjoy a delightful symposium every Sunday evening in the junior common-room; if studious to have free access to the best books and best lectures on any given subject; to belong to a famous debating society; to become a member of the Oxford University Dramatic Society; . . . all these things combine to make life at nineteen just about as good as it can be.[17]

"A College Wine," Oxford.

The lighter side of university life is depicted in this painting of 'A College Wine' at Oxford in 1904. (Oxfordshire Photographic Archive, Centre for Oxfordshire Studies)

At university friendships were forged which lasted a lifetime, while academic work imposed a relatively light burden on all except the most ambitious or scholarly. During the winter there were plenty of opportunities for hunting and in the summer for cricket or perhaps, as with Richard Verney, for learning to drive a coach and four. Richard emerged from New College with 'an easy degree, cricket, hunting and driving four horses; the last three being very necessary accomplishments to the life that seemed to be indicated for me, a life from which I do not believe I could have escaped even if I had tried.' No profession was ever suggested to him, although he was 'presently to be given a chance in the House of Commons'. In 1895 he became Conservative Member for the Rugby Division of Warwickshire and held the seat until the general election of 1900, when the increasing ill-health of his father caused him to retire.[18] This gave him more freedom to engage in fox-hunting, the real love of his life. From this rural world he was to emerge in 1906 to do bitter battle, as a member of the House of Lords, with the newly-elected Liberal Government. (See Chapter 7).

The career of another young aristocrat, George Cornwallis-West, followed a different, though equally traditional, path to that of Richard Greville Verney. At first Cornwallis-West was sent for a year to study languages at Freiburg in Germany, after leaving Eton. The intention was that he should enter the diplomatic service, but he managed to combine his linguistic pursuits with agreeable fishing and walking expeditions, to say nothing of social encounters with students at the nearby university and mild flirtations with some of the local girls. On his return to England in June 1892, he was chagrined to discover that his father had decided, without consultation, that he was to abandon a

Richard Greville Verney Lord Willoughby de Broke. He was an enthusiastic foxhunter but in the period 1906 to 1914 became one of the then Liberal Government's most implacable opponents in the House of Lords. (Lord Willoughby de Broke, *The Passing Years*, 1924)

career in diplomacy in favour of the Army. Because George was too old for Sandhurst, Mr Cornwallis-West, as Lord Lieutenant of Denbigh, arranged for him to be commissioned into the Third Battalion of the Royal Welch Fusiliers. It was a means of entry which he himself labelled as getting in by 'the Back Door'.[19] The following winter was spent at the depot at Wrexham, where he enjoyed hunting with Sir Watkin Wynn's hounds. Then followed cramming for his military examinations at Jersey and Camberley.

> Three happy years slipped by, owning an old chestnut mare, making new friends, and learning to gamble at cards. From Camberley it was possible to catch a late train to London and still have . . . time in town. Fancy dress balls at Covent Garden, which were attended by many stage beauties of the day and required only masks and dominoes . . . were a favourite amusement.[20]

After passing his examinations, George was gazetted to the Scots Guards in July 1895. He had previously spent two months at Chelsea barracks learning the necessary drills and in his spare time, bicycling in Battersea Park – this last being a popular late-Victorian High Society pastime.

> An hour's exercise, and then we would breakfast at a little restaurant in the park; afterwards more 'biking' or a row on the lake. I am sure many of the engagements and

entanglements of that day were brought about through teaching girls and young
married women how to ride a bicycle. . . . The life of a young officer in the Foot
Guards in my time was very pleasant. Soldiering was not taken too seriously; indeed,
it was purely a matter of routine. . . . [T]he young officers were not encouraged to
think for themselves. . . . In the Mess, . . . [the] concrete subjects we discussed were
almost entirely to do with sport.[21]

The reminiscences of other officers confirm this cavalier approach. For, as Sir Ian
Hamilton put it, it was considered 'not good form to be keen'.[22] Hence Lord Ernest
Hamilton, a son of the Duke of Abercorn, gave as one reason for joining the 11th
Hussars the fact that they had only just returned from India and might therefore be
expected to remain in the United Kingdom for some ten years or so.[23] When his
regiment was stationed at Hounslow in the early 1880s he and fellow subalterns would
drive to the many race-meetings held in the surrounding area and play cricket on the
barrack square. 'We had everything . . . the heart of a soldier can desire, except
hunting.' That included frequent trips to the Gaiety Theatre in London to admire the
leading ladies, and on one occasion some of the Gaiety chorus girls were invited to
Hounslow to attend a regimental dance. This escapade caused 'a most desperate stir',
although Hamilton maintained that it had all been conducted in scrupulously platonic
circumstances, with the ladies spending the night in officers' rooms which their owners
had vacated. 'We, on our side, were much incensed at the incredulity of the world, for
. . . were we not before all else officers and gentlemen?'[24]

For most subalterns, soldiering in the late Victorian and Edwardian years was an
agreeable mix of polo, parties, and pleasure. Time was devoted to 'exercise, companionship and enjoyment, but little else. Good breeding and good manners mattered
much more than rigorous training or technical expertise. Hunting, shooting, and fishing
took more time than routine regimental duties.'[25] There were, of course, exceptions, but
they were relatively few in number. Even those like Viscount Wolseley, who reached the
top of their profession, played an active part in London social life, since by cultivating
the right connections they could promote their career prospects.

These sporting preoccupations also meant that most officers welcomed an Irish
posting because of the availability there of nearly every kind of sport at relatively modest
cost. Hunting was especially popular and George Cornwallis-West remembered that
when his battalion of the Scots Guards was in Dublin during the mid-1890s he and his
friends would often dance until 2 a.m. and then hurry off to catch an early 'hunting'
train. There were also many race meetings within easy reach of Dublin and the battalion
owned a four-in-hand which was used for these excursions. Any subaltern with
pretensions to a knowledge of horse-flesh was encouraged to learn to drive it.

In their differing ways Richard Greville Verney and George Cornwallis-West
conformed to the common view of a young late Victorian aristocrat. But a growing
number of landowners, faced by economic problems, were no longer able to afford to
finance their sons – or themselves – in this carefree way of life. Indeed, Cornwallis-
West's father was in a precarious financial position in the 1870s and for long periods
Ruthin Castle, the family seat, was let, while the shooting rights at Llanaromon, their
shooting box, were for several years leased by the Duke of Westminster.[26]

The Earl of Warwick in the 1890s. He was an honorary colonel of both the Warwickshire Yeomanry and the Essex Imperial Yeomanry. (Frances Countess of Warwick, *Life's Ebb and Flow*, 1929)

Similarly Earl Spencer, who estimated in 1893 that his net rents were around 50 to 55 per cent below what they had been about a decade earlier, decided to take drastic action. As well as selling his valuable library and letting his town house, this involved cutting household expenditure, reducing the domestic staff and giving up the mastership of the Pytchley Hounds. He regarded the latter as 'a bitter thing to do as it is what I care most for as amusement in the world. But I dare not face the cost.'[27]

The Earl of Harrowby was in an even more serious plight. He had estates in Staffordshire, Gloucestershire, and Lincolnshire, and between the mid-1880s and the mid-1890s less than three-quarters of the nominal rent due on his Gloucestershire property was paid. Despite the granting of abatements, tenants' arrears inexorably mounted. There were also heavy arrears on the Staffordshire estate and it was in these circumstances that the Earl wrote to his agent in February 1885, stressing the need for economy:

> I am further reducing household and horses from the present small establishment, but if I had not your assurance that from January, 1885, there is being a complete change as to this large and increasing expenditure, I should probably have been obliged to let our house in London, break up the Garden Establishment at Sandon, and settle abroad or elsewhere.[28]

When he died in 1900 not only was his London residence let but he had cut expenditure sharply on the gardens and grounds at his Staffordshire and Gloucestershire seats, as well as giving up the game rights on Staffordshire. He had also reduced his personal outgoings.

Other landowners followed Earl Spencer's example and began to dispose of non-agricultural assets, including works of art and family heirlooms. In 1890, the Earl of Radnor, concerned to make provisions for the marriage of his eldest son to Julian Balfour, sold several old Masters to the National Gallery for £55,000. Many men, particularly on the eve of the First World War, tried to sell outlying parts of their estates. This decision was inspired, in most cases, by a rational wish to switch from low-income land to some more lucrative commercial investment rather than by fear of imminent bankruptcy. However, it caused the *Estates Gazette* to comment gloomily in 1912, when nineteen noblemen were reported to be seeking to sell large acreages, that such unanimity of action pointed 'to some great change in the condition of affairs in this country'.[29] Certain of the more politically minded owners, like the Wiltshire squire and Conservative activist, Walter Long, who sold a large part of his estate in 1910, sought to blame the Liberal Government for the sales. Long claimed that the Government's hostility to the landed interest and the threat of confiscatory taxes had led to his action. In reality he was responding to a slight but perceptible upturn in the land market during this period, after years of stagnation.

A few hard-hit landlords reacted by withdrawing from the London social scene altogether. As one Kent owner, Major Best, noted wryly in the 1890s, he was 'becoming very economical' to match his reduced income. This meant spending time abroad or in quiet English resorts so that he did not 'have to play the part of squire too constantly'.[30]

A further factor hampering the career prospects of many younger sons of landed families was the growing emphasis on the need for examinations and training in most of the occupations they had formerly taken up. Prior to 1871 it had been possible to *purchase* commissions and promotions in the guards, cavalry and infantry regiments of the Home Army, up to the rank of lieutenant-colonel. After that date, competitive examinations were instituted.[31] Admittedly the already well-established links between the Army and the public schools, coupled with the opportunity for men like George Cornwallis-West to be coached by crammers, ensured that the officer corps remained socially exclusive. But success was no longer merely a matter of nepotism and privilege.

Outside the ranks of the military, similar changes were under way, and many older professions became dominated by middle-class meritocrats. This was true of the law. Up to the 1880s the legal profession still maintained close links with the landed establishment. However, the new emphasis on qualifying examinations and the rationalizing of the court system during the last thirty years of Queen Victoria's reign slowly made it less attractive to old-style leisured patricians. Indeed, in 1872 when final examinations became compulsory for men wishing to be admitted to the bar, loud protests were heard that this would discourage country gentlemen who had trained 'merely to acquire such status and so much professional knowledge as would be useful to them as magistrates, politicians, legislators and statesmen'.[32] Some members of landed families did, of course, continue to come forward. Herbert Cozens Hardy, the second son of a Norfolk squire, became a practising barrister and then went on to become chairman of the Bar Council and MP for North Norfolk from 1885 to 1899. In the latter year he was made a High Court judge and followed this by becoming a Lord Justice of Appeal in 1901. Six years later he was appointed Master of the Rolls and in 1914 he became an hereditary peer.[33] But by the early twentieth century such careers for landed aristocrats or gentry were becoming rare. The vast majority of judges were middle-class professionals and even among the Lord Chancellors, Selborne and Halsbury were the last patricians 'by ancestry or aspiration to sit on the Woolsack'. Halsbury ceased to be Lord Chancellor in 1905; his twentieth-century successors neither were members of, nor sought to join, the landed élite.

In the case of the Church of England the links between the aristocracy and gentry and the profession of clergyman survived longer. But even here there was a loosening of the connection as the economic importance of the Church itself declined. In 1837 the average clerical stipend had been around £500; by 1901 it was just under half that amount.[34] In addition, the growing urban population and the fact that the demand for clergy was greatest in the major industrial centres, rather than in rural communities, made it less attractive to the sons of country gentlemen. Nonetheless, some continued to be recruited from this background until well into the twentieth century. 'The Earls of Devon produced clergymen in successive generations,' writes David Cannadine; 'the fifteenth earl was Rector of Powderham from 1904 to 1927, and the sixteenth was Rector of Honiton from 1907 to 1927.'[35] Then there was Lord Scarsdale, who as Nathaniel Curzon had become rector of Kedleston, Derbyshire, in 1855. The following year he succeeded to the title and although he soon ceased to carry out pastoral duties at Kedleston he never resigned the living. Instead he relied on a series of curates until his death in 1916. Meanwhile he assumed the traditional role of a territorial magnate, including serving as a magistrate, acting as governor of Repton School, and sitting on the local water board.[36]

In the upper ranks of the church a number of patrician bishops were likewise to be found. Among them was the Hon. Augustus Legge, fourth son of the 4th Earl of Dartmouth, who was Bishop of Lichfield from 1891 to 1913. Still more illustrious was Edward Talbot, a grandson of the 2nd Earl Talbot, who was successively Bishop of Rochester, Southwark and Winchester between 1896 and 1923. He was related to both the Marquess of Salisbury and the Gladstone family and frequently visited their country houses. Whilst at Southwark he played an active role in London society, and at Winchester was said to have 'lived like a grand seigneur'.[37]

But these men apart, only at court and in certain sections of the civil service were there still significant openings for those with the attitudes and values of the leisured aristocracy. Already by the 1890s only 7 per cent of new civil service recruits were from landed families, but patronage could still play its part for a select few. In 1881 the well-connected Edward Ruggles-Brise was given a junior post in the Home Office as a consequence of his father making a direct appeal to the Home Secretary. In 1895 Sir Edward Ruggles-Brise, as he had now become, was appointed Chief Prison Commissioner. Similarly, Sir Henry Primrose, a cousin of the Liberal Prime Minister, Lord Rosebery, between 1886 and 1907 served successively as Permanent Secretary to the

Office of Works, chairman of the Board of Customs and chairman of the Board of Inland Revenue.[38] Despite the introduction of open competitive examinations from 1870, traditional methods of appointment were slow to disappear, therefore. As one writer has put it, 'competition tempered with selection was very much the Treasury's style of recruitment.'[39] This is confirmed by the fact that the two senior figures in that Department during the 1900s were Sir George Herbert Murray and Sir Edward Hamilton:

> Murray was a kinsman of the Duke of Atholl. . . . He joined the Foreign Office in 1873, moved to the Treasury seven years later, and between 1897 and 1903 was successively chairman of the Board of Inland Revenue and Secretary of the Post Office. Hamilton . . . a relative of the tenth Earl of Belhaven, was a well-known figure in polite, aristocratic society, and during the early 1880s had been one of Gladstone's private secretaries.[40]

Hamilton's diaries confirm that his Treasury duties in no way inhibited his active participation in the London Season. (See Appendix B) On 20 June, 1889, he noted happily that he was 'doing quite an operatic & dramatic week. Last night I went with Lady Rosebery & the Wilton Phipps to hear "Doris" . . . I have just returned from the Opera, where I heard for the first time "Romeo & Juliet". . . . I dined first at the Revelstokes & went to her box with the Duchess of Hamilton.' Just over a month later he dined at Lady Mandeville's and afterwards attended a ball at Dudley House, where he was entranced by Lady Dudley's beauty. This was:

> quite the wind-up of the Season; which this year nobody can accuse of being a dull one. Most of the big Houses have been thrown open: there have been entertainments without end: the Opera has retained its popularity – everything showing that the revival of better times is beginning to tell. It is probable that never in the history of this country has there been so much money-making as there has been during the last few months.[41]

Hamilton was a close friend of members of the Rothschild family and frequently visited their homes. In 1891, he rejoiced that in London society 'Jewish plutocracy [reigned] by the side of Christian aristocracy'.[42] In his view Mrs Leopold de Rothschild and her sister were leaders in maintaining proper moral standards in society: 'there are no two more popular women in London, who in spite of their simplicity always give a smartness to any party, and who don't know how to do a *risky* (sic) act or say a *risky* thing.'[43]

The nobility and gentry were especially prominent at court, with such full-time appointments as those of Private Secretary, Keeper of the Privy Purse, Master of the Household, Master of the Horse, Master of the Ceremonies, and Equerry drawn from their ranks. The same was true of the large number of minor members of the royal household who attended upon the Queen in rotation. By the early 1880s these included, on the male side, eight lords-in-waiting, eight grooms-in-waiting, and eight equerries. All, except for seven of the eight lords-in-waiting, were appointed by the Queen personally, independent of any party political affiliations.[44]

The creation of a new imperial image for the monarchy, following Queen Victoria's assumption of the title of Empress of India in 1876, led to an increased administrative role for members of the household. That also applied to the permanent civil servants most closely associated with them. They included Reginald Brett, the future 2nd Viscount Esher. In 1895 he became Secretary of the Office of Works, largely as a result of lobbying on his behalf by Lewis Harcourt, son of the then Chancellor of the Exchequer, Sir William Harcourt. It was an appointment which the Liberal Party's Welsh Chief Whip condemned as 'execrable . . . a man with about £6000 a year with five houses in town and country . . . It will be looked upon as Whiggery with a vengeance'.[45] But Brett himself valued the post because of its close connections with the royal family. In the summer of 1897 he helped organize the Queen's Diamond Jubilee and soon his involvement with other activities led to invitations to visit the Queen at Windsor and the Prince of Wales at Sandringham. In late November 1897 he and his wife dined at Windsor castle:

> Gold plate and beautiful Sèvres. Indian servants behind the Queen. A Highlander to pour out the wine. . . . No 'courses'. Dinner is served straight on, and when you finish one dish you get the next, without a pause for breath. Everyone talked, as at any other dinner, only in subdued tones. The Queen was in excellent humour. After dinner . . . the Queen sent for me, and she talked to me for half an hour about her affairs and her family. Finally, she bowed and I retired. By that time it was nearly eleven.[46]

After Queen Victoria's death early in 1901, Esher became a confidant of the new King and was concerned not merely with details of court ceremonial but with much 'fussing' about the private affairs of the King and Queen. During the summer of 1901 he complained in his diary about the numerous commands he was receiving from the King to visit Windsor, Sandringham and Balmoral. They were interfering with the heavy load of administrative work he also had to carry out.[47]

A similar fascination with the minutiae of court life was displayed by Lord Ormathwaite. After years on the fringes of court life he was appointed a Gentleman Usher by Edward VII soon after his accession. A year later be became Groom-in-Waiting. One of his first duties in this new post was to look after a Japanese mission sent by the Emperor of Japan to thank the King for conferring upon him the Order of the Garter. The visit lasted about three weeks and Ormathwaite found the ceremonial involved exhausting. 'Banquets and receptions, army and navy reviews followed each other in quick succession, and as the King had to be informed daily of all that took place, any letter-writing lasted into the early hours of the morning.'[48]

Lord Ormathwaite was promoted to Master of the Ceremonies in 1907. For some days after this, 'the King's entire conversation was taken up in telling me all he wished me to do, and in giving me some very valuable instruction.'[49] His main task was to act as 'go-between' in relations involving the King and the diplomatic corps. Ambassadors seeking an audience of the monarch had first to contact the Master of the Ceremonies and he in turn would get in touch with Edward's private secretary, so that an appointment could be made. As with so many of those holding royal office, it was essential for a successful courtier like Ormathwaite to be equable in temperament and yet possess a capacity for taking infinite pains over tasks which many men would have dismissed as too trivial to warrant detailed attention.

But the man's world in London High Society at the end of the nineteenth century was far wider than that of the pleasure-seeking bachelor at his club, the sports-loving Army officer, and the suave courtier. Already in the mid-1880s attention was being drawn to the growing range of commercial employments which the offspring of aristocratic families were taking up. Trade was losing some of its stigma and according to T.H.S. Escott, younger sons of 'great noblemen' were accepting:

> positions in mercantile and trading houses, sheep-farming, ordinary farming, plantations in the colonies, India, and America. When dukes are willing to apprentice the cadets of their houses to merchants and to stockbrokers, an example has been set which it is well should be widely followed.[50]

Escott described patrician parents who hastened to get their sons into business, and noblemen of illustrious lineage who eagerly embraced 'any good opening in the City which may present itself for them. It is perhaps the younger son of an earl or a duke who sees you when you call on your broker to transact business; it may be the heir to a peerage himself who is head partner in the firm which supplies the middle-class household with tea'.[51] Although these upper-class youths were fitted neither by

She. "THERE'S ALWAYS A CROWD ROUND THE DEAR OLD PROFESSOR. HE'S SUCH A WONDERFUL CONVERSATIONALIST."
He. "LOR'! YOU REALLY THINK SO? I TRIED HIM JUST NOW ON EVERY POSSIBLE TOPIC—HOUNDS, BRIDGE, GOLF, MUSIC-HALLS, *EVERYTHING*—AND HE WAS SIMPLY USELESS."

Gossip about sport or the music-hall was the staple conversation of many young 'men-about-town'. (*Punch*, 1912)

education nor by upbringing for such careers, necessity and a desire for profit had become the driving force.[52]

Commercial ventures by major landowners were, of course, not new in the 1880s. Ever since the industrial revolution a number of territorial magnates had derived substantial incomes from royalties and wayleaves in connection with the mining of coal and iron on their estates. Already in 1881–2 the 7th Duke of Devonshire was earning £112,541 from dividend income on stocks, securities and the like, compared to £180,750 from his landed estates.[53] And by 1914 the Duke of Northumberland's mineral earnings amounted to more than 40 per cent of his gross income. Likewise Lord Sidmouth's Staffordshire collieries and his London ground rents provided around 60 per cent of his gross income at about the same date.[54] Others who benefited in this way included the Earl of Derby, with much valuable urban and industrialized property in Lancashire, and the Duke of Norfolk and Earl Fitzwilliam, who together owned the two largest mineral properties in the West Riding of Yorkshire. The Duke also owned a small but valuable property in the Strand in London and about 20,000 acres in Sheffield. His market rights in that town, together with a modest plot of land, were eventually sold to the corporation for over half a million pounds.[55] Lord Crawford, whom *The Times* described as 'one of the most accomplished members of the peerage', was able to follow his interests in astronomy, exploration, yachting and book and stamp collecting largely because of the coal revenues derived from his Haigh Hall estate in Lancashire.

These business ventures were, however, usually conducted in an 'arm's length' fashion, with the task of ensuring that remunerative contracts were concluded largely delegated to agents and legal advisers. That was not the case with many of the commercial concerns with which landed aristocrats were involved on an ever larger scale from the 1880s.

Income from company directorships and investment in stocks and shares became increasingly attractive to hard-pressed landowners during the agricultural depression years. Already in 1896, 167 peers had become company directors; among them were ten dukes. Thirty-one of the peers were directors of four or more companies and although they included commercial giants like Lord Rothschild, that did not apply to all. The impoverished Marquess of Ailesbury was director of four companies and the Earl of Donoughmore of eleven. But even he was dwarfed by the nineteen directorships claimed by the Marquess of Tweeddale, who was a major landowner in Scotland.[56]

Among those taking up their new avocation with enthusiasm was Viscount Churchill. He became chairman of three railways, including the important Great Western Railway, and according to his son, 'business was his real interest . . . My father's associates seemed to have found out that he had ability, and that as well as his name he himself was an asset.'[57] The same was true of the 3rd Earl of Verulam. Besides investing heavily in a number of companies, particularly those concerned with colonial and other overseas ventures, he had by 1913 become a director of thirteen companies, ranging from a small Essex brewery to a major insurance office, a rubber company in Borneo, and various mining companies. Fees varied from the £50 paid by the Colchester Brewery to the £500 secured from Borneo Rubber. Together they represented a valuable supplementary income. Lord Verulam attended board meetings regularly, and by 1897 fees and dividends formed almost a third of his aggregate income. In 1913 they accounted for over a third. As a result of this additional revenue, he was able to move back to Gorhambury, the family seat, which had had to be vacated when he inherited the estate in 1895.[58]

Lord Shrewsbury was a third enthusiast. He became chairman of three companies and in 1903 told his sister proudly:

> Everyone makes their own Role in Life I have taken up the commercial side & I venture to say there is no Landlord or Colliery Proprietor who knows more about his own business in their respective districts than I do – Commercially . . . [I have] my own houses in Paris, Brussels, Turin, Milan & Nice – 2 Factories in London. 4 Retail Houses also & a Company in Manchester – and as in London alone I had sales of Forty Thousand Pounds in July . . . I am not quite idle.[59]

Lord Cottesloe, too, combined the running of an estate in Buckinghamshire with chairmanship of the Brighton Railway and the Eagle Insurance Company, as well as directorships of the Foreign, American and General Trust Company and the Foreign and Colonial Investment Trust.[60] And an advertisement for Bovril in *The Queen* in May 1897 listed the Duke of Somerset and Earl de la Warr among that firm's trustees; a little later, Lord Herbert lent his name to an advertisement for 'De Reszke' cigarettes which appeared in the *Tatler*.

However, not all of those who embarked on these commercial activities were successful. In July 1891, Sir Edward Hamilton noted that Lord George Hamilton, third son of the 1st Duke of Abercorn, had been seriously affected by the collapse of the English River Plate Bank. As one of the directors he had held over 1000 shares, 'to which there is a liability of £10'. At the time Lord George was First Lord of the Admiralty and Sir Edward considered his misfortune 'ought to bring to the front the very questionable practice of Ministers combining commercial with official business. Men who accept office under the Crown ought to be obliged to give up their directorships'.[61]

Another man who used his 'High Society' contacts to gain a foothold in business, albeit to little long-term advantage, was George Cornwallis-West. George was encouraged to leave the Army by his commanding officer when he married the widowed Lady Randolph Churchill, who was about twenty years his senior. Within months of the marriage the couple's extravagant lifestyle forced him to resort to money-lenders. The former Lady Randolph had a cavalier attitude towards money and even on their honeymoon took the small hamper of unpaid bills she always had with her. 'It made her feel virtuous to set them in order, almost as if she had paid them off.' As her husband ruefully admitted:

> If something of beauty attracted her she just had to have it; it never entered her head to stop and think how she was going to pay for it. . . . Her extravagance was her only fault and, with her nature, the most understandable and therefore the most forgivable.[62]

It was to overcome this cash crisis that he decided to go into the business world. He approached the leading financier, Sir Ernest Cassel, who warned him of possible pitfalls but nonetheless gave him an introduction to the British Thomson-Houston Company. On the strength of this, Cornwallis-West went on to become a director of the British Electric Traction Company and chairman of its subsidiary, the Potteries Electric Traction Company. Other directorships followed and within four years he was earning a reasonable income from these various sources. However, he needed large capital sums to settle his wife's debts and his own gambling losses, and in an effort to secure them went into partnership with a glib north-country speculator named Wheater. The latter had come to London hoping to start 'a sort of minor issuing house'. In Cornwallis-West he saw a gullible young man who moved in the right social circles and had desirable contacts with leading financiers. Even more attractive to this predator was George's willingness to invest a mortgage of £35,000 on his reversion of the family estate. Initially everything went well, with Cornwallis-West using his connections to persuade Lord 'Natty' Rothschild to take a block of shares in one of the companies he was promoting. This induced others to invest and within a fortnight the new firm had succeeded in placing over fifty thousand shares in that enterprise alone.[63] During the first year they made a profit of more than £23,000 but George's optimism that money-making was 'an easy affair' proved sadly misplaced. Soon after the beginning of the First World War the business finally collapsed.

This was not the only dubious venture with which Cornwallis-West was associated. He and his partner took a large interest in a Spanish copper mine which, as he ironically declared, would have been 'excellent . . . if only there had been more copper in it'. Then there was a scheme to culture pearls off the north-west coast of Australia. Unfortunately this foundered when the owner of the secret died unexpectedly. The patenting and manufacture of the West-Ashton automatic gas-operated rifle also fell through when the Small Arms Committee rejected it because they considered 'an automatic rifle would encourage the waste of ammunition by the soldier'.[64]

Such men as he were particularly vulnerable to the blandishments of corrupt company promoters like E.T. Hooley, who launched twenty-six companies with a nominal capital of £18m. between 1895 and 1898, and then went bankrupt with a debt of nearly half a million pounds. He had liberally recruited titled directors to give an air of respectability to his undertakings, and in return for lending their names they had been paid a fee. During the bankruptcy proceedings it was revealed that Lords de la Warr, Winchilsea and Albemarle alone had received about £80,000 to join the boards of three of his companies. When asked why he had recruited them for his prospectuses he had bluntly replied that the aim was to attract subscriptions to the shares. *The Times* condemned the whole sorry business:

> Till now, the name of a peer, or a man of great family, upon the 'front page' of a prospectus, has been valuable, because the public has not ceased to regard these persons as men of scrupulous honour, who would not give their names for secret 'considerations.' We seem to be changing all that.[65]

Hooley was not the only unscrupulous financier to take advantage of the greed – and naivety – of members of the aristocracy and gentry, as the case of George Cornwallis-West shows. Sometimes their gullibility could have dire consequences for their family. Sir Frederick Milner, who succeeded to the baronetcy in 1880 on the death of his elder brother, William, claimed that the latter had 'got into the hands of a lot of sharks'. As a result he was 'ruined before he knew where he was, & as a consequence I am driven from my home, with no chance of ever getting back to it'. William himself had died 'broken hearted' at the early age of thirty-seven.[66] And the family estate had had to be sacrificed to meet his debts.

Although these misfortunes acted as a warning to some, even in 1906 Lady Dorothy Nevill could write disapprovingly of 'the bustle of the Stock Exchange' being imported into the drawing-rooms of Mayfair, and of landed families pressing the new millionaires to assist their sons to establish a career in the City.

> I am told that there are now many scions of noble houses who exhibit nearly as much shrewdness in driving bargains in the City as a South African millionaire himself; whilst, on the other hand, the sons of the millionaires in several instances do not conceal their dislike for business, and lead an existence of leisured and extravagant ease . . . So matters adjust themselves, but in the interval Society has been transformed.[67]

She contrasted the life of a rich man in the early twentieth century with the slower pace of his mid-nineteenth-century counterpart. Then he would probably have spent the greater part of the year on his estate, merely taking a house in town for three months or so for the Season, and supplementing it with occasional foreign travel. Country-house parties were fewer but lasted longer, and entertainments were relatively modest. In the 1900s, it was very different:

> Paris, Monte Carlo, big-game shooting in Africa, fishing in Norway, dashes to Egypt, trips to Japan. In fact, no one knows . . . where he may be any given week. He has, of course, a house in town, but so busy is he that as often as not he is too hurried to go there, and puts up at some fashionable hotel . . . where he can entertain with the greatest possible ease. At the proper time he goes to the country to shoot, more often than not entertaining a large party, who disperse the moment the last shot has been fired and the last pheasant killed. . . . His expenses are in all probability enormous – a wife whose extravagance he is too indolent to check . . . ; children who also spend largely; houses, hotels, horses, motors, pictures, and other works of art, and very likely, in addition to all of these, most costly of all – a yacht.[68]

For their part, many of the *nouveaux riches* were anxious to enjoy the pleasures and the prestige of country-house life without giving up their major business interests. Sir Julius Wernher, the gold and diamond magnate, for example, purchased Luton Hoo in Bedfordshire in 1903, after renting it from its previous owners for several years. He then set in hand a costly programme of renovation and rebuilding which lasted for about three years. But although he, and particularly his wife, enjoyed being able to entertain in style, his main interest in life remained his business concerns. The Wernhers only went to

A house party at Mr Wingfield's Bedfordshire home, Ampthill, in 1910, with, from left to right: Lady Norah Churchill; Lady Dysart; Mr J.E.C. Bodley, a distinguished writer on France; the host, Mr Wingfield; Mrs Alston; H.R.H. Infante Luiz of Spain; and Anthony Wingfield. (The author)

Luton Hoo for occasional Sundays and for a few weeks in the autumn, even though they maintained a large domestic and outdoor staff.[69]

A similar attitude was apparent on the part of Sir Alfred Hickman, the millionaire Wolverhampton steel manufacturer, who built a house in the country and rode with the local hunt. He also entertained on a grand scale in London but he never lost interest in Wolverhampton and its affairs. His regional and national contacts were used to promote its economy. For men such as he, the purchase of a landed estate did not mean a rejection of industrial values, but a careful marrying of the pleasures of gentrification with the 'imperatives of capitalist production'.[70]

However, while the *nouveaux riches* and their imitators combined business with pleasure in a world where the values of the countryside and the counting house increasingly coalesced, this was not true of large numbers of the traditional landed classes. They continued to concentrate on their duty to their estate and its associated communities. For them, life in the public eye meant taking on the role of president of the local agricultural society or membership of charitable boards and bodies, as well as service as a justice of the peace. Such men prided themselves on their concern for the welfare of those living on their properties. And this was a theme taken up by T.H.S. Escott in the mid-1880s:

> What is the daily life of a territorial magnate . . . , even in London, when the season is at its height? As surely as ten o'clock comes each morning he will seek his library, where his correspondence is spread on the table for his perusal. The letters are written by all kinds of people. . . . Some are from tenants on his estates, who want repairs done, or apply for permission to make alterations in their holdings; others are from

bailiffs and stewards. . . . Others are mere begging letters from a legion of mendicant correspondents. . . . On the back or margin of each he will note down the nature of the reply to be sent.[71]

In Escott's view, for those who carried out their duties conscientiously, there would be 'as few spare minutes as a merchant's clerk . . . They are charged with the administration of a miniature empire'.[72]

This preoccupation with the detailed running of an estate applied to the 3rd Lord Leconfield at Petworth, Sussex. Not only did he take an active part in the planning of the annual fêtes of the local friendly society which were held in the grounds of his house and which included a church service, a procession of members through the park, a dinner, and a cricket match, but he maintained a personal interest in applications for admission to an almshouse he supported at Tillington. He was also concerned with the payment of pensions to long-serving employees, as well as with the distribution of charity and the holding of various communal celebrations.[73]

At Compton Verney, too, Lord Willoughby de Broke claimed that estate workers had 'certainty of employment for as long as they chose to work. They were looked after when they were sick. They were pensioned when they could work no more. . . . And above all, there was a mutual bond of affection that had existed for many generations between their families and the family of their employer, a bond that cannot be valued in terms of money.'[74]

The general approach was summarized by the Duke of Richmond, the fourth largest landowner in the country (with 18,000 acres in England and 268,000 acres in Scotland), when he declared in 1884: 'I look upon myself and the tenantry as members of one large, vast, and I am happy to be able to add, united family . . . It is my duty . . . to look after the interests myself . . . individually, of the humblest crofter on this estate as well as the wealthiest tenant.'[75] Unfortunately, as the agricultural depression intensified, many less affluent owners were unable or unwilling to conform to this vision of a miniature welfare state. But most appreciated that it was the goal at which they should aim.

Finally, for those men who were married, there were domestic duties and responsibilities to take into account. In accordance with prevailing views on the 'separate spheres' of males and females in upper-class society, few fathers took a major part in the day-to-day upbringing of their children. This was seen as the task of their wife or, more accurately, of the nursery staff whom they employed. Often, when they were in London a husband would go to his club for a few hours while his wife carried out her domestic and family role. Sir James Reid, former resident medical attendant to Queen Victoria, regularly retreated into a male world of clubs and committees when he found the endless comings and goings of his wife's numerous relatives tedious. Likewise the diaries of Lady Frederica Loraine reveal that during the 1890s while she took the children to the Zoo or the Botanical Gardens, her husband, a retired admiral, would go to the Navy Club or attend the races.[76]

Fathers, in these circumstances, often came to be regarded as remote, authoritarian beings, who took little interest in the doings of their offspring, once they had secured an heir to succeed to the title, or estate.[77] Clayton Glyn, an Essex landowner, found his children so unappealing that he even refused to travel on the same train as his two daughters when they were small. Special arrangements had to be made at Durrington, the family home, to keep all nursery sounds and smells from his notice.[78]

The 2nd Viscount Esher, too, displayed a lack of affection for three of his four children which his biographer describes as 'almost pathological'. But in his case the situation was complicated by his strong homosexual tendencies and by the unhealthy passion he developed for his younger son, Maurice, when the boy was at Eton. Esher's relations with Maurice led to resentment and suspicion among the other three children, who were excluded from all paternal interest.[79]

Lord Randolph Churchill, younger son of the Duke of Marlborough, was another cold and distant father. 'He treated me as if I had been a fool; barked at me whenever I questioned him,' wrote his elder son, Winston, sadly.[80] Surviving letters written by the boy from school reveal a pathetic desire to please his father – an aim he notably failed to achieve.

Some men broke this expected upper-class mould of paternal strictness and aloofness. One who took a deep interest in his children's welfare was Charles Wood, 2nd Viscount Halifax, who took them for rides and romped with them in a loft over the stable. He read aloud stories and wrote many affectionate and amusing letters. Sometimes he pretended to be a witch or a gipsy and would then stage a 'raid' to capture a small boy.[81]

The 2nd Lord Leconfield also showed genuine affection for his children. In a letter sent to his wife in 1899 whilst she was in Ireland nursing one of their sons, then seriously ill, he gave many domestic details: 'Bumps has returned (from school) looking very well and with a good report. Edward's is of course a very disappointing one . . . Maggie has immensely improved in her playing.'[82]

Lord Carrington was another father who shared in the upbringing of his children, despite a busy political and social life. In April 1893, on his eldest daughter's birthday, he took the youngsters to a guard mounting at St. James's Palace, followed by a visit to the Crystal Palace. 'We . . . went in the Swings and Switch Back Railway, and all came home to tea.' On another occasion he accompanied them to 'Captain Boyton's' water show. 'We came down in the "Chute" & made Captain Boyton's acquaintance.'[83] On Sundays he, rather than Lady Carrington, often took them to church and when they were at Wycombe Abbey, their country home, he joined in many walking, riding and boating excursions. On 1 April, 1894, Lady Carrington noted that he had even looked after the latest baby when the nanny took the older children to church and he 'again took her up the hill in the afternoon'.[84]

Nevertheless there were periods when Lord Carrington's outside activities kept him away from home and family for weeks at a time, and the children were left at Wycombe Abbey with nursery staff, while their parents were in London. In late August 1892, for example, he went to Osborne House on the Isle of Wight to kiss hands on taking up appointment as Lord Chamberlain to the Queen. From there he went to Lincolnshire and then joined his wife and children for a few days in Norfolk before visiting his sister-in-law in Northumberland. This was followed by a trip to Scotland, where he combined politics with pleasure and joined a shooting party. He returned to High Wycombe on 16 September and almost immediately he and his wife prepared for a shooting party of their own.[85] Both his diaries and those of Lady Carrington confirm regular attendances at race meetings, dinner-parties, balls, the theatre and various official functions connected with his position as Lord Chamberlain. They also include details of his participation in sessions of the London County Council – of which he was a member – and of his contributions to debates in the House of Lords.

The daily round of men such as Lord Carrington was in marked contrast to that of the pleasure-seeking 'idle' rich like Hugh Lowther, 5th Earl of Lonsdale. Hugh succeeded to the title in the early 1880s when he was twenty-five. Within three years he had 'started collecting horses like a schoolboy collects postage stamps'. He dressed his servants in a distinctive livery, and himself always appeared in the height of fashion; when in London he often changed his clothes four times a day. During the spring of 1885, when his wife was ill and so was unable to attend late-night balls and dinner-parties, he went out to music halls, the Gaiety Theatre, and boxing matches. His liaisons with actresses became notorious and for a time his extravagance was such that the estate trustees insisted he must give up hunting. But the economies proved short-lived. His personal entourage numbered over a hundred and when he moved from one house to another – he had at least three country seats – a special train was reserved for the household. If he travelled overnight, one first-class sleeper was set aside for him and another for the dogs.

With expenditure on this scale his annual 'pocket-money' of £80,000 soon disappeared. It was small wonder that on the Lowther estates in Cumbria, particularly around Whitehaven, where the Lonsdale wealth was based on coal and iron-ore mining, Hugh's extravagances and absenteeism were resented. 'One thing is certainly not intended, namely that the Earl shall do Whitehaven the justice of residing and spending his money there for a short time,' declared the normally loyal *Whitehaven News* in the mid-1880s. 'His Lordship may be proud to learn that there is an analogy between himself and Royalty, though the instance is not so creditable as it might be. The depression in London would be mitigated if the Queen would once more hold Court at Buckingham Palace. The depression in Whitehaven might disappear if the Lonsdales held Court at the Castle and circulated the money they take from the town amongst the towns-people.'[86]

Hugh ignored these strictures. Only with age did he learn discretion, if not thrift. At the end of the century, his biographer comments, his capacity for spending money:

> remained in full flood, but the general pattern of his life was beginning to emerge in more solid form. He spent the social season with Grace [his wife] in London. In July after Goodwood he would go to Lowther for the grouse shooting before taking up residence at Barleythorpe [his hunting box]. . . . As his finances started to mend, . . . he found himself devoting more and more time to . . . hunting perhaps three or four days a week . . . all over the country.[87]

Men as extravagant as Lord Lonsdale were nonetheless the exception even in the plutocratic world of the later Victorians and Edwardians. Partly from financial necessity and partly from a sense of duty, most male members of High Society at the turn of the century spent at least part of their time personally involved in looking after their estates and pursuing their professional and business interests. 'Life was free-and-easy up to a point,' wrote George Cornwallis-West in 1930, 'but there was much more attention paid to the idea of what people might say . . . Possibly owing to their upbringing, the young men and women of that generation had less self-confidence and, in consequence, less individuality; but we hadn't that cold-blooded wish to experiment with life in all its aspects that is so often seen now.'[88]

CHAPTER THREE

Daily Round: The Woman's World

Lady Warwick takes a broad view of the duties of a *chatelaine*, both at Warwick Castle, and at her own place, Easton Lodge, in Essex. She is on the Board of [Poor Law] Guardians of the former place. . . . Her interest in all matters affecting the welfare of women is sincere. . . . Of Society Lady Warwick is so brilliant an ornament that people are sometimes incredulous about her good works and her philanthropy, genuine as they are. She dresses in the best taste, dances beautifully, skates gracefully, and is never more charming than as a hostess, her fascinating manner agreeing well with her beautiful face and kindly eyes in expressing her hospitality. The Countess drives a four-in-hand with grace and skill, hunts regularly with the Warwick-shire and Essex packs, rides her bicycle about the country lanes, and gave . . . [in 1895] a wonderful fancy ball at Warwick Castle.

Country Life, 18 Sept., 1897, 286.

Country Life's flattering portrait of the Countess of Warwick depicts an archetypal upper-class society lady, as seen through the eyes of admiring contemporaries. Concern for dress and appearance, complemented by a display of the appropriate social graces, was combined for her, as for many others in her position, with involvement in philanthropy and communal responsibilities. Significantly, most charities at that time sought to have at least one titled lady on their management committee, and at a local level, as Consuelo Marlborough drily observed, there were always agricultural and horticultural shows to attend or prizes to distribute at nearby schools. 'The cinema star had not yet eclipsed the duchess and archaic welcomes were still in line.'[1]

Yet the account of Lady Warwick was a very selective version of the truth. It carefully ignored such delicate questions as her personal extravagance and her sexual entanglements, even though both provoked gossip and press comment at the time. In the 1890s her friendship with the Prince of Wales was notorious and a few years earlier her infatuation for Lord Charles Beresford had brought her to the brink of divorce.[2] On the eve of the First World War her financial difficulties were eventually to lead to some

A shooting luncheon at Easton Lodge, home of the Earl and Countess of Warwick, October 1895. H.R.H. the Prince of Wales stands in the middle; at this time Lady Warwick was one of his closest female companions. Other guests included Blanche, Countess of Rosslyn, Lady Warwick's widowed mother, Lord Rosslyn, her young half-brother, and her half-sister, Lady Angela Forbes. (Frances Countess of Warwick, *Life's Ebb and Flow*, 1929)

dubious money-making ventures, verging in one case at least on blackmail.[3] As she herself disarmingly admitted, 'Money is something I have never been able to keep.' Worth frocks were purchased in Paris at a hundred guineas each, 'and often his gowns were half as much again . . . For day gowns and lingerie one went to Doucet. I had my special saleswoman . . . at Doucet's.'[4] *Country Life*, however, preferred to ignore these weaknesses and to focus on the superficial attributes of beauty, charm, and graciousness which were deemed essential for a gentlewoman carrying through her role as a social arbiter and an amusing and congenial companion.

The then current 'separate spheres' view of society required women to 'cultivate their characters, minds and abilities for the benefit of those around them'. They were to 'adorn the home, and . . . bring order and harmony to it'.[5] Even if many did not live up to this ideal, all were expected to aspire to it:

> In her role as mistress of the household, a wife was responsible for presenting her establishment as a stage for the family's dealings with the world, for ensuring that the elaborate furnishings, meals and services needed to demonstrate conspicuous consumption were plentifully provided and ordered. Though a housekeeper might run everything, the lady of the house was ultimately responsible for its reputation . . . Participation in society was a serious, valid function which a woman could perform for her family; it could even become a career, to which she gave 'the same energy, devotion and work that a man [gave] to politics'.[6]

Sometimes the concern for family and status could led to unwelcome displays of vanity and pride. The young Lady Emily Lytton commented sharply on the way in which a cousin, Lady Derby, was 'fearfully annoyed if anyone seems to be above her. I think she treats Mother very rudely . . . and is always airing her great position as compared to Mother's. . . . The whole thing is very ludicrous. I do think ambition is the most absurd passion.'[7] The Derbys were one of the wealthiest landowning families in the country, and their principal seat, Knowsley, was among the four or five largest houses in the country.[8] Both of these facts doubtless contributed to Lady Derby's arrogance.

More common than this, however, was the women's anxiety to conform to the accepted rules of etiquette and to maintain appropriate social connections. Much emphasis was placed on apparently trivial matters like leaving visiting cards and paying calls. Without careful observances of such rituals, warned the anonymous author of the *Manners and Rules of Good Society* in 1910, 'intercourse between friends and acquaintances would be uncertain and chaotic'.[9] Card-leaving was a 'privilege' placed in the hands of 'ladies to govern . . . their acquaintanceships and intimacies, to regulate and decide whom they will . . . visit, whose acquaintance they wish further to cultivate and whose to discontinue'. Those who neglected this 'gate-keeping' role disrupted the smooth flow of social life. For as *Etiquette for Ladies* pointed out in 1900, 'good Society' was 'a complicated machine', and like all such machines it would not work 'smoothly and pleasantly unless every wheel and component part' were geared in with its surroundings. 'Hence many of those conventionalities which some sneer at, are founded on the common-sense views of the necessity of some uniform system of regulation.'[10]

So firm was the social discipline imposed that the need to be present at 'important' events during the Season overrode many of the women's own inclinations. Lady Warwick was 'bored to tears' by the 'stilted, expensive, extensive and over-elaborate garden parties that made up Ascot, and lasted for four days on end', but she still attended.[11] A reluctant Mary Gladstone similarly visited Ascot in 1880 and bemoaned in her diary both the tedium of the journey there and the dullness of the races themselves: '[They] only last 1 minute and about 6 hours between. . . . Lady Salisbury and the Bradfords in our pew, and it was terribly smart all mixed up with the Royalties . . . Got home with racking head, dined at Lucy's in misery, dressed, struggled to [a] party, and felt very sick and went to bed as bad as possible.'[12]

For those girls who were awkward and shy, the close intimacy of a country-house visit could create particular misery and embarrassment. At Knowsley in the autumn of 1893, eighteen-year-old Emily Lytton ruefully recognized that Lady Derby considered her 'very dull and spiritless and a great muff in all ways . . . and snaps a good deal at me. Although I only want to laugh, it does not make one feel happier.' Shortly after Emily and her mother prepared to move on to Lathom House, the home of another relative and a change which she anticipated with trepidation: 'I . . . dread beginning again in a new house.'[13] In the close confinement of a house-party it was easy for backbiting and ill-feeling to creep in among female members of the party, especially if the weather were bad and they had to stay indoors.

Another important female ritual was the 'At Home', when ladies were formally available to receive their friends. Molly Bell, later Lady Trevelyan, remembered that during the London Season her mother's 'At Home' day was on a Friday, from 4 p.m. She

Mary Gladstone in about 1880. (The author)

and her sister, Elsa, had to help pour out the tea and entertain the guests. 'Sometimes a dozen people would come, men as well as women. . . . These were the people whom we afterwards met at balls, or whom we invited to our balls.' But there was calculation as well as hospitality attached to the issuing of such invitations. Some people were asked to parties 'because we wanted to see them – some because we owed them an invitation, having already been to a party at their house. Some were invited because we thought it likely that they might be giving a dance to which we young people would like to be asked. There was a definite system between hostesses of inviting and being invited. The social phrase, "Cutlet for cutlet", was well understood and carefully followed.'[14]

Elsewhere, as with Lady Augustus Hervey, these encounters were a means of assessing the suitability of a potential marriage partner for a son or daughter. In March 1885, Lady Augustus told her second son, Frederick, that she was dining with Mrs Campbell of Craigie the following Friday because she had a 'daughter with money, growing up – & I want to see her for *you*. I have my attention quite fixed on such fiancées for you & Charlie', Charlie being her eldest son. A few days later she reported the result of the meeting. Mrs Campbell was a 'nice woman', but her son was probably unsuitable for Lady Augustus's daughter, Maria.

> *Yet* – we may have to take worse!! he is a bit of an ass – I did not see the girl as she is only 15 – but she is the £100,000-er! . . . Tomorrow I have another iron in the fire – I

am going with Mrs Gladstone the Curate's Wife by train over to 'Firle' – to make the acquaintance of Mrs Gage – but *really* to see the place & take stock of her son Lord Gage & see if he might do for Maria![15]

For those women who were mistresses of a large town household and of one or two establishments in the country, the domestic duties and responsibilities attached to their position were considerable. With the help of senior servants, the migrations of family and staff from home to home had to be arranged, as well as the recruitment of additional temporary servants when needed. Someone said of the Earl of Derby that he was a man 'who had eight houses and no home', for he and the Countess rarely spent more than ten or eleven weeks in a year even at Knowsley, their principal seat.[16] They were also surrounded by relations and dependants, who had to be accommodated, and by an indoor staff of thirty-eight domestic servants, who had to be directed and controlled. Their lavish style of living is confirmed by the fact that before the First World War household expenditure amounted to nearly fifty thousand pounds a year.[17] All of this it was Lady Derby's duty to oversee.

Once the family had settled into its new location there were such routine matters to deal with as the drawing up of menus, in consultation with the housekeeper or the cook, and the allocating of rooms to guests. Julian Lady Radnor went each morning to discuss domestic matters with the housekeeper and to approve the day's menus with the cook,

Lady Leconfield at around the time of the First World War. Even in old age she remained a central figure in the life of her family. In 1911, her daughter-in-law, Gladys, asked her advice on pension arrangements for a former caretaker at her London town house. 'It would be *very* kind if you would arrange whatever you think best & let me know who I pay the money to,' Gladys told her. (Lord Egremont and Mrs P. Gill, Archivist, West Sussex Record Office)

while at Petworth, Lady Leconfield and her youngest daughter, Maggie, attended to many day-to-day household details.[18] In Lady Violet Greville's view, a large country house resembled a popular hotel, with people arriving and departing every day. In many cases, including Leigh Court near Bristol, a visitors' book was kept which each person signed and against which the number of the room allocated was noted.[19] While at Kingston Lacy in Dorset such details as the times of arrival and departure of the post, the times of meals for guests and servants, and the cost of hiring a fly from the Station Hotel at Wimborne were prominently displayed. Breakfast for family and guests was served at 10 a.m., for example, but for 'shooters' at 9 a.m., while luncheon was at 1.30 p.m, tea at 4.30 p.m. and dinner at 8 o'clock.

Sometimes, as Mary Curzon discovered, there were also problems when expected guests failed to arrive at dinner-parties or country-house weekends, and thereby upset the numerical or gender balance of the guests. On 17 July, 1896, the Curzons had invited twenty-four guests to dinner, but three of these failed to appear on the night, even though they had accepted the invitation. Five nights later, they had another dinner party to which they had originally asked sixty-one people. Twenty accepted, but one failed to attend. In her Dinner Invitation Notebook Mary excused the numerous refusals on the grounds that she had only issued the invitations a week before the dinner was to be held – a quite inadequate notice, given the full social programme arranged by hostesses during the Season.[20]

Among less fashionable or less wealthy chatelaines domestic preoccupations were carried still farther. At Hodnet Hall, Shropshire, Gladys Heber Percy not only ran the house but the gardens and the stables as well. Each day after breakfast orders were given to the various heads of department in her office and menus were discussed with the cook. The stud-groom was told which horses and ponies were needed for riding, and which young horses were to be broken in. 'There were guests to be met at the station. The head housemaid must get the oak room and dressing-room ready . . . The head gardener must supply flowers for the house, fruit and vegetables.' Stores were ordered by the crate from Harrods and were issued once weekly. Mrs Heber Percy would also go to her husband's study while he was interviewing the estate agent to ascertain if there were a pig ready for slaughtering, or to inform him that more fuel was required or more fodder for the horses.[21]

Towards the end of the nineteenth century the development of the 'aesthetic movement' under the influence of William Morris and his disciples encouraged a few fashionable women to take up 'housekeeping from an artistic point of view'. Leading Society figures like Madeline Wyndham and her friends busied themselves with table settings and the redecorating of their homes, 'collecting fabrics on their foreign travels and cutting up chair and sofa covers for their servants to sew'.[22] Madeline's daughter, Pamela Tennant, whose father-in-law, Sir Charles Tennant, was an immensely wealthy Scottish businessman, followed her mother's interests. She, too, purchased William Morris chintzes and carpets and, from time to time, indulged her whim for 'the simple life' as advocated by Morris. Sometimes she made jam, or sprinkled grain for the chickens, or dead-headed the roses in the garden, but the presence of a substantial staff of indoor and outdoor servants ensured that she need only exert herself when she wanted to. In her fantasy of the simple life she also took her children caravanning down the lanes near their Wiltshire home, 'and made fairy stories real for them'.[23]

But most ladies regarded this kind of detailed domesticity as too dull to occupy their attention for long. Certainly that was true of frivolous socialites like Lady Sitwell, who rarely rose before midday and spent the morning reading newspapers, writing letters and considering what to wear.[24] Lady Annesley, too, enjoyed the pleasures of London society and was bored by the daily round on her husband's Irish estate at Castlewellan. When resident there she would walk for miles over the surrounding countryside in order to escape its confining atmosphere. Her principal consolation was the correspondence she sent and received and which kept her in touch with friends and admirers in the outside world. According to her daughter, her letters were 'the backbone of her life at Castlewellan'.[25] The fact that she was a second wife and got on badly with some of the domestic staff, especially the butler, added to her difficulties. 'He made my mother's life hell,' her daughter wrote, years later. 'He did everything in his power to annoy her – and she, in her impetuous ignorance, did everything to offend his idea of fitness.'[26]

Where there were young children in the family their welfare, too, had to be taken into account, although at this level of society day-to-day responsibility for them was normally delegated to the nursery staff and the governess rather than taken by the mother. Motherhood was not considered a major part of the society woman's life, since the physical and emotional care of young children was 'a distraction from the more important business of wider family and social duties'. Hence the comment in *Lady's Realm* in 1909 concerning Lady Beauchamp and her children. Although she apparently preferred their company and the pleasant surroundings of her gardens at Madresfield and Elmley House to 'the amusements of London life', as a member of the Grosvenor family she was aware that she must not shirk her broader responsibilities:

> had it not been for the death of her little nephew . . . the series of political entertainments planned for the weeks following the opening of Parliament would have taken place . . . These are, however, only postponed, and will be resumed early in the season.[27]

Such social preoccupations could easily create a barrier between mothers and their children. Lady Emily Lytton felt inhibited from telling her mother of her problems. Instead she confided in an elderly clergyman friend of her late grandfather. As a child Emily said that she:

> resented bitterly my helplessness, my dependence, the fact that so many people in the shape of nurses and grown-ups stood between me and my mother, and that no child was believed, or treated with respect.[28]

Relations between the 6th Earl of Carnarvon and his mother were still more fraught. This may have been compounded by the fact that the Countess's own antecedents were somewhat dubious. She was the illegitimate daughter of Alfred de Rothschild and on her marriage to the 5th Earl her father had not only provided a substantial dowry of about half a million pounds but had paid off her husband's debts, which themselves amounted

A FILIAL REPROOF.

Mamma (to Noel, who is inclined to be talkative). "HUSH NOEL! HAVEN'T I TOLD YOU OFTEN THAT LITTLE BOYS SHOULD BE *SEEN* AND NOT *HEARD?*"
Noel. "YES, MAMMA! BUT YOU DON'T *LOOK* AT ME!"

Maternal indifference to the feelings of the children is pinpointed by *Punch* in 1896 in this picture of a socialite at home.

to about £150,000.[29] Her son's clearest childhood recollection of her treatment of him arose from a visit he paid as a small boy to a Buckingham Palace garden party given by King Edward VII and Queen Alexandra. In his excitement he inadvertently ran into the King and knocked him over. He then compounded this gaffe by accidentally dropping a raspberry ice on the white satin dress of the King's granddaughter, Princess Mary. As soon as his mother learnt of the mishaps she bore down upon him in fury, seized him by the arm and dragged him to the Palace entrance where her carriage was waiting.

> I was thrust inside to receive the first instalment of her anger. It was the fashion at that time to wear very pointed shoes and throughout the journey . . . my mother never for a second left off kicking me in the shins. During the performance she punctuated her pent up fury with such expressions as, 'You little beast' – kick – 'you disgraceful boy' – kick – 'you shamed me today' – kick.
> By the time we reached the front door of our house, I was sobbing.

Lady Carnarvon gave orders that her son was to be kept in solitary confinement in an attic room for forty-eight hours and was to be fed nothing but bread and milk. The following morning two incidents took place about which he learnt nothing until years later. The first was that Princess Mary sent a note, enclosing a jade paper knife, and stating that she hoped the little boy had not been too upset over the accident to her dress.

The second was the arrival of a carriage from Buckingham Palace, containing a sack of toys and a message from the King, hoping that the mishap had not marred his enjoyment of the afternoon. 'My mother, however, never allowed me to see the toys and they were despatched forthwith to a children's hospital.'[30]

To the Earl, these incidents exemplified the 'great gulf between my parents and me and give some insight into the life of an aristocratic family at the turn of the century.' Even at Christmas he and his sister were mostly in the company of their nanny and the other servants. Gifts were delivered to the nanny for inclusion in their stockings, but they were chosen with little regard for the youngsters' tastes. After luncheon they might be sent for to be shown off briefly to the house guests, but were then dismissed 'so that the adults could get down to a serious game of cards'.[31]

This lack of enthusiasm for maternal duties was confirmed by Lady Warwick. She frankly admitted that although she and her friends were 'good mothers . . . [we] preferred to keep our children young, for the younger generation, we knew, would date us. Time was the one thing we could not control, and consequently it had power to inspire us with fear.'[32]

Happily, however, there were many women, like Florence Bell, Molly's mother, Consuelo Marlborough and Cecilia Carrington who enjoyed close relations with their children and spent as much time as they could with small sons and daughters. This meant not merely having them brought down by the nanny to the drawing-room during the 'Children's Hour' at around tea-time, but sharing in their games and pastimes. Molly's mother read aloud for hours to her three offspring, and played cards, dominoes, and cat's cradle with them. She wrote small dramas for them to act and from time to time played duets with her daughters on the piano. When they were ill she nursed them.[33]

Years later, Molly herself continued this tradition of personal involvement in the children's upbringing. At Wallington, the Trevelyans' family seat in Northumberland, charming examples of her needlework still hang on the nursery walls. One embroidered panel, dated 1908/9, depicts the nursery rhyme 'Hey-diddle-diddle, the cat and the fiddle', etc., and shows three Trevelyan children standing in the courtyard at Wallington watching the cow jumping over the moon, and the dish running away with the spoon. When they were older, there were parties, dancing, games and charades, in which Molly would take part, playing 'vigorously and untiringly' on the piano for the country dances.[34]

The Duchess of Marlborough also seized every opportunity to be with her children, especially at Blenheim Palace. When possible they joined their parents for luncheon, and if she had no engagements in the afternoon she would take them for drives in her electric car. 'They learned to wield a cricket bat and also how to box. In the evenings, dressed in velvet suits, they came down to tea and I read to them or we played games of the Old Maid variety . . . But the best part of the day came at six when together we went to the nursery, where a bath and supper awaited them; then they said their prayers as I tucked them into bed.'[35] Consuelo regretted that the presence of the governess, the head nurse and the groom, with whom they rode out on their ponies, meant there was 'little time left for mother'.

Lady Carrington interspersed a busy social round in London during the Season with periodic visits to her youngest children at Wycombe Abbey, where they spent much of

The Duchess of Marlborough with her younger son, Lord Ivor Charles Churchill, in the summer of 1901. (*The Tatler*, 21 August, 1901.) (British Library Newspaper Library)

the time with their nanny. The older girls, who were in London, went with her to dancing classes and French lessons conducted in the homes of friends. There were also such mundane matters as visits to the dentist.[36] Typical of the mixture of maternal and social duties is the entry in her diary for 23 June, 1892:

> Went to hear Maud Sullivan's Band play, & fetched the children from their French class at Mrs Bo Grosvenor's. The Prince of Wales dined here, & the Duke of York with CC [her husband] who asked Sir F. Leighton, Archy Campbell, the Duke of Fife, Lord Cork, Sir Julian Pauncefoot to meet HRH.[37]

It was with this social round in mind that Lady Cynthia Asquith lamented how during her youth her hospitable mother, Lady Elcho (later the Countess of Wemyss) never seemed free to enjoy the pleasures of her country house, Stanway, in the Cotswolds. Instead she was occupied with her various responsibilities as chatelaine of an attractive, although not particularly comfortable, mansion.

> [I]t is a fallacy to suppose that any woman who ran a large . . . country house ever had a *light* job. . . . True, the well-to-do hostess did not need to do any actual housework herself, for servants were easy to find. . . . But being human, however efficient and obliging, they always tended to quarrel with one another, so that domestic politics were often inflamed and very preoccupying. . . . Morning after morning I would find my mother what we called 'coping' – her breakfast tray pushed to one side, her bed littered with sheets . . . of paper scribbled all over with tangled plans for the day. . . . The plan of the bedrooms would be pored over until some way of packing fourteen guests into ten square rooms was devised. . . . Mamma never seemed . . . able to enjoy the immediate present. . . . I knew that she had a remarkable talent for drawing; but what with family, incessant village duties . . . visitors, neighbours and household, how seldom did she have a disengaged hour in which to exercise this talent, and how few books she managed to get through in a year.[38]

When royalty was to be entertained or important dinner- and house-parties arranged, the anxieties of the hostess were considerable. Even Lady Carrington, who had grown up in the ambience of the court and whose parents were members of the Prince and Princess of Wales's circle, was nervous on these occasions. In the autumn of 1894, while the Carringtons were in Scotland for the shooting, there was great excitement when Queen Victoria announced that she would be 'coming *to tea* at 5' in order to see Lady Carrington's youngest daughter, who was her godchild.

> We prepared the dining room as well as we could & the Indian servant [Queen Victoria's personal manservant] arrived early. Pss. Beatrice, Prince Henry & Prince Christian Victor arriv. at 5 p.m. walking & Her Majesty & Lady Ampthill & Count Mensdorff at 10 min. past 5. . . . The Queen very gracious & after tea asked for her godchild . . . I fetched the 3 children & dear little Baby stood at attention before the Queen for quite 5 min. & did everything she was told & gave the Queen her photograph & made a curtsey down to the ground. The Queen gave her a present of a

A visit by King Edward VII to Blenheim Palace in the early 1900s. (Oxfordshire Photographic Archive, Centre for Oxfordshire Studies)

doll, in a red box. . . . H.M. gave me a Balmoral tartan shawl & wrote her name in the [visitors'] book – leaving . . . at 6 o'clock.[39]

Less experienced or less well-connected hostesses found the strain far greater. Some, like May Harcourt, tried to obtain the aid of an older friend to help with the planning. 'I wrote to Mrs Russell at your suggestion about . . . the arrangements for the King's dinner but she said her engagements prevented her coming,' May told her step-mother-in-law, Lady Harcourt, in 1906. 'I think the dinner was a success except for the heat. . . . We played Bridge after – one long rubber which the King & I managed to pull off mercifully so it ended all right as H.M. hates losing.'[40]

A decade earlier Consuelo Marlborough was on tenterhooks when the Prince and Princess of Wales visited Blenheim, with other members of the royal family, for a shooting party. There were over a hundred people in the house, of whom thirty were guests, and as the party lasted from Monday to Saturday, Consuelo had the Prince as her neighbour for two lengthy meals throughout that period. This was an ordeal 'for one so unversed in the politics and gossip of the day as I was, since he liked to discuss the news and to hear the latest scandal'.

Frequent changes of dress were required – something which the young Duchess regarded with disfavour. Even breakfast, which was served in the dining-room at 9.30 a.m., called for an elegant outfit in velvet or silk.

> We next changed into tweeds to join the guns for luncheon, which was served in the High Lodge or in a tent. Afterwards we usually accompanied the guns and watched a drive or two before returning home. An elaborate tea gown was donned for tea, after which we played cards or listened to a Viennese band or to the organ until time to dress for dinner, when again we adorned ourselves in satin, or brocade, with a great display of jewels. All these changes necessitated a tremendous outlay, since one was not supposed to wear the same gown twice. That meant sixteen dresses for four days.

Small wonder that lady visitors were accompanied by mountains of monogrammed luggage.

Nor was this all. Much attention was paid to matters of protocol, and Consuelo recalled ruefully how on one occasion she was reproved by the Prince of Wales because she had attended a dinner in his honour, and that of the Princess, wearing a diamond crescent instead of the prescribed tiara. 'Luckily I could truthfully answer that I had been delayed by some charitable function in the country and that I had found the bank in which I kept my tiara closed on my arrival in London. But such an incident illustrates the . . . importance attached to the fastidious observance of ritual' was her tart conclusion.[41]

When entertaining large house-parties, mistresses of prestigious households had to ensure that their guests were pleasurably entertained, with excursions or other amusements arranged for those who did not go out with the 'guns'. For the dinners, menus with many courses were the order of the day.

> Two soups, one hot and one cold, were served simultaneously. Then came two fish, again one hot and one cold, with accompanying sauces. . . . An entrée was succeeded by a meat dish. Sometimes a sorbet preceded the game, which in the shooting season was varied, comprising grouse, partridge, pheasant, duck, woodcock and snipe. In the summer, when there was no game, we had quails from Egypt, fattened in Europe, and ortolans from France, which cost a fortune. An elaborate sweet followed, succeeded by a hot savoury with which was drunk . . . port . . . The dinner ended with a succulent array of peaches, plums, apricots, nectarines, strawberries, raspberries, pears and grapes, all grouped in generous pyramids among the flowers that adorned the table.[42]

The aim was to have the meal served within an hour. This was a feat which required a well-organized kitchen as well as efficient servants. At its end the hostess would rise and lead the ladies into the drawing-room or, at Blenheim Palace, into the Long Library, whilst the men remained behind to smoke their cigars.

One especially accomplished chatelaine was the Countess of Warwick. According to Elinor Glyn, the novelist wife of a minor Essex landowner, Easton Lodge in the 1890s was the centre of 'all that was most intelligent and amusing in the society of the day'. Lady Warwick's personal prestige and her close connections with the Prince of Wales made 'every invitation an honour, not lightly refused by those fortunate enough to receive it'. Lady Augusta Fane, another frequent visitor, recalled that special trains were kept in readiness at the nearest railway station to take those interested to race meetings, while in the winter, hunters were lent to all who desired to ride with the neighbouring packs. 'Breakfast started at 9 a.m. and finished at mid-day. Lunch faded into tea, and dinner – supposed to be at 8 p.m. – rarely commenced until an hour later.' Perhaps most disconcerting to the unwary guest was Lady Warwick's love of animals. According to Lady Augusta, the house was overrun with dogs and 'monkeys of all sizes leapt from chair to window-curtains, or from the tops of pictures on to the shoulders of alarmed visitors'.[43]

Unlike many large country houses in those days, Easton Lodge was always pleasantly warm and well lit. The guests' bedrooms were luxuriously appointed, with exquisite furniture and hangings, and comfortable armchairs and sofas. There were shaded lamps to make reading 'as you rested a joy . . . On little stands within easy reach of the sofa lay books of travel, biographies, and the talked-about new novels'.[44] Flowers were arranged on the dressing-tables and just before dinner Lady Warwick's eldest son would be sent to every lady's room with a magnificent spray of flowers for her corsage. The men each received a buttonhole.

After dinner, some of the guests elected to play bezique in the billiard-room, but most sat around on comfortable sofas and talked, or listened to one of the 'brilliant men who were always there'. There were opportunities to engage in discreet flirtations, which might subsequently develop into serious friendships. 'Easton Lodge,' wrote Elinor Glyn, ' . . . was the most delightful of all the houses in which we used to stay. Many others were larger, more stately, and possessed finer art treasures, but none of them had so enchanting and beautiful a hostess, or such absolute perfection of organization and comfort.'[45]

Women from less assured backgrounds than the Duchess of Marlborough and the Countess of Warwick sometimes entertained friends at their country house as a preliminary to embarking on a conquest of London Society. That was true of the American-born Lady Cunard. At Nevill Holt, her husband's Leicestershire home, the new friends she wished to impress were cosseted and entertained. From this base she advanced to become a leading figure on the London scene. In the process she left her staid, sports-loving husband and their only child behind in the country, for she had little taste for the pleasures of motherhood or of rural life. 'My picture of Holt is one of constant arrivals and departures during half the year,' wrote her daughter, Nancy, years later: ' . . . beautiful and exciting ladies moved about in smart tailor-mades; . . . Summer-long, in shot silk and striped taffeta they strolled laughing and chatting across the lawns.'[46] As at Easton Lodge, there were romantic encounters between the guests, with Lady Cunard herself playing an active part. Her long-standing liaison with the conductor, Sir Thomas Beecham, was notorious. But there was also much good conversation, which the hostess promoted by her own 'airy, fantastic wit . . . [T]he times at Holt evoke words like "spacious, comfortable and leisurely".'[47]

Even pregnancy rarely interrupted the routine of most of these women. Only when a miscarriage was feared or some other illness threatened did they normally withdraw from the social scene. Victoria Sackville-West suffered severe discomfort during her menstrual periods from youth until late middle age, but apart from spending the first day of each cycle in bed, she normally carried on, despite feeling generally weak for several days.[48] Consuelo Marlborough even attended the famous fancy-dress ball held at Devonshire House in Queen Victoria's Diamond Jubilee year when she was about seven months' pregnant. She stayed on until the early hours of the morning before walking back through Green Park to Spencer House, where she and her husband were then living, as dawn broke.[49]

May Harcourt, too, continued many of her usual activities whilst expecting her children despite feeling 'seedy' on occasion. 'We had a very pleasant week at Wynyard,' she told her step-mother-in-law in late October, 1901. ' . . . Saturday we help to marry the Gladstone–Paget parties & then go to Venetia James for Sunday. Monday I go to the Hay–Waring marriage & Wednesday we go to the Lockwoods for 2 days shooting.'[50] Her second daughter was born just over five months later. Most of these wives seem to have accepted Lady Diana Cooper's maxim that to complain of illness was 'common'. Only housemaids had pains![51]

But if women's importance as social arbiters was generally recognized, from an early age they had to accept two other, less palatable, facts of life. The first was the need to acquire 'accomplishments' which would smooth their entry into the adult world and ensure that they married speedily and well. Lady Violet Greville expressed the common view when she pronounced that marriage was 'the chief end and object of the Gentlewoman in Society', not merely on social grounds but on economic ones, too:

> Owing to those arrangements whereby daughters as a rule are but slenderly portioned, and professional occupations are out of the question, married life remains [the] only possible goal. . . . The existence of an aristocratic spinster, accustomed from earliest youth to every luxury and comfort, and turned out in middle age to endure grinding poverty and wearisome idleness, is . . . most pitiable. She must either lead a very cramped, lonely, and uncongenial life, or resign herself to a state of dependence which to an active mind must prove intensely galling and repugnant.[52]

She claimed to know unmarried women of forty who had no income beyond a meagre dress allowance and who were unable to travel or to engage in any independent activities without special permission from their relatives. But even younger spinsters could experience rejection. Amalia Sackville-West lived with her father, Lord Sackville, her married sister, Victoria, and her brother-in-law at Knole, the splendid Sackville mansion in Kent. But she was unhappily aware that she was in the way and that even her father found her uninteresting compared to her brilliant elder sister. On one occasion she confessed sadly to Victoria that she felt 'loved by no one'. She eventually left home in 1896 when she was in her late twenties, with an income of about £270 a year. Her niece remembered her as a 'vinegary spinster' but eventually she married a French diplomat, after what must have been a lonely and embittered youth.[53]

In these circumstances it was small wonder that mothers were concerned to ensure that their daughters were settled in life, even if this meant braving the 'hot oppressive mazes of the London ballroom' or pursuing a potential son-in-law to 'Cowes, Germany, and the country house'.[54] Efforts to secure a particularly eligible bachelor could give rise to many sharp rivalries.

Some unmarried daughters, in the meantime, were given the task of deputising for their mother in carrying out philanthropic or other duties. Rosalind Countess of Carlisle regularly despatched her daughter, Dorothy, to investigate the eligibility of cottage families for charitable aid. 'My mother did not . . . carry out her charities by personal visiting,' observed Dorothy. 'It was done by lieutenants: . . . There were visits for the purpose of taking stock – was the house clean and tidy? There were visits on which we [her brother, Michael and herself] presented one blanket, or two, or my father's oldest suit, or tea, or an order on the grocer, or an order for milk . . . In course of time Michael flatly refused to go on any more charitable errands, and thenceforth I went alone.'[55]

The duties of Lady Jersey's daughters included writing letters for their father – a task made difficult by his habit of making false starts as well as by his uncertain temper. Their mother also insisted that her second daughter, Mary, accompany her on afternoon drives, despite the fact that she was often carriage-sick.[56]

A second unpalatable realization for girls was that they were considered biologically

A river boating party, June 1901. Molly Bell (the future Lady Trevelyan) stands second from the right, facing the camera. On the extreme left is Jack Pollock, later Sir Jack, 4th baronet, historian, author and journalist. In the centre, stooping slightly, stands Francis Henley, later 6th Baron Henley. (The Trustees of the Trevelyan Family Papers)

inferior to the menfolk. Any suggestions that the sexes could be intellectually equal were greeted with considerable hostility. As *The Manners of the Aristocracy*, an etiquette manual published in the 1880s, firmly pointed out: 'A woman cannot learn too early that her first social duty is *never to be in the way*.'[57]

This gender bias was manifested in some families during infancy. Lady Constance Annesley discovered that at her birth her mother had hoped for a son; hence the little girl's arrival was 'a bitter disappointment'.[58] Helena Brabazon congratulated her nephew, the future 4th Marquess of Bristol, on the birth of his first child in October 1898, but then added: 'I fear you will be a little disappointed that it is not an heir. The next will fulfil your desires and make you both happy.'[59] In the event, there was to be no heir and the title subsequently passed to the Marquess's younger brother.

May Harcourt likewise in October 1905 reported that 'Bridie Stavordale' was 'the proud possessor of a son & heir & they are all off their heads with joy. I am *so* glad for her.' Pauline Clay 'on the other hand has a girl'.[60] May herself was destined to bear three daughters before the much-desired heir appeared in 1908.

Sometimes, as with Lord Esher's two daughters, parents' preferences were demonstrated in a particularly painful fashion. Sylvia, the youngest child, confessed that from the time she could think she had been obsessed by the idea she was unwanted. Her mother had eyes only for her husband, who was 'the substance and body of her existence, her *raison d'être*'. She stood meekly in his shadow and allowed herself to merge into the background. In the meantime Sylvia and her sister, Dorothy, were made aware that:

> women were only brought into the world to become the slaves of men. Every morning it was our duty to lace up our brothers' boots, so that even now I can never look at any little boy with that particular footwear without having an intense desire to smack his . . . bottom. . . . It even seemed to me that my father's voice altered when he spoke to me, as if he were forcing his words through cubes of ice.[61]

The general acceptance of girls' intellectual inferiority was reflected in the education they received. Serious scholarship was eschewed. Instead emphasis was laid on such 'accomplishments' as learning to play the piano, to speak a little French and German, to acquire a superficial knowledge of history and geography, and to learn to draw and paint. They were to play 'a sort of waiting game until the right (or wrong) man came along'.[62] In the early 1890s the young American heiress, Consuelo Vanderbilt, later the Duchess of Marlborough, was surprised to discover how scanty was the knowledge of the Marquess of Lansdowne's younger daughter, when they compared notes on the books they were reading:

> It was still customary for [English girls] to have, sometimes inherited from a previous generation . . . a 'good homespun' governess. They read Miss Young's (sic) *History of Greece*, but Virgil, Gibbon, Hallam and Green were all equally unknown to them. I pitied the limited outlook given by so restricted an education. . . . Later . . . I was to find that English girls suffered many handicaps, and I came to realize that it was considered fitting that their interests should be sacrificed to the more important prospects of the heir.[63]

Molly Bell, another victim of this kind of superficial instruction, would have agreed with many of Consuelo's strictures. When she discovered that a friend had managed to get to Cambridge she decided to see if she could follow suit. But once she obtained a copy of the syllabus of studies for Girton College she realized it was impossible. 'I could never make up for the years I had lost in the schoolroom learning nothing. All I could do *now*, at the age of eighteen, was to read the great literature of our country, as well as that of France and Germany.'[64] Although she and her sister loved their parents, when it came to lessons she was 'bored all the time, except when our mother came in to teach us music and French, or when we learnt History with Gertrude [her step-sister]'. During the Season the girls accompanied their mother to London and were able to attend lectures at Queen's College in Harley Street, when they were fifteen and sixteen, respectively. But Molly's weak academic background meant she derived little benefit from them. Years later she recalled wryly that her mother's

> idea of the equipment required for her two daughters was that we should be turned out as good wives and mothers and be able to take our part in the social life of our kind. We must speak French and German perfectly and be on friendly if not intimate terms with Italian. We must be able to play the piano and sing a bit, we must learn to dance well and know how to make small talk. . . . The more serious side of education did not take any part in the plans my mother made for us. Science, mathematics, political economy, Greek and Latin – there was no need for any of these. No girl that we knew was trained for any career or profession, nor did girls of our class go to school.[65]

The young Molly Bell at a metalworking bench in her workshop at Red Barns, Redcar, the Bell family home, *c.* 1901. She continued to pursue the hobby in later life, working in silver and copper, as well as doing furniture repairs, upholstery and needlework. (Trustees of the Trevelyan Family Papers)

Those females who did break through class and gender stereotypes and insisted on taking up a career were regarded as unfeminine and unnatural. When Lady Constance Lytton began to review books for various newspapers and to write articles for a women's paper, her younger sister, Emily, was shocked. 'I cannot myself understand how she can bring herself down to such a level. If there was any real necessity and we were starving, I can understand sacrificing one's pride for the sake of one's family, but when there is not the smallest necessity, as there certainly is not in Con's case, I could not bring myself to associate with such a vulgar paper.'[66] It did not occur to her that her sister was simply anxious to develop her journalistic talents. In the event, as Constance admitted ruefully years later, these literary initiatives 'finding no favour, had . . . eventually to be repressed'. In her late thirties she found herself with 'neither equipment, training nor inclination' to lead an independent life.[67] It was in this mood that she discovered the women's suffrage movement and became a committed suffragette – thereby arousing further family hostility.[68]

The objections to girls seeking academic outlets were bolstered by current medical opinion, which warned mothers of adolescent daughters not to allow them to 'dissipate their "feminine" energies' by undertaking serious study. Both mental and physical exertions were held to damage womanly functions. An educated girl would 'unbalance her resources so that she would be unable . . . to nurse her children successfully', just as an athletic girl would become 'spare and thin or overmuscular, but in any case misshapen'.[69] In October 1891 these concerns were voiced by Mrs Lynn Linton in an article in the *Nineteenth Century*. In it she condemned girls' growing participation in 'violent' sports like golf, cricket and hunting – this last indicating 'an absolutely unwomanly indifference to death and suffering'.[70] The so-called 'rational dress' which many sportswomen favoured was also criticized, with divided skirts for cycling, shirt-waist blouses, and boaters.[71] Such attire did not conform to the desired image of a demure, biddable young female, anxious to please her elders.

In financial matters most women were dependent on their family, and particularly on its male members, for support. This became a particular problem in landed circles when incomes fell during the years of agricultural depression at the end of the nineteenth century. One victim was Mary Elizabeth Lucy of Charlecote Park, Warwickshire. When her son's rental income declined in the 1880s and he had a number of farms untenanted, she jokingly claimed that she was 'quite a pauper widow, for I can get no money, as my son has 9 Farms on his hands, and gets little or no rents from those that are let'.[72] The Lucy family remained short of cash up to, and beyond, Mary Elizabeth's death in 1889.

Even some women with ample marriage settlements or private means, like the American-born Elizabeth Harcourt, second wife of the leading Liberal politician, Sir William Harcourt, felt it necessary to apologize to their husbands for incurring extra expenditure. Elizabeth was taking a 'cure' at Harrogate. 'I have ascertained that my whole expenses will be £12. 8. 6 a week, that is, board, lodging & maid,' she told Sir William in the summer of 1902. 'This can be reduced 10/- a day by giving up the sitting room . . . but living alone . . . it is much pleasanter to have it . . . Dearest I feel a great humbug & hate this expense for myself.'[73] However, in her case the cash was available and economies were unnecessary.

Nevertheless, a growing number of younger women were becoming impatient with this 'derivative' female role and were demonstrating an increasing willingness to assert themselves. This took the form not only of efforts to earn money on their own account or, more rarely, to enter the professions, but in a readiness to engage in the outdoor sports so deplored by Mrs Lynn Linton and her friends. Already in 1892, Lady Violet Greville was attributing the growing unpopularity of tight-lacing to the energetic lifestyles of modern girls. 'Women cannot ride all day in a tight habit, or row, if their lungs are impeded, or walk uphill and use a gun, . . . or wield a salmon rod, unless they are perfectly at their ease.'[74] According to Lady Violet, fashionable young women hunted, rode, or skated all winter, played tennis and danced during the London Season, and in the autumn went to a bathing-place, where they swam or played tennis for several hours a day. Later on they migrated to Scotland, where they walked over the moors with the grouse-shooters or sat beside friends during partridge drives, occasionally trying their hand at a shot.[75]

In the late 1890s the Marchioness of Londonderry remembered the popularity of bicycle riding, with invitations to house-parties encouraging guests to bring their machines. 'Society travelled about with footmen in those days – it really was a necessity,

The enthusiasm for bicycling in the 1890s promoted the sale of special bicycling costumes – as in this advertisement in *The Queen* of 5 June, 1897. (British Library Newspaper Library)

in order to clean the bicycles that the visitors brought with them . . . You rode with consummate skill up and down grass slopes and banks, round fountains and flower-beds.'[76] Bicycling was especially important in giving girls both exercise and independence, since it was not possible to have the otherwise inevitable chaperon in tow on a bicycle ride. It also encouraged the wearing of lighter and looser clothing.

For older women, gardening increased in popularity, even if the hardest tasks were normally performed by the paid garden staff. Lady Tweedsmuir remembered older friends and relatives out among the flower beds with hands 'stoutly gloved for tying up of roses' and with a wide gardening hat on their head.[77] But most of them confined their activities to dead-heading the roses and pinks, and discussing with the head gardener the plants they wished to have set, or the changes in lay-out to be introduced.

According to *Lady's Realm* many of these sporting activities also served a useful purpose by bringing together country neighbours. Whereas in the mid-Victorian years ladies had relied on afternoon calls and occasional hunting excursions as a way of meeting acquaintances, by the early twentieth century that was no longer necessary.[78] Hunting, golfing, bicycling and motoring all encouraged friends to gather informally and to exchange greetings and gossip.

Among the 'new women' were Mary Elizabeth Lucy's granddaughters at Charlecote. Although their grandmother had distinct reservations about their activities and also about the 'masculine' fashions of hard hats, collars, and ties which they favoured, the girls themselves enjoyed their freedom to play tennis, to go fishing, to take part in ladies' cricket matches, and to attend picnics on the river, wearing straw 'boaters' and strumming banjos.[79]

In achieving financial independence, however, the women's advances were far slower. Nonetheless, even here some of them were able to use their ingenuity to earn a livelihood as writers or, more rarely, as proprietors of their own businesses.

Gertrude Blood, who as Lady Colin Campbell was to be involved in a notorious divorce case in the mid-1880s, was one such pioneer. Not only was she an accomplished singer, who gave many charitable recitals, and a painter who frequently exhibited her work, but she was also a talented writer. Her literary career began in the early 1870s when at the age of fourteen she published an article in *Cassell's Magazine*. Other works followed and in 1878 a short children's novel entitled *Topo, a Tale about English Children in Italy* appeared. It proved one of the most popular juvenile books of its day. Significantly when Lady Colin's marriage broke down it was as an author and editor that she was able to earn her living. In 1889 she became arts editor of the popular society magazine, the *World*, and late in 1894 she helped to found a weekly journal called the *Realm*. It paid especial attention to the doings of High Society but also covered the arts and other topics of general interest. Although it soon ceased publication Lady Colin was undaunted. Not only did her own literary output continue, but in 1901 she became editor of *Ladies' Field*. She resigned from this post in 1903 on grounds of ill-health and died eight years later, having been confined to a wheelchair for the last five years of her life.[80]

Another exception to the accepted view of female economic dependence was Victoria Sackville-West, who subsequently became Lady Sackville. As her grandson has recorded, from an early stage she was the family's strategist, speculating successfully on the Stock Exchange when money was short and opening a shop in London called Spealls. This sold lamp-stands, stationery and knick-knacks suitable for presents. Despite her eccentric management it proved popular. However, if her friends were slow to pay their bills or attempted to return goods they did not want, as they would have in an ordinary shop, she regarded this as a personal affront. One of her elderly admirers, Sir John Murray Scott, also subsidized the running of Knole, the family seat, and by the time he died in 1912 had provided £84,000 for this. In London he purchased a house in Hill Street for the Sackville-Wests to use during the Season, and Victoria was able to borrow a carriage from him when she needed it.[81] It was through her persuasiveness, drive and initiative that the family kept its financial head above water.

Elinor Glyn and her sister, Lady Duff-Gordon, likewise proved the mainstay of their respective households when their husbands ran into difficulties. Elinor became a prolific writer from the beginning of the 1900s. In 1907 her book *Three Weeks*, with its account of adulterous love, scandalized reviewers but became an enormous popular success. Within nine years it had sold two million copies and although its publication led, for a time, to Elinor's exclusion from High Society, the ban proved only temporary.[82] A year after its appearance she discovered that her husband's health was failing and that he was in dire financial straits, having spent his capital and begun to borrow heavily. She devoted her savings, and also signed away her marriage settlement, to keep him from bankruptcy, and for the next seven years was the family bread-winner.[83] Her sister, who had gone into business as a dress designer in the 1890s, trading under the name of 'Lucile', was equally successful in her career. According to *Lady's Realm*, by 1909 she was 'not only . . . the most enterprising dressmaker in London, but . . . an artist in her own particular line . . . she has had more influence upon fashions in London than any one else of her generation. . . . She is a personal friend of nearly all the smart women whom she dresses'.[84]

Another aristocratic entrepreneur was Lady Angela Forbes, half-sister of the Countess of Warwick, who ran a florist's shop. When a large fancy dress ball was thrown at Claridge's in May 1911 by Lord Winterton and the leading Conservative politician and lawyer, F.E. Smith, it was Lady Angela's shop that supplied the floral decorations.[85]

There is little doubt that Lady Sackville, Lady Duff-Gordon and Lady Angela Forbes used their social contacts to promote their business interests. Other women faced with a cash crisis turned those social contacts into more direct monetary benefit by becoming what were known as 'social godmothers'. It was an approach recommended by *Lady's Realm* and the *Tatler*, among others. In an article on 'Incomes for Ladies' the former magazine suggested that women of 'position' should 'let it be known that they are ready to take young girls in hand, initiate them into the complexities of the social code, give them opportunities of exercising these arts in social gatherings', and in this way find 'lucrative employment'. According to the author there were already 'ladies who procure introductions and other valuable privileges to wealthy clients – and who also . . . bring together the rich and socially inferior, and the poor and well-born'.[86] The *Tatler* also suggested that ladies in the upper ranks of society who were anxious to have the use of a motor-car might be able to borrow one in return for introducing 'well-to-do people struggling to obtain a foothold' in High Society to some of their friends.[87]

One woman who used her contacts in this calculating fashion was Lady Augustus Hervey, sister-in-law to the 3rd Marquess of Bristol. She was perennially short of money and when she decided to bring out her daughter in 1885 she agreed to introduce the Gilstrap family to society, in return for the offer of accommodation in London and the provision of some of the court regalia she and her daughter needed to attend the Queen's Drawing-Room. 'Did I tell you that old Gilstrap paid our court trains and [Maria's] ball dress . . . The *bill* shut him up,' Lady Augustus informed her second son, Frederick. A month or two earlier she had triumphantly recounted that the Gilstraps had 'asked us to go for a "few days" to Grosvenor St. – & I have accepted – so far so good. As a set off I am going in company with Mr & Mrs Gilstrap to the Drawing-room! but will get the Bristols to send us in their carriage.'[88]

Subsequently Lady Augustus mentioned an American-born acquaintance named Mrs Ronalds who added to her income by arranging 'lets' of aristocratic London town houses to wealthy Americans. Lady Augustus suggested that her son, now 4th Marquess of Bristol, should use Mrs Ronalds' services to secure a letting of his own unwanted town house: 'it's *certainty* if she undertakes it that she *will* do it.'[89] But the Marquess preferred to persevere with his existing conventional agents, and as a result the house remained untenanted.

Other Americans, such as Consuelo Duchess of Manchester, Lady Randolph Churchill, and Minnie, Lady Paget, took on a 'social godmother' role in return for rewards in cash and kind. It was Lady Paget who brought out Consuelo Vanderbilt in the 1890s and who firmly informed Mrs Vanderbilt that her daughter must be able to compete 'at least as far as clothes are concerned with far better-looking girls'. Tulle had to give way to satin, the 'baby *décolletage* to a more generous display of neck and arms, naïveté to sophistication. Lady Paget was adamant.'[90] The Duchess of Manchester took up her sponsorship role when her husband was declared a bankrupt after he had succeeded to the title, while a decline in the fortunes of Leonard Jerome, Lady Randolph's father, led to a sharp reduction in the cash he remitted to her and her two sisters and made money-making ventures desirable.

Some of the more determined or avaricious women took this commercial exploitation of their aristocratic links to extreme. The *Realm* in March 1895 condemned an advertisement which had appeared in a weekly paper announcing that: 'A lady in the smartest society in London wishes to chaperone a young lady. Terms £1,000 for one year. Highest references given and required.'[91] But a more common reaction by impecunious insiders was to sponsor the *nouveaux riches* in return for gifts of carriages, accommodation, or payments to charity in their name. Others simply used the money to pay dressmakers' bills.

On rare occasions these campaigns went disastrously wrong. Of none was that more true than of Lady Ida Sitwell. As a result of her notorious extravagance her husband had reluctantly settled a number of heavy debts on several occasions. But by 1911, despite all promises to reform, she was again in debt for the substantial sum of £2,000. Through a friend of her elder son she became involved with a dubious American-born financier who agreed to help. He knew a Miss Dobbs, who was both eccentric and extremely rich, and who wished to enter 'good society'. She was in return prepared to lend Lady Ida £6,000 at 5 per cent interest for a limited period of about six months. This was agreed to, although by the time the middle-men had taken their cut, Lady Sitwell received far less than the £6,000 for which she was responsible. Once embarked upon this course, she found it impossible to deviate. By the spring of 1912 she faced a growing mountain of debt and deception. On one occasion she appealed in desperation to her American adviser, Julian Field:

> Is it not possible to get hold of this woman you told me about? Of course, I will do everything in my power to get her into the society she requires. That lies in the hollow of my hands . . .[92]

In another case an improvident young Yorkshire cricketer named Wilson agreed to guarantee a loan of £4,000 for her in return for an outright payment of £300 and a promise to persuade her brother, the Earl of Londesborough, to propose him for membership of the prestigious Marlborough Club.[93]

As a consequence of these activities Lady Sitwell had become liable for debts amounting to £12,000 by July 1912 and was facing threats of exposure from Field, who had added blackmail to his money-lending pursuits. Although her husband, Sir George Sitwell, agreed to settle some of the debts he refused to deal with that involving Miss Dobbs because of the irregular way in which it had been arranged. This led in March 1915 to Lady Ida appearing at the Old Bailey charged with conspiring to defraud Miss Dobbs. She was found guilty and, with her reputation in shreds, was sentenced to three months' imprisonment in Holloway.[94] Happily, very few 'social godmothers' found themselves in such a desperate plight.

For a small group of gently born but impecunious members of the aristocracy a position at Court might be secured as a means of livelihood as well as status. Susan Baring was one such beneficiary. Her family had been hit by the financial disasters experienced by the merchant banking firm of Baring Brothers in the 1890s. When her father died in 1897 Susan's future seemed bleak and she was delighted to receive a letter from Louisa Duchess of Buccleuch, who was Mistress of the Robes, inviting her to become maid-of-honour to the Queen. She immediately accepted, relieved to have found a position which offered a measure of financial independence, since she was to receive a payment of £300 a year as well as her board when in waiting. In return she was expected to speak, read and write French and German fluently, and to be prepared to play or sing when required. 'It was taken for granted that she could sketch, do needlework and be conversant with the usual indoor games (such as backgammon, *vingt-et-un* and bridge).' Discretion was essential and she had to be a good conversationalist as well as keep herself informed on current affairs.[95] Susan met all these conditions and carried out her duties successfully until in November 1899 she married Sir James Reid, the Queen's doctor.

The Countess of Airlie was another who benefited in this way. She was left in dire straits after the death of her husband in the Boer War. 'My income was strained to the utmost limits by the upkeep of the castle,' she wrote. 'In spite of its enormous acreage Cortachy had never been a rich estate . . . I often spent sleepless nights after going through the accounts with John Black, the loyal old factor.'[96] Despite some initial

A house party in the conservatory at Luton Hoo, 23 November, 1887, the home of the de Falbes. In the centre sits the stately figure of Princess Mary Adelaide Duchess of Teck and standing at the back, second from the right, is her daughter, Princess May, the future Queen Mary. When Princess Mary Adelaide died in 1897 Lord Balcarres described her in glowing terms: 'Her character was admirable and her grace and dignity truly royal . . . it will be impossible to find anyone to take her place.' She was a first cousin of Queen Victoria. (Luton Museum and Art Gallery)

reservations that it might disrupt her family life, it was with relief that at the end of 1901 she accepted an invitation to become lady in waiting to the Princess of Wales, later Queen Mary.

But most female members of High Society had no such opportunities to exercise their independence, at any rate before the outbreak of the First World War. As the Countess of Selborne noted drily in 1902, attitudes to women's emancipation were quite illogical:

> the English seemingly hold the opinion that it is not fitting for women to shoot, but that it *is* fitting for them to hunt & fish. For some inscrutable reason laundresses' work is considered a very feminine employment, though it is so exhausting that only a minority of women are able to do it, while until a few years ago a clerk was held to be necessarily a male, although the ordinary clerk's work can be done by a woman just as well as by a man. Till about 20 years ago a woman doctor was a shocking thing, although a woman nurse was quite correct. I think we must admit that our ideas on these subjects are purely traditional, & require to be examined in the cold light of reason.[97]

The one area where women's organizational abilities were accepted and welcomed was in their role as 'Lady Bountiful'. Not only was this seen as an extension of a long-established female function as carer of the sick and needy, but, through these ministrations the poor could be made aware of the interest – and the condescension – of their social superiors. At the same time the women themselves benefited, particularly those who were elderly spinsters or widows, by being made to feel that they had a useful task to perform in the world. 'Only as Lady Bountiful,' writes Jessica Gerard, 'did they have opportunities for independent action and unfettered power over the lives of others. Women of intelligence, energy, and initiative, those with a thirst for power, found in philanthropy a socially approved outlet for their talents and needs.'[98] For the *nouveaux riches* with ambition charity could also be used as a way of extending the range of their acquaintances and of making contact with social superiors. It was the future Lady Wernher's experience of organizing charity concerts, bazaars and balls during the Boer War which gave her a taste for entertaining on a grand scale both at the Wernher town house at the corner of Piccadilly and Bolton Street and at Luton Hoo.[99] Every Christmas she also gave a 'Happy Evening' to some 150 poor girls in London, and at Luton she was associated with the opening of a new secondary school and of new wards at the hospital. For women such as she philanthropy became a means of confirming their social status.

Others saw charitable work as an expression of their religious beliefs. Laura Tennant, for all her flirtatiousness, unconventionality and vivacity, had a deep, even morbid, religious faith. 'Life is humiliating, Death exalting, and it is good to . . . have the truism "You are of no consequence" drummed into your ears by those who are of consequence,' she wrote on the night following her presentation at Court.[100] It was in this context that she took up social work in the East End of London, starting a crèche, organizing a working-girls' club, and teaching in a school.[101]

It was widely believed by contemporaries that the superior manners of these lady volunteers would have a beneficial effect upon those whom they were helping. Their 'words, their ordinary manners, their dress, their voice, the numerous . . . suggestions and instructions which they carry unconsciously . . . into the houses of the poor, exercise a power far greater than any'.[102]

Even in the new century these attitudes persisted despite the development of a more investigative approach towards the relief of poverty, particularly in urban areas. Some girls, like Susan Tweedsmuir, moved with the times by offering their services to bodies like the Charity Organization Society. This sought to co-operate with local authorities by trying to eliminate poverty through an examination of an individual's family circumstances. 'I don't imagine that I can have helped them much,' admitted Lady Tweedsmuir, 'as I worked as a kind of dog's body licking envelopes in [the] office, but I gratefully acknowledge how much good they did to *me*.'[103]

But most High Society ladies preferred to continue the traditional role of a Lady Bountiful. According to Violet Greville by the 1890s there was virtually no philanthropic, artistic, or political movement in which women did not take an interest. Almost every great lady had adopted some scheme which was designed to benefit her less fortunate brethren. Among the ventures she had in mind were a little orphanage for boys, 'recruited from the poorest and most miserable classes', which was supported by

Lady Breadalbane; a women's hospital in one of the poorest districts of the East End of London, founded and supported by voluntary subscriptions and run by a committee which included Lady Waterford, Lady Stafford and Lady Wimborne; and a society for sick-nursing which covered almost all the East End parishes:

> nearly every lady has her Sunday-school or her Bible-class; and a few aspire to artistic needlework, like Lady Brooke with her school at Easton. Everywhere societies for the help and encouragement of every species of industry, art, and manufacture are being multiplied; and it can hardly be said that, if the ladies of England are wrapped in luxury, they are idle as well.[104]

Nor was charity a 'snug little duty' which the women carried out at home. Although some confined themselves to attendance at charity bazaars or the distribution of Christmas gifts to the cottagers on their family estates or the indigent poor in the local workhouse, many others ventured into the homes of the very poorest and encountered the squalor and deprivation of their lives at first hand. Margot Tennant was much mortified when in 1880 she helped her sister, Laura, set up an East End crèche and was so badly bitten on the face by fleas that she had to hide away until the tell-tale marks had disappeared.[105] Lady Waterford, too, according to her daughter spent all her dress allowance on kind deeds. As a result neither she nor her daughters were well dressed: 'her usual reason for going to any dressmaker at all was the fact that the latter was starving, probably because she was so bad that no one else would go to her.'[106] And Lady Jeune not only supported country holiday schemes and charity dinners for children attending elementary schools in the poorest parts of London but she visited the schools regularly to discuss with head teachers the social problems of the area.[107]

Consuelo Marlborough did not take her devotion to charitable causes as far as this. Nonetheless when she and the Duke decided to separate in 1906 it was to charity that she turned for consolation and occupation. With the help of a friend, Prebendary Carlile, who was head of the Church Army, she set up a hostel to help the wives of first offenders whilst their husbands were in prison. Two houses were leased in Endsleigh Street, London, and were equipped with laundries and sewing-rooms, where the women were employed for a standard wage. Their babies were cared for in the attached day nursery, and Consuelo herself closed each day's work with a prayer. She also interviewed the husbands when they came out of prison so as to help them find employment. 'When one plunges into philanthropy it is not long before one becomes submerged,' she wrote years later. Soon she became involved in other activities affecting the welfare of women and children. They included a recreation home for working girls, a lodging house for poor women, and the honorary treasurership of Bedford College, a women's college attached to London University.[108]

In this way she, and many other women, found some compensation for the frustrations and the limitations of many aspects of the 'female world' in late Victorian and Edwardian England.

CHAPTER FOUR

Drawing-Rooms, Levées and the Marriage Market

I was just seventeen and a half when I was presented at Court – with the usual paraphernalia of white satin and ostrich feathers. I made my curtsey to King George. . . . Poor man! He did look bored. . . . During the whole of the London season . . . I never could find anything in the world to say to the ordinary 'Guardee' – as we dubbed most of the young officers who were our partners at dances. And so it went on: – lunches, tea-dances, balls, . . . the same people, the same talk, the same eternal round of so-called gaiety. . . . I'll swear I never met an intelligent man during my whole London Season.

LADY CONSTANCE MALLESON, *After Ten Years* (1931), 47–8. Lady Constance, the youngest daughter of the 5th Earl of Annesley, was born in 1895.

When girls reached the age of seventeen or eighteen it was accepted that they must leave the seclusion of the schoolroom to enter the adult world. Hair was put up and skirts lengthened, so that years later Lady Cynthia Asquith could 'still remember the thrill of hearing the whisper of my first long dress pursuing my heels down the stairs, and the queerness of suddenly no longer being able to see my own feet'.[1] A new and extensive wardrobe was acquired, including outfits for walking, visiting, playing tennis, boating, bicycling and attending garden parties, dinners, and evening balls. There had even to be a few black garments for 'sudden family or Court mourning'. Small wonder that in the early 1890s Lady Violet Greville should complain of the 'complication of costumes to suit all seasons and occasions' which had become 'a burden on the memory'.[2]

For some girls the coming out process was preceded by a brief spell at a finishing school in France, Germany or Switzerland. One débutante who followed this pattern around the turn of the century remembered Dresden as 'practically under the occupation of English schoolgirls', so numerous were the young ladies attending there.[3] She spent eight months receiving instruction in drawing, art history, music and German, and followed it up with a brief stay in Paris before returning home. Around two decades earlier, Margot Tennant had pursued a similar course, although in her case she herself drew up the timetable to be followed. She lodged in a pension run by a genteel widow and each morning at 6 a.m.:

> I woke up and dashed into the kitchen to have coffee with the solitary slavey; after that I practised the fiddle or piano till 8.30, when we had the pension breakfast; and the rest of the day was taken up by literature and drawings. I went to concerts or the opera by myself every night.[4]

It was Margot's first taste of independence, free from family and chaperons, and she relished it. Indeed, her habit in later life of travelling by train alone, without a maid, and her practice of not taking a maid with her on country-house weekends caused some raising of eye-brows among more conventional contemporaries, as did her habit of smoking.[5]

The wistful Margot and Laura Tennant soon after they 'came out' in the early 1880s. They were soon to gain a prominent place in High Society. (The author)

But for many débutantes their entry into adult society was prefaced by a series of country-house visits to stay with relatives, or perhaps by attendance at a local hunt ball. A number found the transition difficult. In 1911 Madeline Adeane was described by a second cousin as 'rather in the hobbledehoy state inclined to say rather sharp things', soon after she came out, while an American critic considered most English débutantes were 'still in the nursery . . . still shy, silent, unformed', and without conversation.[6]

These were judgements with which the young Emily Lytton would largely have agreed. In November 1892, on a visit to Hatfield House immediately after her entrance into London Society, she complained of the tedium of talking 'for a week to people whom you do not care about on subjects which do not interest you . . . People suppose you have finished lessons when you come out, but I think the hardest lessons are just then beginning.'[7]

Even the young Princess May of Teck, despite her royal connections and her gregarious mother, found small talk at a dinner-party or on the dance-floor 'agonisingly difficult' when she began to take an active part in public life. This 'conversational incapacity', declares her biographer, made the London Season uncomfortable for her.[8]

The immaturity of many of these girls was fostered by parents' desire to retain their innocence, especially in sexual matters, for as long as possible. This concern was displayed by Mary Elizabeth Lucy of Charlecote Park when her eldest granddaughter, Ada, reached seventeen in the spring of 1883. That was an age 'in *my time* when young Ladies *came out* and were marriageable, but I hope this dear Ada will enjoy life unfettered for some years, she is still a perfect child of nature in innocence and simplicity, ignorant of the world and all its vanities'.[9] A few months later in January 1884, Ada made her début at a hunt ball in Warwick, and her grandmother rejoiced not only in her elegant appearance, in a white tulle dress trimmed with artificial snow drops, but in her 'freshness, joy and buoyancy'.[10] In the event, Ada was not to marry until 1892, by which time her widowed mother had become concerned that she might not marry at all!

The real symbol of a girl's transition from adolescence to adulthood came, however, with what Lady Cynthia Asquith called the 'picturesque rites of . . . social baptism' associated with presentation at Court.[11] Already in the 1860s journals like the *Queen* were lamenting that this important ritual was being devalued as a 'title to social distinction'. Formerly, it declared severely:

> presentations were confined to the true aristocracy of the country, the peerage, the superior landed gentry, persons of distinction in art, science and letters and the holders of offices of dignity under the Crown. . . . It is now no longer so. Presentations are . . . so vulgarized that literally ANYBODY who has sufficient amount of perseverance or self confidence may be presented. The wives of all Members of Parliament are presented and they in turn present the wives and daughters of local squires and other small magnates. There is no knowing where this is to stop.[12]

But such criticisms in no way undermined the popularity of the ceremony. Indeed, the annual total of Drawing-Rooms, at which the presentations were made, increased to four

The wedding in 1892 of Ada Lucy, heiress of Charlecote Park, Warwickshire and Henry Fairfax of Roxburghshire, at Charlecote. Henry was a lieutenant in the Second Life Guards and was the eldest son of Colonel Sir William Ramsay-Fairfax, Bart. (Sir Edmund Fairfax-Lucy, Bart.)

in 1880 and five in 1895, while the number of those presented showed a sharp rise over the same period, advancing from 667 in 1880 to 1,209 in 1897, the year of Queen Victoria's Diamond Jubilee.[13] Although there was then something of a decline, especially with the onset of the Boer War at the end of 1899, the number of those presented in the Season of 1900 still totalled 822, well up on the figure of twenty years before. They included not merely girls who were 'coming out', but ladies who were being presented following their marriage or whose husbands had recently succeeded to a title. Others took part in the ritual merely as part of their normal seasonal round and because they regarded it as confirmation of their superior social status. Before a presentation could take place, the names of those involved had to be submitted to the Lord Chamberlain for royal approval, and only then were the relevant cards issued, signifying that the applicants might attend.[14]

Normally a débutante was presented by her mother or a close relative, but in the case of a bride the role was performed, when possible, by a near relation of the husband. It is 'etiquette that *his* family rather than her own should present the bride', pronounced the anonymous author of *The Manners of the Aristocracy*.[15] However, an examination of

Drawing-Room presentation records reveals that where a girl was marrying into a family of lower standing than her own, it was common for her mother, or a friend of her family, to assume responsibility. That was the case with Mary Gladstone. On 4 March, 1886, about a month after her marriage to the Hawarden curate, Harry Drew, she was presented by her mother at the first Drawing-Room of the Season. Nor was she alone on that occasion in relying upon maternal sponsorship after marriage. In 1886 about one in ten of all the women presented as brides were accompanied by their mothers. By 1897 this had risen to one in six and to about one in five in 1900.[16]

It was customary for brides to wear their wedding-dress for the occasion. Consuelo Marlborough remembered appearing in her bridal gown cut suitably low at the neck, a diamond belt round her waist, a diamond tiara on her head, and 'pearls in profusion'.[17] For Mary Drew additional finery was especially necessary since she had been married in humble muslin. For her Court appearance she added 'Mama's lace, and all my diamonds', as well as the obligatory long satin train worn by all those presented.[18]

Sometimes leading members of Society might present humbler friends as a favour or, if they were short of cash, in return for discreet financial or other rewards. More rarely a mother might elect to present several daughters at the same time, as was the case with Lady Kirk in May 1890, when three daughters were brought out at the same Drawing-Room. In yet another example, in what was a reversal of customary procedure, the Countess Cadogan presented an elderly aunt-in-law, as well as Lady Clonbrock, the wife of a prominent Irish peer. At that time, in 1897, her husband was Lord-Lieutenant of Ireland.

For some, the right of presentation was also a means of underlining their own importance and of emphasizing their position at Court. At the first of the May Drawing-Rooms held in the Jubilee Year of 1897, the Duchess of Devonshire deputized for the Marchioness of Salisbury, the Prime Minister's wife, who was unwell, in making the official presentations in the diplomatic circle. The Duchess, often known as the 'double duchess' because her first husband had been the Duke of Manchester, was described as 'very regal in a lovely costume of violet velvet'. At the next two Drawing-Rooms on 11 and 18 May, she presented a further twenty-three ladies, only one of whom was apparently a relative. The German-born Duchess was one of the most influential of the late Victorian political and social hostesses. According to Margot Tennant, she 'not only kept her own but other people's secrets; and she added to a considerable effrontery and intrepid courage, real kindness of heart'.[19]

Occasionally, those who aspired to a presentation were disappointed. This applied to Mrs Gordon Selfridge, whose husband owned a department store in London. In 1909, she asked the newly-appointed American Ambassador, Whitelaw Reid, for one of the invitations at his disposal, only to be told that although as the wife of an American businessman, she was 'perfectly eligible', as the wife of a 'shop-keeper in London in sharp and aggressive daily competition with other shop-keepers', she could not be accepted. To break the rule prohibiting the presentation of people in trade 'would have offended British retailers and put the court and the Embassy in an awkward position'.[20] For, as a contemporary book of etiquette firmly pronounced: 'Those who are engaged in ordinary retail trade are without the pale.'[21]

Presentation at Court to King George V and Queen Mary, *c*. 1913. From *London's Social Calendar*, published by the Savoy Hotel Company, *c*. 1914. (Greater London Photograph Library)

For members of the royal family presiding over these large Drawing-Rooms was immensely fatiguing. By the 1880s Queen Victoria herself attended only a minority of the presentations, delegating the remainder to the Princess of Wales and other family members. On 9 May 1893, Lord Carrington, the then Lord Chamberlain, reported that the largest Drawing-Room hitherto held had taken place on that day, with 510 presentations and 790 other people in attendance, making a total of one thousand three hundred in all. 'This does not include the Court and diplomatic body. 30 more persons attended than at the Jubilee drawing-room in 1887, and there were 100 more carriages. The last carriage left the palace at 7 o'clock. It lasted 3 Hours and 5 minutes – the Princesses were terribly tired. Their feet swelled so much that they could hardly walk out of the throne room.'[22]

The male equivalent of the Drawing-Room was the Levée. By the 1880s this was conducted by the Prince of Wales or his brothers, and those coming forward were largely Army officers, who were perhaps being presented after promotion or on their return from active service. A sprinkling of those attending were men who had recently succeeded to a title or had been raised to some major legal, governmental or state office. Thus in 1880, Lord Middleton was presented by the Marquis of Ailsa on succeeding to his title, while his wife was sponsored by Lady Ailsa at a Drawing-Room in the same year. In the case of professional men it was customary for them to be presented by a superior in the profession to which they belonged.[23] Those who held important official positions in provincial society might also appear on these occasions. Molly Trevelyan remembered her father attending Court periodically in his capacity as Lord-Lieutenant of the North Riding of Yorkshire. 'He went . . . in a handsome uniform rather like a general's, over which he wore a dark blue cloak lined with scarlet. A cocked hat with a magnificent red and white plume completed his attire.'[24]

The numbers of those presented at the Levées were far greater than those at the Drawing-Rooms. In 1880, the annual total reached 1,674 and by 1897 this had climbed to 1,735.[25] But they lacked the elaborate ritual associated with their female counterparts and were over much more quickly. Presentations were also influenced by events in the wider world, particularly by wars and colonial disputes. In 1880, for example, attendance was swollen by officers returning from the recent conflict in Zululand.[26]

For débutantes, the day of presentation was awaited with a mixture of trepidation and excitement. A special gown had to be purchased and curtseys practised, with some girls anxiously receiving special guidance on the latter from a dancing-master. According to Lady Ethel Raglan, the fashionable M. d'Egville was always 'very "booked up" before a Court, by pupils who rushed to him for lessons'.[27]

The selection of the dress to be worn was of particular concern:

> For weeks previously, the showrooms of fashionable dressmakers are besieged; tables and chairs are strewn with the latest products of the loom . . . , and a bevy of fair and

An army officer being presented to King Edward VII at a levée, c. 1902. (The author)

elderly matrons sit round in anxious conclave. It is . . . a serious matter to choose a Drawing-room dress; a presentation dress is simple, but it must possess features of novelty or artistic arrangement, and must provide two pretty gowns for dinners or balls hereafter; while the cost of the matron's dress, when the wearer is especially rich, extravagant, or fastidious, runs occasionally into three figures. . . . White, of course, is *de rigueur* for the *débutante*, as for the bride.[28]

Many girls, like the young Cynthia Charteris, resented the tedious hours spent 'trying-on'. As she shifted her weight from one foot to another, Cynthia was 'twitching with boredom while portentously solemn women, with their mouths full of pins, and tape-measures slung round their necks, knelt at my feet, conferring with one another and from time to time, appealing to [my mother].'[29]

During Queen Victoria's reign Drawing-Rooms were held in the afternoon, and it was not until the accession of Edward VII that the presentations were transferred to evening Courts. The King revelled in the intricacies of ceremonial and the pageantry at the first State Opening of Parliament of his reign was very different from Queen Victoria's austere public appearances. That love of show was also apparent at the Courts.

The débutantes welcomed the change to evening presentations. In Victorian times many had found it embarrassing to drive through the streets of London to Buckingham Palace in broad daylight, clad in their finery. But, as Lady Violet Greville emphasized,

A débutante with an improvised train, rehearsing a Court presentation under the watchful eye of the famous master of dancing and deportment, M. d'Egville. The two ladies represented the King and Queen, respectively. January 1911. (British Library Newspaper Library)

the general public had enjoyed the spectacle of fine carriages, containing a 'veritable garden of flowers' and attended by servants in smart liveries, driving to the Palace.

> No wonder the populace look, and gaze, and, wondering, doubt . . . whether the inmates of these fine carriages are human like themselves . . . [But] some of the dowagers' noses are red, and some of their waists are large, and some of their faces are cross. It is an ordeal to rise early, to sit for two hours in the clutches of the hairdresser and the lady's maid; to be laced into tight gowns . . . ; to take a hurried luncheon or, more likely, no meal at all; to look after the girls' toilettes; . . . and then, after superhuman efforts of laborious bustle, to be hoisted into a family coach with a vast amount of drapery and strongly scented bouquets, and, in the full glare of the sun, to run the gauntlet of a mob's coarse if good-humoured criticism for the space of an hour or more.[30]

Lady Augusta Fane, the Earl of Stradbroke's daughter, remembered the discomfort of donning her first pair of stays when she came out at the age of seventeen. They were 'fearsome things made of silk and whalebone and laced up at the back'. She claimed, too, that the Drawing-Rooms were held in the afternoon not merely for the Queen's convenience but 'to please the dressmakers and shoemakers, as no old garment or once-worn satin shoe could pass muster'.[31] After a meagre lunch – the new stays preventing any undue appetite – Lady Augusta and her mother mounted the steps of the magnificent family chariot, which was drawn by a pair of greys. The chariot swung from side to side as they moved along but fortunately neither she nor her mother suffered from travel sickness. The coachman was perched precariously on a high seat, covered with a gorgeous hammer-cloth embroidered with silver, while two footmen, each six feet tall, stood on a tiny platform at the rear of the carriage, 'hanging on for dear life to two embroidered straps':

> It was a fine sight to see a hundred coaches and chariots drive down the Mall. . . . The fashionable hairdresser of the moment, M. Rolland, a typical Frenchman, ran from coach to coach, putting finishing touches to his clients' veils and feathers.[32]

Two decades later, things had changed little when Molly Trevelyan came out. She attended a Drawing-Room held in March 1899, and the donning of an 'evening dress in the middle of a March morning was enough to make the stoutest shiver'. Like Lady Augusta, she was presented by her mother, and some of their friends came to admire and encourage them before they set off:

> I wore a white satin dress covered with a tunic of tulle, with little bunches of lilies of the valley sewn on to the skirt at intervals. My train was of white figured satin lined with glacé silk. The train hung from the shoulders where it was firmly attached with hooks and eyes, so that there was no danger of its falling off in the Throne Room. In my hair I wore three white ostrich feathers, small and tightly curled, which were pinned to my scalp in some miraculous manner, together with a veil of white net, a yard and a half long. . . . My train was three yards long, as prescribed by the official regulation for ladies' Court dress. The material came in very handy for a ball gown the following year.

We had lunch at twelve, my mother, my sister Gertrude (who had been presented years before) and myself, and at twelve thirty we set off for the Palace. . . . On our reaching St. James' Park we were absorbed into a crowd of other landaus and broughams, all bound for the same place. It was some time before we ceased to perambulate St. James' Park, for the carriages went at a footpace down the Mall, round by the Horse Guards Parade, up Birdcage Walk, across the front of the Palace, down the Mall again, and so round the whole circuit of the Park, until at a given moment the lines of vehicles halted, and stood still for an hour or more, waiting for the Palace gates to open. . . . It was like a glorified game of Musical Chairs. On this occasion we were very fortunate as it only took us ten minutes to move forward to the gates from where our carriage had halted. Once inside the Palace we went up a long flight of stairs, carpeted in red, to the first floor, where we walked through a suite of rooms and sat down in rows on little gold cane-seated chairs for nearly an hour. Just after three o'clock two footmen came in and took away the elegant wooden hurdles which barred our advance, and we moved forward into the next room, in which there were no chairs. Then another hurdle was removed, and we went forward into yet another room, where we formed [a] single file. It was all very restrained and silent, no one spoke or whispered or moved except in slow measured steps towards our goal. As we neared the Throne room, a flunkey spread out our trains (we had carried them over our arms till then) and I, following after my mother, entered the Presence. I saw a fat little person in black, curtseyed to her and to the Duke and Duchess of York, and then fled. My mother told me afterwards that Princess Christian, to whom I was being presented, was tall and dressed in white. I had never seen her; I don't suppose it mattered much. Once the Presentation was over we could enjoy ourselves and talk to our friends. In the room beyond the Throne Room we were among people we knew, as many of our contemporaries were being presented that day. No refreshments were provided at a Drawing-Room, and it was a great relief to get home and have tea, to which many of our friends came, to admire our dresses and to hear how we had comported ourselves in the presence of Royalty. We called this function 'a Drawing-Room Tea'.[33]

Despite her nervousness she at least seems to have been more fortunate than an anonymous 'Peer's Daughter' who wrote to *Lady's Realm* to complain that in the general crush 'three or four people' had stood on her dress. By the time she reached the throne room her bouquet was half dead, her new dress a disgrace to her wardrobe, and her dishevelled appearance 'quite undeserving of the gracious smiles and shakes of the hand accorded to me. . . . But the final weary wait in the hall for the carriage was, I think, the worst of all – everyone too tired to talk and preoccupied listening to the calling out of carriages . . . I have known of departure from home at mid-day, and return at 7 p.m.!'[34]

During her first season a débutante was expected to behave with great decorum. Admittedly at the end of the nineteenth century girls enjoyed greater liberty than their mother's generation had been allowed, but there were still strict rules to be observed, particularly over the necessity for a chaperon. Even in her second year Lady Diana Manners was forbidden to be alone with a man 'except by chance in the country. A married woman must bring me home from a ball. For walking and shopping and . . . driving in a taxi, a sister or a girl was enough protection. I could go to the Ritz but to no other London hotel.'[35]

Yet, paradoxically, despite these restrictions, Lady Diana's mother, the Duchess of

Court gowns worn at the Drawing-Room held by Queen Victoria on 11 May, 1897, from *The Queen*. (British Library Newspaper Library)

Rutland, allowed her to accept expensive presents from a dubious American admirer who was already married. He gave her a full-length ermine coat and a small monkey with a diamond waist-belt and chain, among other things, and twice a week, wherever she was, he sent her a box 'the size of a coffin full of Madonna lilies'.[36]

Nor was Lady Diana's own conduct as restrained as her reminiscences sometimes suggest. Periodically she escaped the clutches of her chaperon to visit the night-clubs which were springing up in London on the eve of the First World War. On one occasion Sylvia Henley had escorted Diana to a ball but at 2.30 a.m., when she wished to leave, her charge was nowhere to be found. She subsequently reappeared from a night-club at 4.15 a.m.[37] Later there was an evening party on the Thames when, allegedly with her encouragement, one of the male guests jumped fully clothed into the water and was drowned, together with another man who had attempted to rescue him. A third member of the party was, with difficulty, saved from a similar fate. Small wonder that Diana's frivolity and recklessness were condemned as raffish by staider hostesses.[38]

She also insisted on choosing her own friends, and dismissed the eligible bachelors introduced by her mother with more force than elegance. She regarded them as 'leprous'. Lord Dudley was condemned as 'slothful and somnolent', while 'that bugger Bobbety Cranborne' was quite unacceptable with his 'loose gaping mouth and lean, mean shanks', and the rich and handsome Lord Rocksavage had no conversation beyond 'three words, adaptable to any remark: "Oh", "Really?" "Right-ho!"'[39] Young men came to tea in the ballroom at the Rutlands' town house in Arlington Street and there they played chess or practised the *csárdás* for a fancy dress ball. Not surprisingly, Lady Diana's flirtations became notorious and she herself admitted to having earned the 'hard name of a "scalp-collector"'.[40]

Another débutante to defy convention at around this time was Nancy Cunard. She came out in 1914 but soon tired of the round of parties: 'one ball succeeded another until there were three or four a week and the faces of the revolving guardsmen seemed as silly as their vapid conversation among the hydrangeas at supper.'[41] With the help of a childhood friend, Iris Tree, younger daughter of the actor-manager, Sir Herbert Beerbohm Tree, she rented a room in Fitzroy Place on the fringes of Bloomsbury. There she and Iris escaped to meet their admirers unchaperoned, or to write and paint, and design costumes for a ball. Once the girls were arrested for swimming in the Serpentine at dawn after leaving a party. Iris herself labelled them 'bandits', who escaped 'environment . . . to emerge in forbidden artifice, chalk-white face powder, scarlet lip rouge, cigarette smoke, among roisterers of our own choosing. . . . The first black jazz bands played at all-night parties.'[42] Their lavish use of cosmetics was one aspect of their rebellion against conventional society, since even the use of face powder was regarded by many as suitable only for actresses and the *demi-monde*.

But Nancy Cunard and Lady Diana Manners were not typical of the girls who came out between the 1870s and 1914. For most, being launched upon Society meant attending balls, theatres, picture exhibitions, garden parties, major sporting fixtures and similar events under the careful eye of a chaperon. Some, like Princess May of Teck, also accompanied their mother to charitable functions and attended improving lectures – the Princess's choice being Elizabethan literature and social hygiene.[43] Others, including

Emily Lytton, went to dancing classes or took up drawing – in Emily's case in connection with botany studies at the National History Museum.[44] Music lessons, language classes, or membership of a choral society were other diversions taken up by the young in the interests of self-improvement or merely for amusement.

Less attractive for most débutantes was the fact that at balls they often had to join in a 'sort of slave or marriage market at the door' as they waited for partners. With faces innocent of powder and with 'shapeless wispy hair held by crooked combs', they appeared raw and shy compared to the sophisticated older women. Those with few friends or who 'had been betrayed by a partner, or were victims of muddling the sequences of their dances, became cruelly conspicuous wallflowers'.[45] In order to escape from this humiliating situation, the more sensitive sneaked downstairs to the cloakroom, ostensibly to have 'their dress mended, and hope not to meet fellow-wallflowers in the same predicament. The mothers sat all round the room encouraging or glaring at their daughters' partners.'[46]

Not surprisingly, some of the young men also found it an ordeal. Charles Hervey was so nervous at one ball he attended with his mother that she described him as turning as white as paper. She pretended not to notice but 'waited till he was better & then dragged him into the thick of it – till he got . . . quite at his ease & dancing away like a proper man, with the young Princesses'.[47]

Yet, despite all the superficial gaiety and light-heartedness, débutantes were only too well aware that they were expected to make a match with a partner from their own rank of society – or a superior one – as speedily as possible. This was by no means easy. In March 1885, Maria Hodnett, the widowed mother of Lady Augustus Hervey, bewailed 'the great scarcity of young men in society' at a time when her granddaughter, Maria, was preparing to come out: 'she is likely to be one too many among the lot of girls on the look out – all the desirable and good parties (sic) are now absent.'[48] Mrs Hodnett's fears were justified and when Maria did marry at the end of her second Season, her husband was merely the son and heir of a Lincolnshire baronet of modest means.

It was in similar circumstances that Mabell, eldest daughter of the Earl of Arran, experienced a pang of envy on hearing of a friend's engagement shortly before she herself was due to have her first London Season. 'Unless a girl was quite exceptional – which I was not – her fate was decided by her first impact on society,' she later wrote. 'Anyone who failed to secure a proposal within six months of coming out could only wait for her second Season with diminishing chances. After the third there remained nothing but India as a last resort before the spectre of the Old Maid became a reality.'[49]

In the event Mabell received two proposals, both suitable, during her first Season and refused both of them. 'By then I wanted something more than the mere fact of being married'. Like Maria Hervey, she met her future husband during her second Season and was married about six months later, at the age of nineteen.[50]

Some girls were hampered when they first came out by a lack of influential friends. This was true of the strong-willed and vivacious Margot Tennant and her sister, Laura. Laura came out first, but her Season proved disappointing because her mother knew too few people. On the night of her presentation at court she wrote gloomily: 'I suppose all Days teach us a lesson. This one has preached a regular sermon to me. Among those hundreds of important, influential, bejewelled and brilliant people, what was I?'[51]

When it was Margot's turn things were at first little better. The magnificent dance thrown by her father to launch her into Society was attended by too many of what she dismissed as 'middle-aged men' in their thirties and forties. At her next ball she 'danced a quadrille "with a mediocre member of Parliament" and for the rest of the evening she and Laura . . . stood watching, wondering if they were always to be cast for the role of wallflowers.' The breakthrough came when Margot went to Ascot with her brother. With some difficulty they obtained tickets for the Royal enclosure and there met Lady Dalhousie, who knew of Margot's passion for horses. She took the girl to the paddock where Margot was presented to the Prince of Wales. They discussed the runners and he was impressed by her shrewd comments. An invitation to luncheon followed and he subsequently presented her with a gold cigarette case. But more to the point, from a social angle, was the fact that once her friendship with him became known invitations flooded in. In those days, she wrote later, the Prince and Princess were 'the leaders of London society; they practically dictated what people could and could not do . . . and we vied with each other in trying to please him.'[52]

Part of that competition consisted in dressing well, and during her first Season Margot acquired a large and fashionable wardrobe, many of her outfits being ordered from the Parisian couturier Charles Worth. Worth was now well established on a career which had transformed him from a shop apprentice at Swan and Edgar's in London to a position as the most important dress designer in Europe. To his Paris salon came wealthy and fashion-conscious women from all over the world:

> before him princesses discrown themselves, duchesses tremble, countesses bow their aristocratic heads in mute acquiescence, and citizenesses of the Transatlantic Republic humbly abnegate that self-assertiveness which is one of their most prominent characteristics,

declared the British journalist, George Sala, in 1880.[53] To Margot Tennant, Worth gave the self-assurance needed to compete with the established beauties who dominated the society of her day.[54]

Some girls, including Frances Maynard, the future Countess of Warwick, were able to achieve the desired objective of an engagement at the end of their first Season. But many did not. Apart from the social barriers which had to be overcome by daughters of the newly-rich, like Margot and Laura Tennant in their early days, another problem was the growing tendency of upper-class men to delay marriage. This was especially true of younger sons, who were anxious to become established in a career before they took on the responsibilities of a home and family. It has been estimated that one in three of the peers' sons born between 1870 and 1879 never married at all, and while the carnage of the First World War may have contributed to this, the personal choice of the men themselves was also significant.[55] By 1911 even the *Tatler* was commenting on the apparent unpopularity of marriage among well-to-do men.[56]

Another difficulty was the growing competition which English débutantes were encountering from eligible foreigners, particularly Americans, at a time when many hard-pressed British landowners and their sons were seeking wives with substantial cash resources. American brides first appeared in aristocratic circles in the 1870s and were

A dancing lesson given by M. Louis
d'Egville in 1911. (British Library
Newspaper Library)

regarded, according to Lady Randolph Churchill (who was one of them), as 'strange and abnormal . . . with habits and manners something between a Red Indian and a Gaiety Girl. Anything of an outlandish nature might be expected of [them].'[57] However, during the peak years for transatlantic marriages, between the mid-1890s and the early 1900s, not only were they accepted but they became the subject of jealous comments by aggrieved English matrons, who resented their competition in the marriage market. Because a large proportion of them could command handsome dowries there were allegations that they were buying titles with the aid of parental fortunes. The crusading British journalist, William T. Stead, condemned as a 'degradation of the idea of . . . womanhood' the practice of regarding matches with American girls as a means of:

> replenishing the exhausted exchequer . . . Indeed, it is not too much to say that when there is no love in the matter, it is only gilded prostitution, infinitely more culpable from the moral point of view than the ordinary vice into which women are often driven by sheer lack of bread.[58]

Some young Americans, such as Belle Wilson, daughter of a wealthy banker and railroad promoter, bitterly resented the patronising approach of the English upper classes they encountered. In 1886, while she was staying in Cowes for the yachting week, Belle met 'a certain Mrs Cust, a hateful old woman' who greeted her by saying 'she thought America must be a dreadful place, she had heard no one had any servants there.'

I told her one or two families *had*. Then she said, 'Oh she thought no one had a lady's maid and she would hate to be without a lady's maid.' I begged her pardon and said I knew someone who had a lady's maid. 'I thought Americans did not like to be servants' she replied. 'They don't' I answered *all our working class are English*!!!' That finished her.[59]

Although Belle felt that she had 'scored one' by this riposte, it is clear that she found the whole experience distasteful and irritating. However, none of this prevented her from marrying the Hon. Michael (later Sir Michael) Herbert two years later. He was a brother of the 13th and 14th Earls of Pembroke. (See also Appendix A).

Mary Curzon, the former Mary Leiter, was similarly conscious that people were annoyed at her marriage to the eligible eldest son of Viscount Scarsdale. 'My path is strewn with roses, and the only thorns are the unforgiving women,' she confessed ruefully to her parents, soon after her marriage. Already pregnant with her first child, she was depressed at the mean strategems they adopted to upstage unwanted rivals like herself. 'London life is a continuous . . . striving . . . , the little people praying to be noticed by the great, and the great seldom lowering their eyelids to look at the small.'[60] One aspect of this was their cold-shouldering of her dinner-parties. On 26 June, 1895, when she held her first dinner in honour of the Prince of Wales, twenty-three of those invited attended but a further fourteen refused. They included such grandees as the Westminsters, the Devonshires, the Londonderrys and the Salisburys.[61] She probably saw this as a deliberate snub.

Not all American brides fell into the 'heiress' category applicable to Belle Herbert and Mary Curzon. But a sufficiently large proportion did to give credence to the belief that impoverished peers who wished to salvage family finances should cross the Atlantic in search of a wife. By the end of the century the American press was commenting acidly on English fortune-hunters who sought a wealthy partner in the United States. That accusation was levelled at both the 8th and 9th Dukes of Marlborough when they married. 'It has been generally understood that Mrs Hammersley married the Duke for a title and that the Duke married her for her money,' was the uncharitable conclusion of the *New York Times* on the wedding between the millionairess widow, Lily Hammersley, and the 8th Duke in 1888.[62] Of the engagement between Daisy Leiter and the badly-off 19th Earl of Suffolk it commented similarly that as a result 'his estate . . . in Wiltshire [would] be restored to the glory of its former days.' Daisy's elder sister, Mary had by then been married to George Curzon for nine years.[63] In 1898 she had become Vicereine of India and thus one of the highest ranking women in the British Empire.

Another reputed fortune-hunter was Lord Acheson, later the 5th Earl of Gosford. He was linked with at least two wealthy Americans before he eventually married a third. In 1905 the Minneapolis *Tribune* reported his efforts to win the 'heart and hand' of Miss Gladys Mills. 'The earldom, which is an Irish one, is not rich, and the Mills' fortune would be very useful in burnishing up aristocratic bearings that have been tarnished for lack of gold.'[64] Although this foray proved unsuccessful, a year later Acheson was again in the news when his alleged interest in the daughter of the American Ambassador to London, Whitelaw Reid, was firmly rejected by her father. Finally, in February 1910 he became engaged to Mildred Carter, the daughter of an American diplomat. They married in that year and were divorced in 1928.

In all, between 1870 and 1914, 102 American women married peers or the sons of peers and by the early 1900s they accounted for nearly one in ten of all peers' marriages.[65] It was this which caused resentful English mothers to complain of the predatory instincts of the transatlantic interlopers, while the *Tatler* noted wryly in 1908:

> Those who are always carping at the tendency on the part of our young peers to take unto themselves wives from among the heiresses of America will be glad to hear that there is a suggestion in the United States that a graduated tax, increasing according to the size of the lady's fortune, should be levied on all rich American brides who marry titled foreigners.[66]

Three years later, however, it described in flattering terms the young Lady Ancaster, formerly Eloise Breese of New York, who had married into the peerage in 1905. She was said to wear 'delightful "picture" clothes of Paris cut', to possess 'the frail, big-eyed, eggshell appearance at present the vogue', and to be 'a keen rider to hounds and an excellent horsewoman'. She had also demonstrated her commitment to her new homeland by becoming an active member of the Women's Tariff Reform Association, a Tory-backed organization seeking to end Britain's free trade policy, and one supported by a number of landed families.[67]

Far greater reservations were felt in aristocratic circles concerning the trickle of marriages between peers or peers' sons and actresses during these years. Overall there were twenty-one marriages between peers and players over the period 1879–1914, with seven of the brides being American.[68] Many were Gaiety or Gibson girls, who had been carefully groomed not only in their speech and deportment but in their dress sense as well. 'The Gaiety girls,' wrote one enthusiast, 'were the embodiment of the Romance of London . . . To take a Gaiety girl out to supper, to drive her home in a hansom through the summer night, to propel such a divinity in her laces and silks in a punt at Maidenhead . . . what more could life offer to a man of that time?'[69]

Among those who successfully made the transition from stage to country house was Sylvia Storey. She was one of the prettiest of the Gaiety girls and came from a theatrical family. When she met the young Earl Poulett in June 1908 she was already established as a musical comedy star. Three months later they were married, amid general approval. Indeed, after the honeymoon the couple were greeted at Hinton St. George, the Poulett family seat, with triumphal arches, mottoes in flowers, songs, flags and widespread rejoicing.[70] The marriage proved a success, with an heir born less than a year later and Sylvia settling down happily to her new role as chatelaine. However, tragedy struck ten years later when the Earl died from pneumonia in July 1918.

Few marriages between peers and actresses went as smoothly as that of the Pouletts. One which did not involved Belle Bilton, the daughter of a Royal Engineers recruiting sergeant, and Lord Dunlo, heir to the Earl of Clancarty. Before meeting Dunlo, Belle had already borne an illegitimate child, the father being a confidence trickster with whom she had set up house. Despite this lapse it was generally accepted that Belle was in no way promiscuous. In the spring of 1889 she met the twenty-year-old Dunlo, who was

Camille Clifford, one of the Gibson girls. In 1906 she married the heir to the 2nd Lord Aberdare, but he was killed in action in December 1914. Camille remarried in 1917. (The author)

two years her junior. Despite the bitter opposition of the Earl of Clancarty, they were married at Hampstead Registry Office a month or two later. Subsequent attempts by the enraged father to break up the marriage by sending his son on a world tour and seeking to collect evidence for a divorce on the grounds of Belle's alleged adultery proved unsuccessful. In the meantime Belle continued her theatrical career and it was while she was on tour in Plymouth in May 1891 that news came that the old Earl had died. Immediately she set off to meet her husband in London and together they went to the family seat in Ireland. There Belle entered on a new life as the Countess of Clancarty. Twin sons were born in 1891 (one of them dying in infancy) and three other children followed. Belle rapidly took on the responsibilities of her new position and earned a reputation as a skilled horsewoman. According to the *Tatler*, she spent most of her time in Ireland where she was 'very popular with her husband's tenantry'.[71] Despite its inauspicious start, therefore, the marriage proved successful until Belle's death in December 1906, at the early age of thirty-nine.

A rather different outcome occurred in most of the seven marriages involving American actresses. Five ended in divorce, and in two of them this was granted on grounds of the wife's adultery. One involved May Yohé, who achieved her first hit in

London in a play entitled 'Little Christopher Columbus'. According to the Duke of Manchester, who was then a teenager, all the men raved about her, although some 'were rather shocked at her habit of using bad language'. At the height of her fame, in 1894, she married Lord Francis Hope, later the Duke of Newcastle. After the wedding she continued her career and it was during an engagement in New York that she had an affair which ended the marriage in 1902.[72]

Another ill-fated match was that in 1905 between the actress Anna Robinson and the spendthrift Lord Rosslyn, half-brother of Lady Warwick. This was Rosslyn's second marriage, his first having ended in divorce in 1902 when his wife ran off with a chauffeur.[73] At the time he was himself trying to earn a living on the stage and he envisaged Anna as his leading lady. But the marriage ended on her petition in 1907, amid bitter recriminations. Rosslyn called the whole affair 'an act of rash folly' perpetrated when he had been 'madly attracted by her beauty and insanely in love'.[74]

However, such liaisons were in no way typical of High Society marriages in late Victorian and Edwardian England. As had been the case earlier in the nineteenth century, much stress was laid on the need for compatability in both rank and background between bride and groom. Hence in 1888, when Edward Stanley, the future 17th Earl of Derby, became engaged to Lady Alice Montagu, youngest daughter of the Duke of Manchester, she was vetted by the family before the marriage went ahead. Edward himself was not present at the ordeal but his aunt told him reassuringly after it was over that Alice was 'what she should be . . . I assure you it would have done you good to see from behind a curtain how well the trial went off . . . I am *quite quite* satisfied.'[75] The young couple were married less than two months later.

Through such marriages the major landed families were able to strengthen kinship networks and to consolidate property holdings. The farflung nature of many of these

The young Earl of Rosslyn with his half-sister, Lady Warwick, in the 1890s. (Frances Countess of Warwick, *Life's Ebb and Flow*, 1929)

family ties is illustrated, for example, by the seven daughters of the 1st Duke of Abercorn. All married earls or above, while two of his seven sons married the daughters of earls. Of the remaining sons, two married into gentry families and three were unmarried. There was a great deal of visiting between these different households, with some of the children of the marriages staying with relatives for weeks at a time: 'we grew up more or less as one gigantic family . . . with a plurality of residences,' was how one of them remembered it.[76]

Before a marriage took place care was taken to arrange appropriate financial settlements to ensure that the couple would be able to live in the station of life to which they were accustomed. The importance of these considerations was made clear in the marriage negotiations involving Lady Emily Lytton and the young architect, Edward Lutyens. At first Emily's widowed mother had refused to countenance the union. In a blunt letter she warned Edward that her daughter had:

> nothing but a very small allowance which I give her, and even at my death will have only a small sum of settled capital which her father left her, and therefore I must beg you not further to seek Emily in any way.[77]

Although Lutyens had a comfortable annual income from his profession this did not meet Lady Lytton's requirement for a substantial capital contribution to the settlement. In the end the problem was overcome by the prospective groom taking out a life assurance policy, and the couple were finally married in August 1898.

Two of the principal purposes of marriage settlements were to protect a wife's financial position and to make provision for any children the couple might have. A husband's right to dispose of property which his wife brought into the marriage was also curtailed by the Married Women's Property Acts of 1870 and 1882. But often the business side of the settlements involved lengthy negotiations between the two families, as well as the employment of solicitors to deal with the legal intricacies involved. Mary Elizabeth Lucy, whose eldest surviving son, Spencer, married the Scottish-born Christina Campbell, commented sourly on the difficulties experienced with the lawyers over the settlement:

> Mr Beith, the Scotch man, looked like a bird of prey and Mr Martin, the Englishman, a piece of old dried parchment (as if he had been nourished on old deeds instead of the milk of human kindness). The many questions they asked – and required to be answered; it was enough to puzzle Solomon himself and weary out the patience of Job.[78]

As the Lutyens' case showed, a bridegroom's earned income was not taken into account in the negotiations. Instead both sets of parents were expected to provide as much capital as they could reasonably afford, and, 'ideally, equal amounts'.[79] However, that did not apply to some of the wealthy American brides mentioned above. In these cases, the disparity between the parties could be considerable. Thus when Mary Leiter married George Curzon in 1895, she brought £140,000 into the settlement, while his family contributed £25,000.[80]

Once the legal formalities had been settled, plans for the wedding could be finalized. The most popular time for this was during the latter part of the Season, when families were still gathered in London, since the most fashionable weddings took place in the capital. The costs involved could be formidable. Frances Maynard, the future Countess of Warwick and an heiress in her own right, was allowed £2,000 by her trustees to spend on her trousseau when she married Lord Brooke at the end of April 1881.[81] The ceremony was conducted at Westminster Abbey and there were twelve bridesmaids, including Frances's sister and her three half-sisters. Among the guests were the Prince and Princess of Wales; the Duke and Duchess of Connaught; Princess Louise Marchioness of Lorne; and Princess Mary Adelaide Duchess of Teck. Among the less illustrious guests was Mary Elizabeth Lucy of Charlecote Park. She also attended the wedding breakfast which was held at the bride's home, 7 Carlton Gardens, and was taken to see the display of wedding gifts:

> First there was china, countless beautiful tea services, etc. etc., then plate – gold and silver – then jewellery; the most dazzling costly array: the inhabitants of Warwick gave a diamond necklace . . . the Prince and Princess of Wales, a splendid bracelet of diamonds and sapphires. . . . Then there was a quantity of rare articles of vertu. In short there was more than enough of precious things to confuse the eye and defy description.[82]

The Brookes spent their honeymoon at Ditton Park, which was lent to them by the Duke and Duchess of Buccleuch. There in lovely spring weather they spent a fortnight, enjoying many pleasant boating and canoeing excursions on the river. They were also commanded to dine at Windsor Castle on the day after the wedding, and Frances was requested to wear her bridal dress, 'orange blossoms and all!' As she remembered wryly, this 'worldly honour . . . demanded all our self-possession'. However, the Queen's kindness 'went far to soothe the shyness of a bride in her teens. The Queen took from my corsage a spray of orange blossom to keep as a souvenir and said many charming things about the beauty of my frock'.[83]

For many girls in this rank of society, ignorance of the physical facts of married life added to the stresses of their new relationship. A few, like Emily Lytton, may have taken the precaution of finding out what they could by pumping the servants. 'I . . . pretended to know more than I did in order to draw them out. A cousin and I made a bargain to find out all we could and report our discoveries to each other'.[84] But most, as Lady Warwick admitted, were 'unbelievably ignorant . . . Marriage – their goal, their destiny, their desire – was all in a rosy haze. Afterwards, as wives, they accepted without question the code of their day'.[85]

This was true of Sylvia Brett, Viscount Esher's youngest child, who married in 1911. The first part of her honeymoon was spent at Nuneham Park, Oxfordshire, which had been lent by the Harcourts, and Sylvia's principal memory of her first evening of married life was of her fear as to what was to happen to her:

> When I undressed that night, my trembling fingers would hardly unfasten my clothes. I put on my bridal nightgown of pale pink chiffon and lace, and looked in the mirror, to meet my own terror-stricken eyes and chalk-white face.[86]

Her ignorance extended to pregnancy itself and when a few months later she began to feel sick she was at first unaware of the reason.[87]

Lady Airlie's honeymoon in the late 1880s was mostly passed in feeling extremely ill. 'I, who never feel ill as a rule, did nothing but faint . . . I was nearly frightened to death and suffered *tortures*!'[88] Even when she and her husband returned from their honeymoon and were greeted with flags and evergreen arches and cheering crowds of tenants on the vast Airlie estate of Cortachy, she was unable to share in the festive mood. Only slowly over the months did she grow accustomed to her new position and learn to cope with an autocratic widowed mother-in-law. Her first baby was born thirteen months after her marriage but, as she ruefully commented, to start with the little girl did not mean very much to either parent. She was too preoccupied with self-pity. 'It was an unsettled phase for both of us, and one that I imagine a great many young couples must pass through. But in my youth there were no easy divorces – even a separation was considered a terrible disgrace. Husbands and wives were forced to have patience with each other.'[89] Happily the Airlies resolved their differences and forged a good relationship until Lord Airlie's early death in the Boer War.

Furthermore, despite Lady Airlie's pessimistic conclusion, it is clear that most High Society marriages got off to a better start than this. The diary of Victoria Sackville-West shows that she rejoiced in the pleasures of physical love, with many entries recording the number of times she and her husband had sexual intercourse in a day.[90] On one occasion she referred to him as a 'stallion'. Molly Trevelyan, too, recalled the pleasures of her wedding night when she found out 'what a man's love was'. Five years later she regarded it as 'a very perfect state of things that we are not ashamed of our love and of our desire'.[91]

Laura Tennant and Alfred Lyttelton also seem to have enjoyed an idyllic honeymoon when they married in May 1885. Shortly after the wedding, Laura confided to Alfred: 'How wonderful it is that 5 weeks should graft our souls so close to each other.' Alfred responded: 'I never expected to be so happy as I have been since our marriage.'[92] Tragically, eleven months after she married Laura died in childbirth.

The speed of conception involved, if not this sad outcome, was common among High Society brides, for whom it was seen as a duty to produce a son and heir as quickly as possible. Out of a sample of three hundred married or widowed peers in the 1910 edition of *Burke's Peerage and Baronetage*, two-thirds had had a child within two years of their marriage. And if childless peers are excluded, the proportion rises to three-quarters with a child born in the first two years of married life. A number of brides, like May Harcourt, became pregnant on their honeymoon or immediately after. This was true of Lady Hastings. She married on 11 February, 1907, and her son was born the following 12 November, while Mary and George Curzon, who had married on 22 April, 1895, had their first daughter on 20 January, 1896. Lady Brooke, too, suffered a miscarriage about five months after her marriage but within a further three months she was again pregnant. Her first child, a son, was born on 10 September, 1882, after a painful labour which lasted seven hours.[93]

Significantly, when Consuelo Marlborough did not conceive immediately, she was quickly reminded of her duty by her husband's family. At her first meeting with his

Molly and Charles Trevelyan, walking at Salcombe, Devon, Easter 1905. (Trustees of the Trevelyan Family Papers)

grandmother, the Dowager Duchess of Marlborough, she was subjected to a searching personal examination. The old lady bestowed a welcoming kiss 'in the manner of a deposed sovereign greeting her successor' and then fixing cold grey eyes upon Consuelo she continued:

> 'Your first duty is to have a child and it must be a son, because it would be intolerable to have that little upstart Winston became Duke. Are you in the family way?' Feeling utterly crushed by my negligence in not having insured Winston's eclipse and depressed by the responsibilities she had heaped upon me, I was glad to take my leave.[94]

Consuelo's first son was born about eighteen months afterwards, in September 1897, and her second son appeared a year later. 'Thus having done my duty', she wrote, 'I felt I should now be allowed a certain measure of the pleasures of life.'[95]

Molly Trevelyan was equally anxious to conceive. She had married early in January 1904 and by July of that year her husband, Charles, was visiting their doctor to ask why Molly was not yet pregnant. She then 'tried the dodge of not being at all active' for two or three months to avert the danger of an early miscarriage. This, too, was unsuccessful and it was not until the beginning of 1905 that she was at last able to report her pregnancy. Her first child, a daughter, was born the following October. In all, she was to have six children, as well as to experience a serious and very unpleasant miscarraige.[96]

However, correspondence between Molly and her sister-in-law, Janet Trevelyan, confirms that by the end of the Victorian era some younger women were beginning to question the merits of unrestricted fertility. Although many thought contraceptive devices were not quite 'decent' because of their association with prostitution, or objected to them on religious grounds, by December 1906, Molly and Janet were debating the merits of the condom as a means of family limitation. Each had given birth to a child in both 1905 and 1906 and Janet was anxiously reporting the comment of her maternity nurse, Nurse Robbie, that condoms were unreliable. 'She has had ever so many babies thr' them, whereas the other things have never failed'.[97] The two women also complained about the doctors who had attended them and their friends during labour. In November 1907, Janet reported visiting one friend whose maternity nurse had arrived only '5 minutes before the baby. The brutal doctor hadn't given the poor thing a single whiff of chloroform.'[98] Six months later, she discussed the birth of a son to another friend:

> Eleanor . . . says Geoffrey appeared with very little trouble – 'about 10 long yells on my part and hardly any chloroform because when we sent for the doctor from his repose on the drawing-room sofa he thought us a pack of alarmed women, as he just decided there was a good 3 hrs. sleep ahead of him.' Doesn't it make your blood boil? Why couldn't the idiotic nurse have given it her. Tell Nurse Robbie she's the only nurse in the world who knows her business, as far as I can make out & that I shall require her services some time in February next year.[99]

Although the Trevelyan women seem to have had limited success in restricting their family size during these years, it is clear that contraception was becoming increasingly accepted in High Society circles. It has been estimated that of those landed aristocrats who married in the 1830s an average of about 7 births per fertile couple was recorded. By the 1870s this had fallen to between 4 and 5 births to each marriage, and in the 1880s to just over 3, with the trend continuing down, to average between 2 and 3 births per marriage on the eve of the First World War.[100] In part the trend was a product of the growing concern to promote women's well-being and the fact that with declining infant mortality it was no longer necessary to over-compensate for the potential loss of an heir by having several additional children. In part, economic pressures induced by the agricultural depression and the competing demands for cash to enjoy the pleasures and luxuries of late Victorian and Edwardian society also made family limitation desirable. The women, for their part, were anxious to minimise the physical suffering associated with too frequent pregnancies and, often enough, the threat to life and welfare which these represented. Maud Yorke, Lady Leconfield's second daughter, was typical of the younger generation when in December 1899, she gloomily confessed to her mother soon after marriage that it was 'rather a bore beginning [a child] so soon, & it will be a great bore all through the hot summer, but it cannot be helped & I shall not mind so much if it is a boy.' A few days later she referred in another letter to the way in which Lady Leconfield herself had borne nine children in the first twenty years of her married life. 'I feel quite *appalled* at the amount of experience you have had! How perfectly *dreadful* it must have been, you can hardly ever have been without it!'[101]

Even the passionate Victoria Sackville-West was so shocked by the very bad labour she experienced with her first child that she was terrified of again becoming pregnant. She and her husband took 'precautions' but it seems likely that their sexual relations were inhibited by her fear. After they had been married for just over ten years he virtually ceased to sleep with her, and sought consolation elsewhere.[102]

A similarly drastic decision in favour of sexual abstinence was taken by the former Margot Tennant after a fifth baby was born early in 1907. Almost thirteen years before she had married the leading Liberal politician and future Prime Minister, Herbert Henry Asquith, as his second wife. Her first child was born in May 1895 after a long and painful confinement which nearly killed her. Although the baby was born alive, it died a few hours later, and a similar fate was to await another two of Margot's babies. After the fifth birth, which reduced her to a mere shadow of herself, the doctors warned that there must be no more children. From 1907 onwards, she and her husband occupied separate rooms and the sexual aspect of their relationship was at an end.[103]

The tragic fate of Margaret Spencer, wife of Viscount Althorp, was a warning of the dangers attached to childbirth among the well-to-do in the early twentieth century. Margaret had married in 1887 but shortly after giving birth to her sixth child, in July 1906, she died of heart failure at the early age of forty-one. Her husband, always delicate, never completely got over the loss and it was their eldest daughter, then just seventeen, who took responsibility for the running of the household and the overseeing of the younger children. She was aided by advice from her mother's married sister, Lady Reid.[104] Similarly Mary Curzon, who died in 1906 ostensibly from heart failure, never fully recovered from illness associated with a miscarriage in the summer of 1904. This had itself occurred a few months after the birth of her third daughter. To her husband it was a bitter blow. 'I am not fit for society,' he told a friend, 'and desire only to hide my head.'[105]

However, problems connected with sexual relations and childbirth were not the only causes of marital difficulties. Incompatability of personality or eccentric conduct on the part of one of the partners could also lead to marriage failure. Despite the fact that the 1857 Matrimonial Causes Act had made divorce easier for all sectors of society it was still frowned upon in aristocratic circles. Hence out of a sample of 350 peers in 1910 only eight had been divorced – including the 5th Earl of Rosslyn, who had been divorced twice. In a ninth case the 6th Lord Walsingham had married a divorcée as his first wife, but she had died in 1906 and he had then remarried. Of the eight divorced peers, six had had their marriage ended between 1901 and 1910 and only one – the 15th Lord Zouche – had been divorced before the mid-1890s.[106]

But if divorce was regarded with disfavour, judicial separation was also considered questionable. Often enough, husbands and wives who did not get on merely went their separate ways within the large houses in which they lived. They continued to practise 'a polite observance of the deference each owed the other' when they met in public, but otherwise had little contact with one another. Sometimes, however, this attempt at normality created so much tension that separation was decided upon. It was in these circumstances that the former Consuelo Vanderbuilt became judicially separated from the 9th Duke of Marlborough in 1906. As a consequence she was excluded from Court but with the support of her mother-in-law (who had herself been divorced from the 8th Duke in 1883) and of her own family and friends she was able to maintain a place in London Society.[107]

Other women followed the example of the young Baroness De Forest, who left her husband for a time in 1910 because of his ill-treatment; he had reputedly beaten her on two occasions.[108] But there was no formal separation between them.

A far more dramatic example of personal incompatability arose when the eccentric future 5th Marquess of Anglesey married his cousin, Lilian Chetwynd, in 1898. About nine months later he succeeded to the title and immediately embarked on a massive spending spree. This included purchasing a large and valuable collection of jewellery. His preferred way of admiring this appalled his young wife. Each night he made her undress and then covered her naked body with precious stones 'until she stood before

Lady Blandford, mother-in-law of Consuelo Duchess of Marlborough, and the divorced wife of the 8th Duke of Marlborough. She was fond of practical jokes and is here shown driving a miniature cart drawn by a tame pig at Mr Wingfield's home, Ampthill, in June 1908. (The author)

him dripping in emeralds, rubies and diamonds. He then forced her to sleep wearing those jewels'. He seems to have had no sexual interest in her and the marriage was never consummated. Eventually she left him and the marriage was annulled in 1900. After that, the Marquess immersed himself in the theatre, acting in productions himself and organizing expensive tours. By June 1904, when his trustees intervened, his reckless conduct had brought him to hopeless insolvency. Arrangements were made to auction his belongings to pay the enormous debts. This included the disposal of his collection of jewellery as well as a vast range of other effects; the sale of his clothing alone took three days. Nothing of value was spared. Even his Coronation robes went under the hammer. After the sale the Marquess retired to France and died from pleurisy at Monte Carlo in March 1905, at the age of thirty.[109]

A less bizarre but more puzzling example of marital breakdown involved the highly respectable Margaret Cowell Stepney, youngest daughter of the 2nd Baron de Tabley. In 1875 she married a former Foreign Office official and Welsh landowner, Arthur (later Sir Arthur) Cowell Stepney. Although at an early stage he displayed certain eccentricities of conduct, their marriage was at first happy. In September 1876 a daughter was born, apparently to the father's great joy. However, less than a month later he left home, without explanation, and never cohabited with his wife again. He subsequently made certain allegations against her (including a charge that she had married him for his money), but when these were investigated by his friends they were found to be groundless. Indeed, Margaret was determined to accept as little money as possible from him once they had separated.[110] Although he was given treatment for mental delusions and in 1877 and 1878 travelled on the Continent with a doctor, he steadfastly refused to be reconciled with his wife. Yet in other respects he appears to have been quite sane and to have mixed freely in society. From August 1876 to May 1878 and again from July 1886 to 1892 he served as a Member of Parliament for the Carmarthen district. He acted as High sheriff in 1884 and was a magistrate and deputy-lieutenant for Carmarthen during these years.

For Margaret, meanwhile the sudden breakdown of her marriage was devastating. A year after her husband had left she was still in a state of shock. Only her little daughter gave her any consolation. Gradually, however, she accepted her situation and began to create a modest social life for herself, often in company with her great friend, Mary Gladstone. From the mid-1880s her husband paid fleeting visits to her and her daughter so that he might see the little girl, to whom he was apparently much attached. When he arrived his wife was careful never to ask for any explanation of his conduct. Eventually Sir Arthur went to the United States and on 1 January, 1901, he wrote to inform his daughter that he had become an American citizen. He then asked her to manage his Welsh estates. Soon after, he seems to have contemplated remarriage and to this end he initiated proceedings for a divorce in Idaho. A decree was granted in March 1903 on the grounds of his wife's desertion, since it was claimed she had refused to accompany him to the United States! However, her lawyers contested its validity, claiming that he had no permanent residence in Idaho. Margaret herself now reluctantly applied for a judicial separation and this was granted in May 1903. Sir Arthur, in the meantime, remained in the United States and in 1909 he collapsed and died at a railway station in Yuma,

Arizona. Apparently he had suffered a heart attack brought on by the excessive heat, but to his wife this sudden end was the final blow in their ill-starred relationship: '*just now,*' she confessed to a friend, 'the tragedy and the pathos and the utter *un*necessariness of our two wrecked lives are heart-breaking – and . . . I always had just a hope that when either of us was dying the other might come.'[111]

Fortunately few brides suffered the fate of either the Marchioness of Anglesey or Lady Cowell Stepney. For most couples, the breakdown of a marriage was concealed from prying eyes by an outward display of harmony. Only intimate friends were aware of the true state of affairs. As Lady Warwick put it: 'The . . . thing that mattered was that there should be no scandal; everything was all right if only it was kept quiet, hushed up, covered.' Where children were born as a result of extra-marital infidelities they were frequently brought up in the husband's family as his own children. This was the case with two of the Duchess of Rutland's daughters, for example, while the Duke consoled himself with 'a series of jolly little actresses'. A similar process of assimilation was applied to the little daughter born to Lady Cynthia Asquith's mother, Lady Elcho, as a result of her liaison with the notorious philanderer, Wilfrid Scawen Blunt. She was reconciled with her husband before the birth and the following year they had another son.[112] By such means the wheels of society were kept running smoothly, despite hidden turbulence.

CHAPTER FIVE

Taken Care Of!

. . . as for ladies' maids, they ruled their mistresses with a rod of iron. The latter were helpless without them; they could not even do up their own hair. . . . [M]y mother's generation and Granny's . . . were too helpless for words, and I do not believe they would have known how to boil an egg if they were starving. They never even took their own tickets at a railway station – a footman went on and did it, having the carriage engaged, and all the rugs and hand-luggage settled in there by the maid who went with him. . . . One travelled first-class with a maid, though she went in the second-class carriage next door.

LADY CLODAGH ANSON, *Victorian Days* (1957), 264–5.

In the opulent world of the later Victorians and Edwardians, when much emphasis was laid on luxury and ostentation, the demand for services of all kinds increased sharply. Of none was that more true than of personal service, despite a growing reluctance among many younger people to take up what they often regarded as the drudging and restricted routine of indoor servants.

The importance of domestic staff was underlined in the household manuals of the day, such as the *Servant's Practical Guide* (1880) which stated firmly: 'Without the constant co-operation of well-trained servants, domestic machinery is completely thrown out of gear, and the best bred of hostesses placed at a disadvantage.'[1] This was a view which Lady Cynthia Asquith largely shared. She lamented the humiliating dependence of upper-class women on maids even to help with the putting on and taking off of the dresses 'we were for ever changing . . . Either they laced up at the back, or they fastened with quite un-get-at-able intricacies of hooks and eyes.' When she was in her teens she had her own maid and 'what with perpetually making, mending, washing, darning and packing . . . she was . . . no idle woman. She also played the part of duenna and took me about London.'[2] Nevertheless, although she regretted the way that she and her friends had been so dependent on maids, she believed that 'there was never . . . any virtue other than necessity in keeping only one instead of several servants'.

Sometimes, especially in the case of middle-aged and elderly women, this reliance on domestics extended to the selection of the clothes they wore. According to Lady Clodagh Anson, her grandmother, the Duchess of Beaufort, had all her clothes made by her lady's maid:

> She would . . . say, 'Will you put on your new gown, your Grace?' and produce one that Granny had never seen or thought of – could anything be more uninteresting? . . . If a maid makes some of your clothes the expense in thread alone seems to come to as much as if it were bought in a shop, . . . while the sight of little bits of the stuff lying about everywhere has sickened you of the whole garment long before it is finished.[3]

A valet offered a similar personal service to the male members of the household. Not only did he need an equable temperament and an efficient appreciation of the intricacies of his master's daily routine, but he had to ensure that the appropriate attire was always ready for wear, that boots were polished, and brushed hats kept glossy. Often, as with Henry Moat, Sir George Sitwell's valet, it was upon him that the employer depended for companionship on foreign travels and for nursing during sickness.[4] His knowledge of the details of court dress was also necessary to prevent the more careless employers from appearing improperly clad. Thus on one occasion the then Prime Minister, the Marquess of Salisbury, suddenly realized that he was required to attend a Drawing-Room. He hastened to his Arlington Street home and dressed without the help of his valet. When he arrived at the Palace, however, he was found to be wearing the tunic of an Elder Brother of Trinity House; the hose of a Privy Councillor; his Garter was over the wrong shoulder; the lace around his throat was misplaced; and he had 'an incongruous hat and curious old-fashioned shoes with strangely wrought buckles'.[5] The Prince of Wales, who was meticulous over sartorial matters, was horrified at his appearance. He flew into a passion, complaining that Salisbury was 'dressed like a guy . . . twenty ministers and ambassadors looking on . . . what can they think of a premier who can't put on his clothes?'[6] Had the Prime Minister's valet been consulted the contretemps would doubtless have been avoided.

But aside from the issue of dependence, the employment of retinues of servants, especially male servants, was regarded as a symbol of a family's social standing. To have a footman in fine livery with plush breeches, silk stockings, and a supercilious expression to answer the front door was a form of display which few socialites could resist.[7]

A similar spirit lay behind the refusal of some of the great houses to employ commercial breweries or laundries to supply the beer and clean linen used in running the household. At Longleat, for example, callers at the back door were usually offered a glass or two of home-brewed ale, and leather flagons of that liquid, together with plates of bread and cheese, were left standing on the table in the servants' hall for anyone to help himself.[8] At Blenheim Palace, too, even in the early 1890s the Marlboroughs kept a separate dairy and laundry to cater for household needs, while at Compton Verney, Lord Willoughby de Broke recalled the extravagant use of coal in the kitchen. A ton was consumed each day and 'I have had the privilege of seeing the sirloin hanging

New Footman. "I SUPPOSE THERE ARE A LOT OF NOBS 'ERE TO-DAY, MR. BLOUNT?"
Butler. "A FEW MY LAD, A FEW. BUT MOST ARE THE SECONDARY CROWD THAT WE 'AS TO ASK ONCE A YEAR."

'Duty' entertaining. The snobbishness of senior servants is pinpointed by *Punch* (1911)

by a chain slowly turning round and round and being basted by the stout kitchen wench, whose face was quite as red and nearly as hot as the huge open fire in front of her'.[9]

But elsewhere economies were under way. In 1909 the Sackvilles of Knole Park began sending washing out to the Darenth Laundry and in the same year they cut the size of their female domestic staff by four. It is likely that some of these were laundrymaids. The Duke of Bedford, too, utilized the services of the Tavistock District Laundry each summer while the family were staying at Endsleigh, one of their country houses. At Woburn a local baker began to supply bread and later cakes and buns to the big house from the early 1900s – probably for the servants' hall. And in order to economize in the use of seamstresses, in 1910 the Bedfords for the first time ordered ready-made print dresses for the housemaids from Harvey Nichols. The order was regularly repeated thereafter.[10]

Many of the grander owners kept dual establishments staffed by a nucleus of permanent servants in both town and country. Usually these consisted of a housekeeper, who also carried out caretaking duties, and one or two housemaids to look after the rooms while the family was away. Thus in the early spring of 1891 the Marquess of Salisbury kept an indoor staff of eighteen at his London home, 20 Arlington Street, and a further five servants at his country mansion, Hatfield. As an indication of the role of technical change in the running of households it is interesting to note that two of the London servants were electrical engineers.[11] Similarly the 11th Duke of Bedford had two large houses in Belgrave Square, as well as his principal seat at Woburn Abbey. According to his grandson, he kept:

> four cars and . . . eight chauffeurs in town, eating their heads off. They were responsible for the first part of the journey down to the country of any guests. The town car used to take you as far as Hendon, where you had to get out and join the car which had been sent up from Woburn. You never travelled with your suitcase, that was not considered the thing to do. It had to come in another car, so you had a chauffeur and a footman with yourself, and a chauffeur and a footman with the suitcase, with another four to meet you. Eight people involved in moving one person from London to Woburn.[12]

On the largest estates the staff employed might run into hundreds. At Woburn the army of fifty or sixty household servants was supplemented by a vast array of outdoor workers. This large band of retainers was employed from the time the 11th Duke succeeded in the early 1890s until his death in 1940. They included one man whose sole duty it was to trim and keep filled the large number of oil lamps which were still in use. To add to the problems of maintaining – and modernizing – Woburn, the Duke refused to allow any workmen to be seen in his presence. If he appeared in the distance they would duck out of sight, if necessary in a cupboard, until he had walked past.

At the 1st Duke of Westminster's Eaton estate near Chester in the 1880s and 1890s there were over three hundred people employed, including ground staff. The Duke, as the wealthiest landowner in the country, could afford to have his slightest whim attended to. Hence thirty-five workers were engaged in keeping the cluttered rooms dusted, the oil lamps cleaned and trimmed, and the bedrooms supplied with cans of hot water for baths. A French chef presided over a large kitchen staff, there were thirteen laundrymaids, and seven male employees manned the estate fire brigade. Fifteen men worked in the stables, seventy were employed under the head forester in the woods and coppices, and a further forty worked on the home farm under a bailiff. There was a stud manager as well as a stud groom with his attendant staff. The gardens, too, were lavishly supplied with labour, the head gardener presiding over a staff of forty, some of whom lived in a bothy with their own cook and housemaid to look after them. So great was the importance attached to the comfort and convenience of the family and their guests that the estate was 'as self-contained as any small town . . . all the services were there to supply whatever might be needed at a moment's notice. Plumbers, cabinet-makers, painters, glaziers, electricians – their skills were permanently available.'[13]

At Welbeck Abbey in the early 1900s the Duke of Portland employed a staff of around 320 divided among sixteen different departments, including the gardens, gymnasium, racing stables and golf course as well as the house itself. Among them were fourteen housemaids and thirty-eight men and women employed in the kitchens and associated departments. As in all large households there was a clearly established hierarchy among the domestic staff, with the juniors under the direction of the head of their own department. Frederick Gorst, who went to Welbeck as a young footman around the turn

Servants employed by Lord Windsor at St Fagans Castle, Cardiff, in the 1880s. From the end of that decade the family spent a large part of every summer in Wales, with a full complement of household staff present, many of them coming from the Windsors' seat in Worcestershire. At that time between 45 and 50 servants might be at work, but when the family went away the housekeeper was left in sole charge of the house, with a small number of maids to help her and an 'odd man' to do the heavier work. (National Museum of Wales: Welsh Folk Museum)

of the century, received his orders from the steward. His first task was to learn the geography of the massive house, including where the pantries were located, where the silver was kept, and where the bell boxes were situated.[14] He found himself working alongside 'scores of people' whom he did not know.

Gorst also recalled the problems involved in moving the family and their retainers to London for the Season and from London to their estate in Caithness for the shooting. Many of the senior servants and some of the juniors regularly travelled around with their employer. It required a special train to carry them to Scotland. 'We referred to it as the "iron caravan",' wrote the footman. During the long journey the Duke and Duchess occupied one carriage, which was divided into bedrooms, a sitting room, and a dining area. The next carriage was occupied by the children and their governess, while the senior servants (nicknamed the 'Upper Ten') rode in the carriage after that:

> then the footmen, the chef and his helpers, and chauffeurs; and the final passenger car was reserved for [the] stillroom maids and housemaids. The rest of the train was a long string of wagons, each one housing an automobile.[15]

Every time the train stopped the Duchess's personal footman ran forward to see if she wanted anything, even though she had her lady's maid travelling with her.

At Longleat, the Marquess of Bath's domestic staff was more modest than that at either Eaton or Welbeck but there, too, about forty-three servants were employed. Fifteen were male (including the steward and a French chef) and twenty-eight female, of whom the most senior were the housekeeper, two ladies' maids and the nanny, There were also fourteen men employed in the stables. When the family moved to London for the season they took seventeen of the staff with them, together with eleven horses and five stable men.[16]

The limited size of town houses meant that London establishments were normally much smaller than their rural counterparts. Often contacts were maintained between town and country, with the despatch of hampers of dirty linen by rail from London to the country-house laundry, and its return by a similar route. Garden produce, too, was sent up from country estates, for it was during the months of the Season that some of the best vegetables and fruit would be gathered. The Earl of Derby, for example, obtained produce for his town house from the gardens at Coworth Park near Sunningdale, while the enormous kitchen garden at Knowsley supplied Stanley House, Newmarket, as well as the Knowsley residents.[17] Similarly, the Nisbet Hamilton family obtained flowers and luxury fruit from Archerfield, their East Lothian estate, while their Engish residence, Bloxholm Hall, Lincolnshire, supplied more routine vegetables and fruit.[18] Produce such as asparagus and beans survived the journey packed and separated by spinach leaves, but fruit required more careful treatment. One head gardener claimed to feel as much pleasure when informed 'of the satisfactory condition of such soft fruits as ripe Peaches and Nectarines after a journey of 800 miles as in winning a well-contested prize at a flower show'.[19] Clearly no expense was spared in satisfying the culinary requirements of ambitious High Society hosts and hostesses.

Furthermore, despite the limitations on the size of town properties, the staff employed in the London houses of the richest and most prestigious families could be considerable. In 1881 the Earl and Countess of Dudley had a resident staff of thirty-three at Dudley House, Park Lane, to look after themselves and their three young children. These included, on the female side, a housekeeper, two ladies' maids, a nanny and nursery maid, five housemaids, two stillroom maids, three kitchenmaids, and a sick nurse, as well as a needlewoman to assist with the household sewing. There was also a housekeeper to look after the stable staff. The male workers were headed by the steward, a valet and an under butler. There were four footmen.[20]

At the Marquess of Lansdowne's impressive mansion at 54 Berkeley Square in the same year the resident staff consisted of twenty-three servants plus a governess. Of these, fourteen were females and nine males; only one of them – the gardener – had been born on the family's Wiltshire estate. The rest, as was common with employees in these large households, came from all parts of the country or even, as in the case of Lady Lansdowne's Swiss lady's maid, from overseas. French and Swiss ladies' maids and valets and French chefs were often recruited by the social élite because they were thought more skilled – and more exclusive – than their home-grown counterparts.

Often the servants in these households obtained their position through personal recommendation from a previous employer, who was perhaps a friend of the family. In other cases they were recruited through advertisements in newspapers like *The Times* or

Servants seeking situations at Mrs Hunt's registry office, Duke Street, London, *c*. 1900. (The author)

by the use of specialist servant agencies. These latter proliferated in the late nineteenth century as they outgrew their earlier dubious reputation as the resort of prostitutes and inferior servants only. By 1898, 122 different agencies were advertising in the London *Post Office Trade Directory*, compared to less than eighty which had appeared in the 1880 edition. The most prestigious of them was Mrs Hunt's office in Duke Street, which claimed to have been in business for half a century and to be able to send 'tested job servants for anywhere in a few hours' notice'. For those who wished to interview potential applicants for permanent positions, rooms were available on the premises. Mrs Hunt claimed to run the largest agency ever established and to have daily letters 'in and out' in excess of two thousand, with an 'average of 136 persons . . . suited every day'.[21]

Sometimes employers also recommended servants to potential masters and mistresses through the columns of the newspapers, so that Lady Fitzwygram inserted an advertisement on behalf of her second housemaid, who had lived with her for three years, and the Hon. Clarice Rendel highly recommended 'E. Mason as Head Housemaid of 3; for town or town and country; leaving solely on account of death'.[22] There are many others in a similar vein.

In most larger establishments the steward or the housekeeper would hire the junior staff. One girl whose family lived on the Lloyd Baker estate in Gloucestershire remembered obtaining her first position with the help of Mrs Lloyd Baker, but she was interviewed in London by the housekeeper when she secured her second. This was for a post as junior housemaid at Ashridge, Lord and Lady Brownlow's mansion in Hertfordshire. She was especially impressed by the fact that the housekeeper wore a black silk dress 'though it was morning, and a black silk apron. I thought "Oh to wear a black silk dress in the morning".' At Ashridge she was instructed in her duties by the head housemaid.[23]

The population census returns for well-to-do households in the fashionable districts of London confirm the substantial numbers of servants employed. Thus at Carlton Gardens in 1881 the Earl of Dalhousie, who lived at no. 1 with his wife and two infant sons, had thirteen servants; next door lived the wealthy banker and landowner, Lord Overstone, with his married daughter and son-in-law and sixteen servants; and at no. 3 Lord and Lady Forrester were attended by thirteen servants. At nos. 4, 5 and 6 there were only servants in residence, acting as caretakers, but at no. 7 lived Lord and Lady Rosslyn, Frances Maynard's mother and step-father. The 1881 census was conducted shortly before Frances's marriage to Lord Brooke and apart from the family there were fifteen servants living in, as well as Frances's much-loved governess, Miss Blake.[24] Small wonder that years later Lady Brooke (then the Countess of Warwick) should conclude that servants were 'as much a part of the household as any member of the family'. She then added complacently, if not entirely accurately, that such retainers:

> would as soon have thought of criticizing their 'betters' as they would have thought of criticizing God. Masters and mistresses were 'different' – a race of favoured beings. . . . [Servants] had pride, too, and an obstinate snobbery. They were often more conservative and greater sticklers for etiquette than their masters and mistresses were.[25]

In practice, of course, many servants were not only ready to criticize their employers but to demonstrate their independence by moving on if they were dissatisfied with their treatment or wished to gain promotion. But some, as Lady Warwick suggested, did form close ties with the family they served. They also enjoyed the reflected glory of their employers' superior social status and for that reason, too, became identified with them. 'The happiest time of my life was from the age of fourteen to twenty-two,' declared one former servant, 'for those years were spent in the stately homes of England before the decline of the real gentry and noblemen set in . . . I feel that I was privileged to have lived in such mansions and to have seen and touched the wonderful treasures they contained.'[26]

Significantly when Lady Maud Cecil married the future Earl of Selborne in 1883 she proudly reported that the upper servants had given her 'a most lovely silver looking glass & brushes'. 'My thoughts keep running on the curious fact that all these superfluities keep pouring in on me,' she told her fiancé, 'while so many want bread & coals. It's not an original reflection I know, but it comes with a new force every now & then & almost stuns one morally.'[27]

Many other reminiscences bear witness to the intimacy which could grow up between members of the family and their servants, and which found expression in such events as the holding of daily prayers for all the household. At Eaton, this made a large congregation and at the end the servants filed out in solemn procession, in order of rank. First came the head female servants and then the housemaids and kitchenmaids in their print frocks and frilly caps, with the men-servants bringing up the rear.[28]

But often it was with the children of the house that the warmest links were forged.

REFLECTED GLORY.

Shopman. "HERE! HI! ARE YOU HIS GRACE THE DUKE OF BAYSWATER?"   Magnificent Flunkey "I HAM!"

The pretentiousness of the flunkey mocked by *Punch* (1883)

Lord Willoughby de Broke regarded Jesse Eales, the head gamekeeper at Compton Verney, as his 'first and . . . best friend' after his parents.

> It was with him that I saw my first fox killed; it was with him that I killed my first pheasant, partridge, duck, hare, rabbit and rook; also my first fish. He showed me my first rat hunt, and escorted me on my first expedition in quest of birds' nests.[29]

He wrote, too, of the 'bond of love between master and man' which existed at Compton Verney and the way in which many old retainers remained 'part and parcel of the establishment'. It is impossible to know whether they shared his sentiments or merely deferred to the wishes of one who so clearly dominated life in their community.

Edith Sitwell, who confessed that her parents 'were strangers . . . from the moment of my birth', relied for childhood affection upon her 'dear old nurse Davis [and] . . my father's valet Henry Moat – whose friendship with my brothers and me lasted until his death'.[30]

Even happy youngsters, like Molly Trevelyan's children at Wallington in Northumberland, regarded Keith, the head gardener, Whitley, the coachman, and Slade, the gamekeeper, as special allies. It was Whitley who taught Pauline, the eldest child, to ride in Rotten Row, while Slade took her and her brothers and sisters on the moors, where he showed them grouse and golden plovers.[31] The housekeeper, Mrs Prestwich, had formerly been nanny to a previous generation of Trevelyan children and she stayed on

Often a nanny was closer to the children of the family than was their mother, and this was especially the case when the parents had marital problems. Mrs Trotter was nanny to the children of John Edward Courtenay Bodley. This photograph was taken in 1906; two years later the Bodleys were divorced. The photograph, and other ones of Mrs Trotter, appear in the album of Mr Bodley's only daughter, Ava. (The author)

with the family until her death. According to Pauline, the staff 'knew their place', but this gave a 'sense of confidence and not of inferiority or unhappiness'.[32]

Still stronger bonds of affection linked Mabell, Countess of Airlie, and her lady's maid, Louisa Roffey. Louisa had joined the household when the motherless Mabell was in her early teens and she quickly assumed the role of 'duenna, companion and friend' to her and her sisters. When Mabell married, Louisa accompanied her to her new home at Cortachy in Scotland. There the treatment she received from the other staff added to Lady Airlie's own unhappiness during the early months of her marriage. For the Cortachy servants continued to regard the forceful Dowager Countess of Airlie as their mistress rather than the head of the family's new young wife. 'This attitude spread through the whole household,' wrote Lady Airlie, years later, 'My own maid – dear loyal Louisa . . . – was treated most unkindly by my mother-in-law's housekeeper. She was given no carpet in her room, and no form of heating all through the bitter cold of January and February. She was never introduced to any member of the staff, and at meals in the servants' hall no one spoke to her. In every possible way she was made to feel an interloper.'[33] But the warm ties between mistress and maid survived and Louisa remained with Lady Airlie, offering affection and support, for the rest of her life.

The Countess of Airlie, however, was not the only High Society bride to experience difficulties with the servants. Mary Curzon encountered even greater problems when she and her husband set up house at 5 Carlton House Terrace in 1895. George Curzon had engaged all the servants before his marriage and Mary soon found their behaviour 'tyrannical'.

> They would do as much work as they thought they were paid to do, and not a stroke more. When she complained that the grocery bills were too high, the cook gave notice. She was served so little food to eat herself, that she had to send her plate back to the kitchen 'three or four times' for a refill. Then the footman ran off with the parlour-maid, and the best of the housemaids broke her leg. . . . Mary . . . found herself haggling over the price of tomatoes in Covent Garden market and queueing up at the Army [and] Navy Stores, because the servants, knowing that otherwise complaints of the cost would follow, insisted that she accompany them.[34]

This thinly disguised insubordination arose partly from the fact that Mary, as a wealthy American, was unfamiliar with the disciplinary procedures needed to manage a household of English servants. Another difficulty was that the staff had too little to do, especially after the Curzons moved to a smaller house at 4 Carlton Gardens. For not only did the young couple rarely entertain but their own personal tastes were very simple. Hence the fourteen indoor servants, plus a coachman and two grooms, had little to do but to wait on one another and defy their mistress. 'English servants,' wrote Mary, 'are *fiends*. They seem to plot among themselves. They are malignant and stupid and make life barely worth living.'[35]

Lady Colin Campbell was another victim of servant malevolence. When she was accused of committing adultery by her husband during a lengthy divorce trial at the end of 1886, the principal witnesses against her were former servants. They had noted not only from whom she received calls but to whom she wrote letters. Her lady's maid claimed that her conduct with Lord Blandford (the future 8th Duke of Marlborough) had been 'the constant topic of conversation amongst the servants'.[36] During the subsequent proceedings the Duke of Marlborough was one of four men cited as co-respondents. Another was a former army officer and the chief of the Metropolitan Fire Brigade, by name Captain Shaw. In this case James O'Neill, a man-servant employed by the Campbells, claimed to have peered through the keyhole of the dining-room door when Lady Colin was entertaining him and to have seen them lying down together on the carpet. Not surprisingly both of them vehemently denied the allegation. Indeed, Lady Colin responded by accusing her husband of committing adultery with the housemaid, Amelia Watson. However, when medical evidence showed Amelia was still a virgin that charge collapsed. Eventually, after a sordid trial lasting for eighteen days, the jury refused to find for either of the parties and no divorce was granted. But it is significant that Lady Colin's counsel, Sir Charles Russell, stressed that virtually the whole of her husband's case against her had depended on the 'gossiping stories of servants'.[37]

Some employers, for their part, treated their domestics with lack of consideration. Lady Londesborough, Edith Sitwell's grandmother, not only forbade her footmen to look at each other in her presence or to speak except in their professional capacity but she herself never spoke to any servant except the butler, Martin, and the old housekeeper, Mrs Selby.[38] They conveyed her wishes to the other staff members.

Even Lady Randolph Churchill, despite her general good nature, showed a quick temper with her maids. 'The evening ritual of dressing for dinner inevitably caused tantrums and . . . hairbrushes, etc., would fly through the air.' Yet despite this, Gentry, her lady's maid, remained with her many years, and after Lord Randolph Churchill's death in January 1895, his valet stayed on and eventually became the butler, while his wife was the cook.[39]

Junior servants, on the other hand, were likely to be firmly disciplined by their own senior colleagues. Mrs D.K. Dence, who began her domestic career in a large country house in Buckinghamshire in 1906, when she was fifteen, recalled that her working day as a housemaid began at 6 a.m. A quarter of an hour before this the housekeeper rang a bell from her bed and this sounded just outside the maids' sleeping quarters.

> Our work was carried out by the light of tallow dips which we pushed along in front of us, as we crept over the carpets with dust pans and brush. . . . The public rooms were dining-room, serving room, study, library, drawing-room, cloakrooms and corridors, and all this had to be finished by 9 o'clock. . . . When the house was full most week-ends I have had as many as 15 fireplaces to clean after attending Church. We were obliged to go to Church all of us, wearing bonnets and black, no 'feathers, flowers, veils, furs or shining jewellery'. . . . There were many restrictions; one must ask to post a letter although the post office was just outside one of the entrances. . . . We were not allowed to speak in the corridors or to the men servants, although we were often working in the same room.[40]

At mealtimes the juniors were not allowed to talk, nor were they given a pudding at the main meal of the day. That was reserved for the seniors, who ate it in the housekeeper's room.

Even at the Trevelyans' Wallington only the senior staff were allowed in the front rooms of the house – that is the drawing-room, dining-room, library and front hall. The younger housemaids and the kitchenmaids never saw the front door or any of the finely furnished principal rooms.[41] It was in such circumstances that Margaret Thomas, a kitchenmaid in a large country house in Yorkshire, confessed to having met her mistress on only one occasion. That was when she was dismissed because the family were moving to Scotland for the shooting. She 'told me they weren't taking me as I wasn't strong enough for the hard life there. I was upset as I had been looking forward to the visit.'[42]

Questions of status and conspicuous display were not confined, however, to the size of domestic staff recruited. They also extended to the servants' appearance and to their skills. It was common for fashionable families to specify the minimum height for the footmen or butlers they wished to recruit. Royal footmen were supposed to be over six feet, and tall men of good appearance were able to command higher wages than less fortunate rivals. Hence the pay of footmen depended 'far more upon height and appearance than efficiency'.[43] According to the social investigator, Charles Booth, a second footman who was only 5 ft. 6 in. tall would earn no more than £20 to £22 a year in London during the 1890s, while one 5 ft. 10 in. and above would obtain £28 to £30.

Similar differences applied to the wages of first footmen, too. The flavour of this is caught by such advertisements as that which appeared in *The Times* of 28 April, 1885, for a footman 'in a nobleman's house in the country. Must thoroughly understand lamps. Height not less than 5 ft. 10 in.'

Even female servants were subjected to these specifications. In 1905 Lady Coleridge recommended 'a tall girl of 19' to act as under lady's maid: 'knowledge of dressmaking and hairdressing.' Four years later Mrs Pritchard of Donnington Manor, Moreton in Marsh, sought an experienced parlourmaid: 'good valet, waitress, carver, plate cleaner; Church of England . . . seven servants; lamps. State age, height, wages, experience.'[44] At Woburn Abbey the 11th Duke of Bedford insisted that the housemaids must all be 5 ft. 10 in. or above in what was clearly another example of the exercise of aristocratic whim.

A concern for ostentatious display lay behind the dressing of footmen and coachmen in elaborate liveries. Even at the beginning of the twentieth century the young Frederick Gorst was surprised to discover that he was expected to wear powdered hair when he became footman to Lord and Lady Howard at 19 Rutland Gate, London. The purpose of this was to make the footmen look as much alike as possible and to create an impression of uniformity when they served together. Gorst was also much struck by the livery he had to wear:

> I had never before put on blue plush knee breeches, white stockings, and pumps with silver buckles. I . . . was expected to wear a claret-coloured, swallow-tailed coat with silver buttons, a claret waistcoat, and a stiff, white shirt.[45]

A still more extravagant régime was instituted by the 5th Earl of Lonsdale shortly after he succeeded to the title in the early 1880s. His male servants were dressed in canary-yellow jackets with dark-blue facings, white beaver hats and white buckskin breeches.[46] He was attended by an entourage almost as grand as the court of minor European royalty. He even had his own Master of Horse and his own Chamberlain. His private orchestra of twenty-five members, under a Master of Music, travelled with him from one mansion to another. This army of officials and servants protected him from the administrative details attached to his large inheritance, and the use of domestic staff to mediate between employers and the outside world was common among members of High Society. In these fashionable households the protective role of servants often reached a point 'where the most intimate human relationships were mediated through servants in order to give maximum time for preparation and minimum unpleasantness in face-to-face contacts'.[47]

The concern with status also influenced the servants' own attitudes. It led to a stress on hierarchy and discipline below stairs and to sharp pay differentials. Thus at Wilton House, Wiltshire, on the eve of the First World War, the Earl of Pembroke paid £60 a year to the housekeeper; £75 a year to the female cook; and £85 a year to the house steward. At the lower end of the hierarchy, the steward's room boy and the fifth and sixth housemaids received £16 a year. At this time, in the spring of 1914, there were thirty-six servants employed, of whom at least fifteen seem to have accompanied their employer when he moved to his London residence in Chesterfield Gardens.[48]

These below-stairs social divisions likewise extended to such matters as where the servants ate their meals and with whom. When Consuelo Marlborough arrived at Blenheim Palace in the mid-1890s she quickly realized that her 'first duty' was to concern herself with the running of the household. At the head of affairs was the house steward whose principal preoccupation was:

> to keep everyone, including himself, in his place. His rule in the men's department was absolute – only the two electricians, who at that time were treated with the respect due to men of science, were his equals. The groom of the chambers ranked next. One of his duties was to keep the numerous writing tables supplied with paper, pens and ink. . . . Marlborough's valet shared the prestige that tails and striped trousers conferred. Such a costume was considered necessary to uphold the standard of elegance of the steward's room, where the valets and [ladies'] maids had their meals, strictly seated according to the rank given their masters upstairs. . . . [The] upper servants remained entrenched in their own dining-room, to which such newcomers as chauffeurs were refused admittance and sent packing to the servants' hall. Next in the servants' hierarchy came the under butler and three or four footmen. There were also humble individuals who were known by the strange name of odd men . . . because they were expected to carry out the butler's wishes however strange they might be. They were kept busy carrying coal to the fifty or more grates; they also washed the windows . . .
>
> On the distaff side, the housekeeper ruled. I felt sorry for her, for she had only six housemaids which was an inadequate staff to keep so colossal a house in order. . . . There were, further, five laundresses, and a still-room maid who cooked the breakfasts and the cakes and scones for our teas. . . .
>
> A French chef presided over a staff of four. Frequent rows between him and the housekeeper ensued over the intricacies of breakfast trays, since meat dishes were provided by the kitchen, and the kitchen and still-room were separated by yards and yards of damp, unheated passages so that the food was often cold.[49]

Consuelo found the constant presence of servants irksome, especially when in her early married life she was attended around the house by a small black page whom Marlborough had brought from Egypt for the purpose. She eventually found an excuse to send him packing but 'with a page in the house, a coachman or a postilion to take me for drives and a groom to accompany my rides, my freedom was quite successfully restricted'.

Later, when her children were born, there was a 'fourth estate', the nursery, presided over by an autocratic and snobbish head nurse. 'Still another important person in the household was my maid. She was with me twenty years and died in my service. . . . She . . . made me the object of a loyal but somewhat hectoring devotion.'[50]

Sometimes below-stairs sensitivities over status could disrupt otherwise harmonious employer/servant relationships. Lady Augusta Fane recalled that a well-bred but untitled girl of her acquaintance was told by her long-serving lady's maid that she wished to leave. On being asked the reason, the woman replied that although she was happy in her post it hurt her feelings always to walk out last from the servants' hall when the upper staff departed, 'so I want to take a situation with a "*titled lady*", or at least with an "*honourable*".'[51] This difficulty arose because ladies' maids and valets were accorded the status of their employer; hence a duchess's maid would always precede that of a countess, and both would be ahead of the maid to the untitled girl whom Lady Augusta knew.

Those who worked in these large households were the 'aristocrats' of the domestic labour force. Most of them enjoyed comfortable living standards, with plentiful meals and varied leisure activities, including servants' balls and periodic outings. At Longleat dances were held in the servants' hall twice weekly, with a pianist engaged from the neighbouring town of Warminster and a buffet supper produced by the kitchen and still room staff. The outside servants also attended, as well as unmarried grooms and gardeners who lived in a hostel, or 'bothy', close to the house.[52] And at Welbeck Abbey, Frederick Gorst had the benefit of a men-servants' billiard hall, as well as a comfortable bedroom, which he shared with another footman and which was kept clean by a housemaid specially assigned to the footmen's quarters.[53]

In return for these amenities servants were expected to perform their duties with unobtrusive efficiency. Sometimes, as in Mary Curzon's case, those expectations were unrealized, but most domestics appreciated that personal promotion and continued residence in an élite household depended upon their satisfying their employer's wishes. Hence one former scullery maid remembered that when there were shooting parties in the autumn she would rise soon after 4 a.m. so that she could be in the kitchen by 4.30 to cut the sandwiches sent out for the beaters and begin preparations for the elaborate luncheon to be served to the guests.[54] Even the well-paid Gorst had to get up at 5 a.m. on some mornings so that he and a fellow footman could go out with the coachman when he exercised the Duke of Portland's magnificent carriage horses. On their return they served breakfast to the family and guests in the dining-room. It was all part of what Gorst called 'the perfect service dispensed at Welbeck', in which he and his colleagues took great pride.[55]

The domestic sphere was, however, not the only area in which members of High Society displayed their affluence through their demands for personal service. The same applied to a wide range of other activities with which they were involved, particularly during the Season. These covered, for example, the bespoke trades of the West End of London, such as tailoring, shoemaking and cabinet making, as well as millinery and dressmaking, confectionery, transport, and a number of minor trades like artificial flower making, leather goods manufacture, and the production of jet bead ornaments for ladies' bonnets. Of the artificial flower makers, Charles Booth noted in the 1890s that while many outworkers were recruited when demand peaked, as it slackened around the end of May only the best of them had anything to do. Even many of the 'indoor hands' were dismissed.[56] Similar seasonal fluctuations applied to the temporary coachmen who were hired at the height of the Season and were discharged in late July, to make a living as best they could. Then there were painters, plumbers, plasterers, upholsterers and carpenters who were called in each spring to prepare town houses for the expected influx of fashionable families from the country. Even West End laundries and bakeries took on extra labour in readiness for the anticipated upsurge in demand.[57]

During the three months of the Season, therefore, while hostesses demonstrated their skills in entertaining and socialites engaged in a wide variety of diversions, a substantial segment of the capital's labour force was occupied in catering for their needs. Florists benefited from the demand for floral arrangements to adorn dinner tables and buffets, while on the morning of a Drawing-Room hundreds of posy bouquets were despatched by shops like Mrs Green's of Crawford Street. Another trade which did well on Drawing-Room days was the photographer's:

> An establishment like Mayall's of Grafton Street had a continual succession of noble appointments coming on from Buckingham Palace . . . Caterers were indispensable for the more elaborate parties – no domestic kitchen could cope with the vast quantities of food and drink which were needed, nor could any house muster the necessary staff. Many caterers were at the same time restauranteurs . . . and thus drew a double benefit from the Season, as did the tea-shops and other purveyors of refreshments.[58]

For numerous West End businesses the Season was the most profitable time of the year. 'Every step that Society took, every invitation it offered or accepted, every function it attended, meant more money in somebody's pocket. Club servants, fan-makers, menu card-holder makers, crossing-sweepers, theatre-programme sellers, flower-sellers in Piccadilly Circus, cab touts, wine merchants – all flourished as at no other time of year'.[59] Printers of visiting cards and theatre programmes also benefited, while the proliferation of garden parties, balls and parties created a demand for professional musicians. Among them was 'Vorzanger's Austro-Hungarian Band', which advertised its services in *The Times* during the summer of 1909 for 'At Homes, Receptions, Dances, Garden Parties, &c.' A few years earlier it was Mitchell's Blue Hungarian Band which announced its arrival and its readiness to accept engagements 'as a Band of either twelve, nine or six performers'.[60] Even military bandsmen profited, since when they were not required for regimental duties they were allowed to play at private parties, or to take employment in theatre orchestras. The fees thus secured (put at 18s. to 21s. per man per engagement by one writer in the late 1890s) were a useful supplement to their ordinary income.[61]

Dancing classes burgeoned, with instructors like the 'West-End Professor (lady) of 20 years' experience in the Court Circle of Society' advertising a willingness to receive 'a young gentlewoman student daily, at a fee of 30 guineas per annum.'[62]

At a murkier level demands for the services of prostitutes likewise increased sharply. Lady Warwick remembered many 'smart young men about town, who had no profession other than perhaps soldiering. . . . They would have died rather than have dishonoured a girl of their own class, but they fixed their eyeglass in the other eye when the woman was married, or when they "looked after" a maid of low degree.'[63] According to her, most bridegrooms had a 'second establishment to pension off or maintain when they married', and if a Society woman met a man (even her own brother) in the park when he was accompanied by his mistress or an actress, 'he would not raise his hat to her. He cut her, and she understood.'[64]

But those who came to the capital briefly for the Season had no such permanent establishment and instead availed themselves of the services of the elegant inmates of fashionable brothels and the frequenters of such venues as the promenade bar at the

Empire Theatre, Leicester Square. During the late 1880s and the 1890s there were attempts by puritan elements to close this latter on the grounds that it was a 'centre of moral contamination', but its supporters demonstrated so vigorously that the efforts failed. Among the protesters in the mid-1890s was a young Sandhurst cadet named Winston Churchill.[65]

As for the prostitutes themselves, a contemporary claimed that at the Empire promenade 'their manner was always unobtrusive, [and] they very seldom spoke to anyone who had not addressed them first.' A number of them were 'fairly educated and of quite a good class', and these advantages, combined with their attractive appearance, ensured that many married well. 'Several eventually found their way into Burke's Peerage.' In the meantime, a sort of 'informal censorship' was applied at the Empire so that 'admission was refused to any woman of a really undesirable kind'.[66]

However, of all the seasonal trades catering for the social élite those connected with dress were the most important. 'In London,' advised Charles Pascoe during the mid-1880s, 'a gentleman should always dress well. He will find . . . that a well-cut coat will gain him admittance to places from which a man who has no eye for a coat is debarred.' For a woman the art of 'displaying her charms to the best advantage' was so essential that 'no sensible lady' would disregard it.[67]

Paris was the Mecca for the most fashion-conscious females. Already by the early 1870s the famous couturier, Charles Worth, employed 1,200 seamstresses to cater for his large range of important clients, and a meticulous index system was kept of the measurements of regular customers. Among them was Lady Lytton. Even in her eighties she still went up to London each year to purchase her 'little bit of finery' from the branch of the House opened there by Gaston Worth.[68] Many other women, however, patronized dressmakers in Regent Street and its environs. The Princess of Wales had her clothes made by Welborn's of Regent Street, while Liberty's came into prominence during the 'aesthetic craze' of the 1880s and 1890s because 'the aesthetic woman's clothes had to be made of Liberty silk'.

Bond Street was the centre for jewellers, milliners and shops selling lace, fans, gloves, and 'every other adjunct of elegance', and this made it a favourite place for a morning stroll.[69]

Other ladies had their own particular dressmakers and milliners to whom they went regularly. Princess Mary Adelaide Duchess of Teck patronized Madame Mangas, a first-rate Parisian dressmaker who did not charge tip-top prices, and who could supply for a relatively modest outlay the smart clothes she and her daughter, Princess May (later Queen Mary) needed for their forays into London society. Madame Mangas came over periodically to London and set up in a tiny *pied-à-terre* which she shared with a French bonnet-maker, Madame Valentine Meurice, in Mount Street. The Duchess considered Madame Meurice to be an excellent worker, too. 'Her prices run from £2.8 to £3.3 or thereabouts,' she told a neighbour in 1888, while £4 represented 'her highest figure and . . . only charged for a very handsome confection with feathers and embroidery!'[70] For everyday purposes the Teck ladies had their clothes made by a local dressmaker in Kingston-on-Thames.

Apparently Queen Mary did not inherit her mother's interest in clothes and when her husband, George V, succeeded to the throne in 1910 *The Tatler* commented waspishly on her rejection of up-to-date fashions:

> she appears on even the grandest occasions in skirts of the mode of the year before last, hats of unknown date, and a waist where the *mondaine* has not had one for years and years . . . In King Edward's time, . . . the more ultra-modish the frock the more chance of notice for the wearer. Times have changed, however, and it is perhaps not too much to say that in this . . . day of grace, it is rather the other way round, viz. the smarter or more remarkable your costume the greater your risk of being barred.[71]

When Lady Cynthia Asquith first came out she received a dress allowance of one hundred pounds a year. At first she felt rich but she soon discovered that the large number of outfits needed outran her income and she was chronically overdrawn. In such circumstances members of High Society frequently delayed paying their bills for months and, on occasion, even years, as they sought to juggle with their finances. The 7th Earl of Shaftesbury was considered sentimental because he never kept tradesmen waiting for their money; such an attitude was exceptional.[72]

Lady Cynthia's favourite shop was an exotic milliner's called Maison St. Louis. It was run by a Miss Louise Piers and years later she remembered the thrill with which she ran up the stairs, three steps at a time, to the showroom. There she and her friends suffered the agonies of temptation and indecision in front of its mirrors until, 'rapturously transfigured' they 'finally emerged from that enchanted shop'.

> Besides hats, Miss Louise Piers made lovely Botticelli wreaths, one of which I nearly always wore in the evenings. She also designed our bridesmaids' head-dresses, and Violet, her deft-fingered second in command, came to our homes to adjust our wedding veils.[73]

For less important fashion items ladies patronized the more select drapers, like Marshall and Snelgrove or Debenham and Freebody, where they would be attended by a favourite assistant. 'At the lace counter in Marshall & Snelgrove,' wrote Lady Tweedsmuir, 'I remember Miss M, who wore a grey false fringe.'[74]

Men, too, had their specialist shops. The principal tailors were located in Savile Row and Clifford Street, while Lock in St. James's Street and Scott in Bond Street were the main hatters. The leading bootmakers included Wildsmith in Sackville Street and Hoby in Pall Mall.

> Truefitt and Douglas, both in Bond Street, and Jasche, in Regent Street, were for long the only hairdressers for [fashionable] men . . . Luggage came from Drew's in Piccadilly Circus . . . Briggs, in St. James's Street, were the sole source of the elegant umbrella. Buttonholes were bought at Solomon's in Piccadilly. Tobacco came from Fribourg and Treyer . . . in the Haymarket . . . Heppell's, the chemist, sandwiched between the clubs in the western part of Piccadilly, concocted the pick-me-up which relieved the morning headaches of revellers. Jewellery for men came from Garrards. . . . The fashionable livery stables were Wimbush and Ricardo. Floris, in Jermyn Street, provided bath salts and essences and sponges and loofahs. . . . Charbonnet and Walker, the chocolate shop in Bond Street, kept lists of the favourite

Debenham & Freebody.

Wigmore Street.
(Cavendish Square) London,W.

Famous for over a Century
for Taste, for Quality, for Value

RACE COATS

All these garments are adapted from the latest Paris models. They are made by skilled men tailors—the quality of the material used is invariably excellent. They are suitable for smart occasions as well as for driving, for motoring and country wear.

Race Coat (*as sketch*) in the new Reversible "Sultan Ottoman" silks, lined silk throughout to tone, turn-up collar of Oriental embroidery. An exact copy of a late Paris Model.

$7\frac{1}{2}$ Gns.

Debenham & Freebody was one of the major drapers patronized by fashionable women before World War 1. This advertisement was published in May 1911. (British Library Newspaper Library)

choices of their women customers, so that male shoppers ordering boxes of chocolates to be sent as presents could rely upon a hundred-per-cent success in their selection.[75]

At the end of the nineteenth century there were said to be only three kinds of outfit in which an elegant man could be seen in London – riding clothes, frock coat, and evening dress.[76]

Gieves, which specialized in providing uniforms for naval officers, also offered other services to regular customers. These included a credit account which could be used in any Gieves branch or by letter from anywhere in the world. Payment by instalment was encouraged – an important consideration when officers were expected to buy their uniforms out of their own pockets without any Treasury assistance except for a small tax allowance. Records were kept of the measurements of regular account customers, which meant that long distance orders could be satisfied, and from the time that the first London branch opened in 1903 much attention was paid to full-dress occasions. Officers were provided with changing rooms when they were due to attend levées or other court functions, and were thus enabled to dress in comfort and also to have the assistance of trained staff to ensure they looked their best.[77] This service was particularly valued by the firm's customers.

The central role of royalty in the social scene is indicated by this advertisement for Horniman's tea using King Edward VII. (The author)

Yet, while so much effort was expended in satisfying the needs of the affluent, there was also emerging a growing unease at the social inequalities which this situation revealed. At a time when nearly a third of the capital's inhabitants were living in need, a fashionable woman might spend over a hundred pounds upon a ball gown or court presentation dress which would be worn fewer than a dozen times. Or, like Lady Dudley, she might purchase an exotic fur tippet made from black fox which had taken four years to collect and cost £240.[78] The researches of Charles Booth and other investigators revealed the appalling living conditions and the low pay of many of those providing the specialist services demanded by socialites. This was underlined in September 1892 when it was reported that garments ordered from prestigious gentlemen's tailors in the West End were in fact made up at 'sweat' shops in the crowded tenements of the East End or in disreputable 'backshops' around Soho, where disease was rampant. The *Star* newspaper complained of 'evil, dark and dirty dens . . . within two minutes walk of Regent Street' where 'the clothing which covers the backs of the dandies of Europe and America is made'. It mentioned a sweat shop in Bridle Lane, where ten people worked in a room, each paying 2s. a week 'for his sitting and here he will bring the work from the best tailors'. The *Chronicle*, not to be outdone, found a former tailoress who had worked in a dilapidated garret in Poplar where, she claimed, 'the Prince of Wales's waistcoats and plush Court costumes used to be turned out'.[79] There were even hints that the premature death from influenza of the Duke of Clarence, elder son of the Prince and Princess of Wales, early in 1892 was in fact the result of wearing an infected jacket![80]

Nor did female customers escape these dangers. According to a witness to the House of Lords Committee on the Sweating System in 1888, ladies who dealt with the prestigious firm of Redfern in the belief that their clothes were being made by skilled master tailors were sadly misled. Instead much of the work was done by poorly-paid girls. In this way clients were duped into paying high prices for garments made by cheap labour.[81] The health question was also important, and there were allegations that a daughter of Sir Robert Peel had died as a result of wearing a riding habit made in a fever den.[82] In 1909 legislation was passed to set up a wages board for workers in the ready-made and wholesale tailoring trade but it did not help those employed in Savile Row, since retail, bespoke tailoring was excluded from its provisions.[83]

Paradoxically, therefore, the Season was associated with both the prosperity and the exploitation of labour associated with many of London's service trades. If for some reason, perhaps because of war or the death of a member of the Royal Family, the Season were a poor one, then the demand for services slumped and their providers were unemployed. It was on these grounds that apologists for the excesses of High Society argued that a valuable role was being played by those who provided work for the less privileged sections of the population. This was a view expressed by Lady Dorothy Nevill in her autobiography, *Under Five Reigns* (1910). She conveniently ignored the wastefulness – and injustice – which such a system encouraged and instead stressed that a successful Season was immensely important to a large number of the poor.

> If a diminution in social gaieties merely affected the well-to-do and the frivolous, there might be some reason for deploring the sums spent on entertainment; but a far wider circle of individuals than is generally supposed suffer from a bad Season, for the money expended in the West End during the summer months distributes itself far and wide amongst the poorer classes of the town, and a dull Season . . . entails much disappointment and even distress. That which affects Belgravia is unfortunately sure to react upon Whitechapel. For this reason those whose circumstances permit them to entertain should do so, even at some sacrifice to themselves, in order to benefit their humbler and more dependent neighbours.[84]

She concluded complacently that the great increase in luxury which had taken place over the previous twenty years had 'without doubt helped to save large numbers of people from poverty, besides affording employment to hundreds, even thousands, of girls, milliners, and the like, who have largely profited by the enormously increased attention bestowed upon female dress.' Such comments ignored the fact that whilst Society's requirements furnished some short-term prosperity, in the long run the variable nature of the demand and its instability aggravated the problem of seasonal unemployment, which was a major feature of poverty in the capital.[85]

For those who took part in the social whirl, meanwhile, the high level of expenditure needed to keep up with other members of their circle was a considerable burden. In 1911, the *Tatler* claimed that it was impossible for a society woman to dress herself on even £1,000 a year:

> she goes to Paris to fit a frock and to New York for a new face treatment. The London season is a costly campaign, and to carry on, say from the middle of May to Goodwood a woman in the swim must have at least six sumptuous evening gowns with a couple of 'little' frocks to act as accessories, and of course the usual lot of Ascot and garden-party gowns with a correct get-up for bridge, days on the river, short journeys, and motoring. And all this without mention of the court gown and train which every year or two are demanded by her position.
>
> Then with August comes yachting and Cowes followed by a trip to Aix, Homburg, or Marienbad. September brings Scotland, with an interlude for Doncaster, while October sees [her] at Newmarket. After this comes a run over to Paris, and November has its round of country-house visits, big shoots, and smart race meetings. Then London again with its merry winter season, and after Christmas . . . the Riviera or . . . Egypt.[86]

A fashionable man, too, would spend at least £1,000 annually on his attire. 'His gloves, waistcoats, ties, and hats are counted by the dozen, his sable coat is of immense value, and his pearl studs mean a small fortune.'[87] This took no account of the expenses involved in racing, yachting, motoring and hunting, which were also part and parcel of male High Society existence, or of subscriptions to clubs and other organizations.

For this reason those landed families who were hit by the prolonged effects of agricultural depression and falling rentals and who lacked alternative incomes from overseas investments, mineral royalties or urban land, faced a dilemma. Was it better to participate in the London scene, albeit on a reduced scale, or ought they to withdraw altogether, perhaps by remaining in the country or travelling abroad? If the former solution were adopted, there was the danger of a loss of face when they mixed with their friends, unless some convincing excuse for the economies could be produced. If they chose the latter, they faced exile from their established social circle.

Some elected to deal with the problem by selling family heirlooms. Between 1886 and 1902 the Earl of Dudley disposed of china, old masters and jewels worth £240,000, while in 1905 Lord Tweedmouth sold old masters for £48,895. Two years later the Duke of Fife, whose wife was Edward VII's eldest daughter, auctioned 150 pictures from Duff House.[88] Many others followed their example.

However, the anxieties which could arise when families were unable, or unwilling, to boost their finances in this way are exemplified by Sir Rainald and Lady Knightley of Fawsley Park, Northamptonshire. The Knightleys' difficulties first became apparent in 1879 when, on their return from a 'cure' at Bad Homburg they were informed by their agent that several major tenant farmers had threatened to surrender their holdings because of the effects of the depression.[89] In the following years, despite the granting of rent rebates and changes in tenancy, some of the farms had to be taken in hand, with heavy expenditure involved in stocking them. At the same time the Knightleys made repeated resolutions to economize and in December 1882 their town house at 4 Grosvenor Crescent was sold. But they continued to rent substantial properties. In May

1889, for example, they paid five hundred guineas to rent a house in Grosvenor Street.[90] Not until August 1890 were they shocked into drastic action. On 6 August Sir Rainald visited his solicitor in order to increase the mortgage on his estate. He returned with the news that as a result of this additional loan the mortgage debt had risen to almost £100,000 and the interest on this of £4,000 a year, represented about half their income. 'Now . . . we *must* retrench & have quite decided after this one more winter to do so,' wrote Lady Knightley in her diary. A few days later she detailed the economies they had decided upon in order to cut their outgoings by £2,000 per annum. They included 'discharging 6 servants & giving up hunting & our winter party. The worst is that R. says we must go away for a year, in order to inaugurate the new system.'[91] This latter proposal arose from Sir Rainald's desire not to reveal to the outside world the scale of his financial embarrassment.

The solution they in fact chose was to bring Lady Knightley's frail 91-year-old mother to spend the winter at Fawsley. In the following March Lady Knightley then undertook the disagreeable task of telling the servants that they would not be taking a house in London for the Season: 'Of course Mother's health . . . is a reason in itself . . . but it is all very painful.' On her brief trips to London for business or pleasure during the ensuing Season Lady Knightley stayed at Claridge's hotel or at her club, the Alexandra. In this way expenditure was pruned with the least possible loss of dignity.

Finally, there remains one area of service for the well-to-do to be considered – that relating to their health. When they were ill, wealthy families normally hired private medical staff to care for them, although a few might enter a nursing home. Hence when Lady Dudley had an operation for appendicitis in Dublin during 1902 the fees amounted to £1,700, including 300 guineas for a London surgeon who arrived too late to operate and 100 guineas to the Court doctor who held Lady Dudley's hand while the anaesthetic took effect.[92]

At this date hospitals still catered mainly for the poor, because of the possibility of cross-infection they offered. However, some of the more prestigious London hospitals sent out their nurses into private homes for a fee. In 1905, the London Hospital alone sent out 160 nurses, for an annual profit of well over a thousand pounds. Overall perhaps 70 per cent of all nurses in the early twentieth century were engaged in private duty work.[93]

Typical of such cases was that of Lord Colin Campbell. When he had various operations to relieve his syphilitic condition, with one exception they took place in private residences. The exception was when he entered the personal clinic of the surgeon, Sir Henry Thompson, and, in practice this more resembled a small luxury hotel than a traditional hospital.[94] At home he was looked after by privately hired nurses, some of whom remained with the Campbells for weeks at a time.

But this 'treatment at home' method was most dramatically demonstrated in June 1902, when King Edward VII was operated on for appendicitis shortly before his coronation was due to take place. A room at Buckingham Palace was prepared for the operation and the King was laid out on a billiard table. Fortunately the operation was successful and the coronation took place about seven weeks later.[95]

Another, albeit less grave, aspect of the 'health question' was the custom of taking 'cures' in various European spas, usually at the end of the Season. As the Countess of Warwick admitted, after three months of indulgence many socialites were suffering from nerves, indigestion, and 'sometimes plain obesity, due to too many meals and too little exercise. . . . Then the cure at a foreign spa became a necessity, and London society was compelled to visit such places as Homburg, Marienbad, or Wiesbaden.'[96] Bad Homburg was made popular by the Prince of Wales, although after his accession to the throne he switched his allegiance to Marienbad. The Prince's gargantuan appetite – his dinner seldom comprised fewer than twelve courses – made periodic slimming treatment essential.[97] According to Lord Ormathwaite, who accompanied him on some later visits, Edward took the 'cure' seriously.

> Water drinking began between 6 and 7 a.m. Then a stroll to one of the numerous little cafés in the woods or on the hills for breakfast, where one looked forward to the excellent cup of coffee that was sure to be provided, and after that a return to Marienbad for a bath or massage. There was a very frugal meal at midday, and after that an expedition to some of the neighbouring country resorts. In the evening one had a slice of ham or a poached egg at some little restaurant, and then to bed between 9.30 and 10 p.m.
>
> No one was more particular than King Edward in seeing that his rules and regulations in regard to food were strictly observed by himself and his entourage, and he used to get really angry if anyone exceeded in this respect.[98]

Those who were chronic sufferers from rheumatism, or bronchial and digestive disorders might take advantage of the cures on offer at Bad Ems. Although Ems was patronized more heavily by Germans and other central Europeans than by English people, there were almost 450 guests from Britain in 1890 out of a total of 10,611 visitors to the spa in that year. They included the Marchioness of Huntley and her servants, the Hon. Mrs Rollo, and Lady Young and her daughter. Most English visitors stayed at the appropriately named Englischer Hof – there were thirty-two British families resident there on 11 June, 1890 – and they normally remained for a month or six weeks.[99] In addition to taking the water and the usual baths there was also a special inhalation and gargling treatment for those with throat and chest complaints.[100]

Bad Nauheim, too, had its devotees. By 1897 it had five bath houses and according to a visitor baths were taken in the morning between 9 a.m. and 12 noon.

> Your own particular bath man or woman becomes quite a friend long before you have finished . . . There are also four other springs at some little distance from the bath houses, which are used for drinking purposes only. To them, in the early morning between the hours of seven and eight o'clock, those people flock who have to drink so many glasses of water a day in addition to taking the baths. The Kur-Kapelle band plays at the "Quelle" (springs) during the drinking hour, while people walk up and down in the surrounding garden . . . and buy roses from the peasants who stand about with baskets full.[101]

There was, of course, more to taking a cure than the rigours of dieting, bathing, and taking the water. It offered to wealthy socialites an opportunity to meet and exchange news and gossip, as well as to display their finery, attend concerts and make excursions

Visitors strolling in the park during a concert at Bad Ems, *c.* 1900. (Stadtarchiv, Bad Ems)

into the countryside.[102] Thus Elinor Glyn, who visited Carlsbad on several occasions to receive treatment for a gall bladder complaint, much enjoyed the 'slow prescribed walks through the Carlsbad woods' and the long conversations with congenial companions whom she met there.[103]

At Marienbad, King Edward VII played croquet and golf, as well as arranging long motor drives. In 1905, one of his fellow guests was May Harcourt, who had gone there for a rest and to lose weight. She was accompanied by her widowed mother and each morning she began her day by rising at 6.15 and drinking a glass of spa water in her room. Then came a walk to the spring where she had a second glass of water, followed by breakfast. Massage, a bath, and a rest followed. After lunch and a further rest, there was another walk to get coffee. Dinner was taken at 8 p.m. and then came bed.

> Throw into the day a certain amount of Bridge & you have a pattern of all our days . . . I enjoyed it enormously, that sort of foreign life always amuses me for a little while. It was pleasanter before the King came as after his arrival there was too much entertaining going on. . . . The King was very kind to Mother & me – we lunched with him one day at his Hotel . . . H.M. took me out in his Motor one afternoon. We were gone over two hours and stopped at a lovely place . . . to have some coffee. I enjoyed it but it is a long time to be alone with him trying to find subjects of conversation. He also dined with us one night. . . . Mercifully HM was in the best of spirits & joked & told stories most of dinner. Afterwards he . . . played Bridge.[104]

So highly did many of the social élite value the medical attention they received at these German spas that they continued to visit them up to the very brink of the First World War. Among the later visitors were Lady Selborne and her married daughter, Mabel, who was being treated for problems following a miscarriage. 'The doctor still cannot say what is exactly the matter,' Lady Selborne told her husband. ' . . . He makes her take exercise, play lawn tennis etc. & live on a vegetarian diet with eggs, milk & cheese thrown in, under which . . . she certainly is improving.'[105] The two ladies apparently left Germany at the end of June 1914. Just over a month later Britain and Germany were at war, and the old spa life – like much else involving High Society – received a blow from which it never fully recovered.

CHAPTER SIX

Sports, Pastimes and Pleasures

Boredom and frustration afflicted the society which revolved round the Prince of Wales. Admirably . . . endowed, as most of its members were, with tradition and an elevated patriotism, comparatively few did themselves justice. Their true quality was obscured in a hothouse world of game preservation, gold plate, jewels and other luxuries, and their sense of complete security was buttressed by the gaping servility of a host of inferiors. Some, in these circumstances, had recourse to gambling and other absorbing hazards. . . . A variety of frivolous stratagems were devised in an effort to charm away the tedium of assembling again and again in the same great country houses; and some hostesses were prepared always to divert their guests, including the Prince, by a discreet allocation of bedrooms in accordance with their known but unexpressed wishes.

PHILIP MAGNUS, *King Edward the Seventh* (1964), 181–2.

A s earlier chapters have shown, the London Season played a central role in the lives of most members of the social élite, with its round of balls, dinners, concerts, perambulations in the Park, inter-regimental polo matches, bicycling parties, and much else besides. But these diversions formed only part of the pastimes and pleasures enjoyed by the well-to-do. By the end of the Victorian era, improvements in transport and growing demands for excitement and lavish display had led to a far more frenetic social life than had applied in the middle of the nineteenth century. In 1906, Lady Dorothy Nevill disapprovingly contrasted the 'slow, rather solemn' annual routine which had applied in her youth with the 'sort of firework' which constituted the existence of opulent Edwardians.[1] And a more recent commentator on the social scene at that time has concluded that no one in the upper ranks of society 'seemed to stay a week in the same place'.[2]

That feverish attitude was epitomized by the annual round of Edward himself, both as heir to the throne and as King. Late December and January were spent principally on his country estate, Sandringham, although this was interspersed with brief visits to London and a week's shooting at Chatsworth with the Duke of Devonshire or at Elveden with Lord Iveagh. February saw his return to London, where he entertained guests or went out to nightly dinner, theatre and supper parties. Early in March he left England for two months' holiday in the sun. He liked to spend a week in Paris incognito, calling himself the Duke of Lancaster and exploring the pleasures of that city. (In the 1890s there was much gossip concerning his over-familiarity with La Goulue, a leading dancer at the Moulin Rouge.[3]) Then came three weeks on the Riviera or at Biarritz. In 1907, for example, he stayed at the Villa Eugénie in the latter resort, in a house built by Napoleon III for the Empress. It had been taken by Edward's friend and trusted financial adviser, Sir Ernest Cassel, and the daily routine revolved around finding entertainment for the King. 'We are his servants quite as much as the housemaid or the butler', declared Cassel's daughter indignantly.[4]

After Biarritz came a Mediterranean cruise in the royal yacht for about a month. Early in May Edward returned to London to preside over the Season. During this time he again dined out or entertained friends every night, and spent each weekend at a country house, or at Sandringham, or at his private quarters at the Jockey Club at Newmarket. In the middle of June he went to Windsor castle for a few days for Ascot Races, and at the end of July stayed with the Duke of Richmond for Goodwood. This was followed by the yachting week at Cowes and then by a visit to Homburg or Marienbad for a month's 'cure'. On his return, there was a brief spell in London before he went north to stay with friends for the St. Leger meeting at Doncaster. From there he moved to Scotland.

When Edward became King, Balmoral, with its grouse and deer, remained his headquarters throughout October, and from there he attended the autumn race meetings at Newmarket, using the royal train.[5] The first week of November he spent in London; the second at Sandringham, for a shooting party which centred around his birthday on 9 November; and the last two weeks were spent at Windsor. The first week of December was also taken up with a shooting party at Sandringham and thereafter, for an entire fortnight he indulged in what his biographer calls 'a round of Christmas dinner, theatre and supper parties . . . to which he looked forward boyishly'.[6]

Yes, despite this royal example not all members of High Society adopted a similarly restless routine. Many preferred to concentrate on the traditional country pursuits of hunting, shooting and fishing. They included, in the 1880s, the Duke of Portland, who hired stables at Melton for the fox-hunting season so that he could go out each week with the Quorn. On one day a week he and some of his friends also periodically chartered a special train from Melton to Derby, so that they could hunt with the Meynell. Over the period 1874 to 1889, the Duke estimated that he had had at least two days' hunting a week during the season with twenty-six different packs of hounds.[7]

Late Victorian and Edwardian England was *par excellence* the era of the sporting landlord, and enthusiastic riders would return to the shires in the autumn and remain there, except for brief forays to London around Christmas or to the homes of friends for shooting parties, until fox-hunting ended. As Lord Willoughby de Broke, for many years Master of the Warwickshire Hounds, solemnly declared, hunting 'four times a week for seven months in the year is not a profession that affords much leisure for entertaining'. It was also an expensive occupation, especially for the Master. In 1911, Willoughby de

Broke estimated that he was spending £1,000 a year over and above the guarantee of £3,500 provided by Hunt members, and this did not take into account his personal expenses.[8] Yet to him, and to those who thought like him, hunting was an all-consuming passion. It is perhaps not surprising that in his autobiography he should put the Master of the Foxhounds as the second most important figure in County society, after the Lord-Lieutenant.[9]

Lady Randolph Churchill and Margot Asquith shared this enthusiasm. For a time in the 1870s Lady Randolph regarded hunting as her principal preoccupation. 'Many were the "tosses" I took . . . but it was glorious sport.' Two decades later Margot went to Leicestershire for the hunting season even when she was pregnant and against the advice of her doctor. For her, it was an 'insignia of freedom'. As her biographer comments, to fly through the air:

> on a big and powerful horse which she could only just handle gave Margot the feeling that she was living life to the full. The excitement of jumping a tricky fence or out-riding everyone else was an experience that went to her head, and once she was heard to say that only fools refused to hunt.[10]

To women of an independent mind and determined character, hunting offered one of the few opportunities for them to compete with men on equal terms and to demonstrate their skills – and their courage.

By 1911 the popularity of the sport was such that there were almost 350 hunts in England and Wales alone; 164 of them were with foxhounds, 81 with harriers, 71 with beagles and foothounds, and 16 with staghounds. There were also 11 drag hunts.[11]

Significantly most of the best hunting country in the midland shires – Northampton, Leicester and Nottingham – had a low level of game preservation, since 'foxes and pheasants were not compatible, and enthusiasm for the one tended to exclude the other.' Hence the complaints of some hunting people in shooting districts that keepers were poisoning the wild foxes because they threatened the game. In certain 'shooting' counties this happened to such an extent that one well-informed journalist claimed in 1908 that hunting had become 'little more than a farce'.[12] In the end the difficulty was solved by gamekeepers being paid to preserve foxes and, in hunting areas, by encouraging tenants who had taken hunting boxes for the season to rent the 'shooting' as well, to ensure that this was not taken by an enthusiastic game preserver. That was the method favoured by the famous Pytchley Hunt under the mastership of Lord Annaly between 1902 and 1914.[13] The conflict between the foxhunter and game preserver was also kept in check partly by the broad geographical separation between hunting and shooting areas and partly by the fact that many sporting landowners both hunted and shot, 'either in succession on different days in the week or in succession in different stages in life, taking to shooting as they became too old and portly to continue riding to hounds'.[14] It was thus not in their interest to let the rivalry between the two sports get out of hand.

Nonetheless tension between preservers and huntsmen became acute in the late nineteenth and early twentieth centuries, when shooting reached a peak of popularity and huge 'bags' became a matter of pride and pleasure. Even the architecture of houses was affected by the cult for game preservation, since it was from the 1870s that the gun room became a feature of country mansions, with its walls adorned by cases of stuffed game and fish, or the heads and antlers of dead animals, and by racks of firearms. Heavy expenses were also incurred in hand-rearing the birds. It was estimated that each preserved pheasant lost its owner about £1, or as a popular saying of the shooting world put it: 'Up gets a guinea, bang goes a penny half-penny, and down comes half-a-crown' (12½p), this last being the market value of the dead bird.[15]

It was in these circumstances, too, that the Earl of Crawford complained in 1913 of mounting expenditure in connection with shooting on estates in Scotland.

> The equipment, the paraphernalia and above all the cost of grouse driving increases every year. There is a growing standard of comfort for instance in the grouse butts, which are now constructed with great care and accuracy in order the better to circumvent the birds: and the wages of the drivers, mostly boys from the surrounding villages, have largely increased. One now pays five shillings a day to these youths, and into the bargain they have to be driven to the moor . . . [but] when the last increase in wages was conceded, their free lunch was knocked off, which is considered a real advantage, as the boys now bring their own frugal bread and cheese with them whereas previously they gorged themselves at their employers' expense, so freely as to find post-prandial walking a hard and uninviting task.[16]

With much heavy investment committed to the sport, landlords inevitably took a stern line with poachers who, in their eyes, were trying to steal their 'property'. Most responded by recruiting more gamekeepers. Between 1871 and 1901 the number of these rose from 12,429 to 16,677, and by 1911 there were more than twice as many gamekeepers as there were policemen in country districts. Significantly, although the

A meet of the Marquess of Exeter's harriers in Northamptonshire, c. 1910. (The author)

number of game law offences dwindled in the last years of the nineteenth century as rural living standards improved and respect for law and order increased, even in 1897 18 per cent of all non-indictable offences committed in Bedfordshire involved the game laws; in West Suffolk, it was just over 13 per cent; and in Norfolk and Northamptonshire around 9.5 per cent.[17]

Ill-feeling arose, too, between the sportsmen and local farmers in a number of counties, with the latter complaining of damage to their crops caused by the game. This applied particularly where an estate was let to a sporting tenant. As an agriculturist from Bury St. Edmunds, Suffolk, noted sourly, 'letting shooting to a stranger was like having two dogs picking off one bone.' Another man declared that in North Devon, shooting tenants and their gamekeepers created great friction everywhere: 'probably they are even more disposed to be arbitrary with comparatively small farmers, such as those in Devonshire, than with the larger farmers in other counties.'[18]

But for the enthusiastic sportsman all this was a price worth paying. He would begin his campaigns on or soon after the 'glorious' 12th of August, when grouse shooting commenced, and would then spend most of the succeeding months indulging his passion either on his own estate or on those of his friends. Men who were experts, like Lord de Grey (later the 2nd Marquess of Ripon), Lord Walsingham, and the Duke of York (later George V) enjoyed considerable prestige. The shooting record books of Lord de Grey show that between 1867 and his death in 1923 he 'bagged' no fewer than 556,813 victims, including 241,224 pheasants and 124,193 partridges.[19] Lady Randolph Churchill witnessed his prowess on one occasion, when she was staying at Panshanger. Out of fifty-four shots fired he killed fifty-two birds, 'and for a bet this was done with one hand. He had two loaders and three guns'.[20] He liked to claim that his success was achieved effortlessly, but that was not strictly true, as another visitor to Panshangar, Edith Balfour, was to discover. One night when she was unable to sleep she went down to the library to select a book. There she was surprised to find the crack shot with his two loaders practising the art of changing guns. As she drily commented, 'he was not too pleased at being discovered.'[21]

This competitive urge and its associated mass slaughter of birds was encouraged by the Prince of Wales himself. Over the years he spent about £300,000 transforming the Sandringham estate into a world-famous shooting property, with a consequent increase in the head of game shot annually from about 7,000 to 30,000. At a shooting party held between 7 and 10 November, 1905, for example, the nine or ten guns who went out each day accounted for 4,135 pheasants, 2,009 partridges, 232 hares, 576 rabbits, 14 woodcock, 275 wild duck, 12 pigeons, and 3 'various', making a grand total of 7,256. The partridge bag for 10 November (1,342) was a record for a single day on the Sandringham estate.[22] The spirit of competition was also fostered by the practice of an equerry questioning each guest at the end of a drive as to how many birds he had shot. These figures were then read out over luncheon, to the undoubted satisfaction of the good shots and the discomfiture of the less successful.

The picnic lunches served at most shooting parties were lavish, which must have made concentration during the afternoon drive difficult. Only genuine enthusiasts like Lord Leicester at Holkham, provided their guests with a spartan sandwich or two, so that no

A shooting party at Wilton House, home of the Earl of Pembroke in September, 1901. Apart from the Earl himself the group includes Lord Ingestre, Lord Herbert, Lord Hyde and the Hon. George Herbert. Lady Muriel Herbert is on horseback at the rear of the group. (*The Tatler*, 25 September, 1901.) (British Library Newspaper Library)

time should be lost in pursuing the birds.[23] More typical was the arrangement at Sandringham, where a sumptuous meal was served when the ladies came out to join the guns. The Prince normally offered two hot dishes, as well as a variety of cold food, such as lobster salad and chicken mayonnaise. If the weather were inclement, there were cottages all over the estate with facilities for entertaining twenty or thirty sportsmen and their wives. An extension was even built on to the royal station at Wolferton to serve as a lunch-room if necessary.[24]

Those landowners who invited Edward to their shooting parties inevitably incurred a good deal of expenditure. In 1910 Lord Balcarres estimated that to entertain royalty for a week in this way might cost 'anything from five to ten thousand pounds'. In certain wealthy families it was even customary to have the royal suite specially refurbished for each visit, while the chef who served 'for ordinary occasions would be replaced by a specialist, whose skill was equalled only by his wastefulness'. There was also the extensive royal retinue to accommodate, numbering as many as sixteen on occasion. Lord Balcarres confessed to having 'an invincible dislike of royal chauffeurs and footmen, the most insolent class of the community'.[25]

Not all hosts had the resources to meet this kind of outlay and yet their social ambitions were such that, according to Lady Warwick, some of them would economize for a whole year, or alternatively get into debt, so that they might entertain royalty for a single week-end.[26] The Walsinghams were one family who regularly entertained Edward both as Prince and as King without having the means to do so. In the 1890s, indeed, the

Prince took the shooting at Merton, one of Lord Walsingham's estates, and 'in a single year, the wine cellar which had been painstakingly built up for generations was exhausted.'[27] Over the years Walsingham's financial problems mounted, as his sporting expenditure increased. In 1912 he was forced to sell two Yorkshire estates, as well as property in London which included the site of the Ritz Hotel, and other valuable assets. He cut back on his own spending, too, and spent the last seven years of his life abroad.[28]

It was in these circumstances that Lady Augustus Hervey warned her son, now the 4th Marquess of Bristol, to think carefully before he invited Edward to Ickworth for a shooting party. The Marquess had married an heiress a few years earlier, but cash was not the sole point at issue:

> There is no doubt that the King will *want* to shoot some day at Ickworth – Himself or others – or – *and* others.
>
> The point uppermost with *me*, has been & is – The physical exertion for *you*. It's an appalling thing to undertake a King – the house, the staff of servants – all seems against you . . . I seem to think Augustus Lumley, an adept as such things, died of exhaustion after only *preparing* his Villa at Cannes for the old Queen. Middle class Entertaining won't do . . . nor really bad shooting. So you see – *with me* it's you against the World.[29]

The Marquess apparently took her advice and decided to postpone an invitation until he had settled the question of death duties on his inheritance and had completed various repairs and renovations to the house.[30]

Not all shooting parties involved the major outlays associated with entertaining royalty. Small parties of family and close friends could derive a great deal of pleasure at relatively modest cost, as the diary of Geoffrey Gathorne-Hardy confirms. While he was still at Eton, he spent the New Year of 1896 on his grandfather's estate, Hemsted Park in Kent. On this occasion shooting expeditions were interspersed with rehearsals for a play which members of the house party were putting on to entertain themselves and their friends. Amateur dramatics were a favourite pastime at many country-house gatherings. Hence Geoffrey's comment on 3 January: 'Went out partridge driving. Shot very badly indeed. Marvellous numbers of jays were killed in one place . . . Coming home we rehearsed "Good for Nothing". I think it will go well, but father must learn his part.' Three days later the play was dominating proceedings:

> Rehearsing and acting took up the whole of the day, except a small part, when we tried to shoot pigeons in the rookery, but without much success. The play went off very well indeed. So did the variety entertainment.[31]

On 8 January the party began to break up, to Geoffrey's regret, with his sister, Isobel, going to a ball at Hatfield House, and other members departing as well: 'we all go at the end of the week.'

Yet however much male members of the shooting parties might enjoy themselves, many of their womenfolk were less enthusiastic. As Lady Brooke wrote acidly to a non-sporting male friend, her husband was due to return home on 6 August and then go 'off shooting on 12th. . . . No women exist – wives or mistresses – after August 12th.'[32]

Amateur theatricals were a feature of many country-house parties. A group of friends at Wakehurst Place performed *The Merchant of Venice* in April 1911. They even had a specially printed programme for the occasion. (The author)

Lady Maud Wolmer took an even stronger line when she firmly requested her husband not to accept any fresh invitations to go grouse shooting in Scotland:

> You see if we go to Faskally we shall get back to Blackmoor [their Hampshire home] about Aug. 20 to 25 & you surely can exist for 5 or 10 days without killing anything & on the 1st of September a kind legislature permits you to slaughter a partridge. If you get an invitation to Bolton or Raby for grouse driving at the end of August I know you will wish immensely to accept it so I don't say anything against that, but don't let us engage ourselves for anything in that detestable northern Kingdom except Faskally, to which we are engaged on the 12th.[33]

Whilst shooting was in progress the females had little to do, since even in the reign of King Edward a woman 'who used a rifle was considered very unconventional'. A few ignored the criticisms, like the Duchess of Bedford who, according to her grandson, became an expert shot, as did Lady Randolph Churchill's friend, the Comtesse de Paris, and Millicent Duchess of Sutherland. Years later, Millicent's niece could remember 'the oft-repeated question, in somewhat bated breath "Does the Duchess really shoot herself?"' Others, including the Marchioness of Breadalbane and Lady Graham, were also skilled in deer-stalking, but these were the exceptions. Even Lady Randolph Churchill had strong reservations about shooting as a female accomplishment. 'The fact is, I love life so much that the unnecessary curtailing of any creature's existence is more than distasteful to me,' she wrote. ' . . . If these things must be done, how can a woman bring herself to do them?'[34] Queen Victoria was equally disapproving. In 1882 she told her daughter that while it was acceptable for a lady 'to be a spectator . . . only fast women shot'.[35]

The feminine duty at most shooting parties was, therefore, to look decorative, add sparkle and gaiety to the conversation and, when opportunity offered, engage in discreet flirtations with fellow guests. In this connection it is significant that during the last decade of Edward VII's life, the Hon. Mrs George Keppel, the last of the King's intimate female companions, was invited to virtually all the houses which he visited. The exceptions were Hatfield and Welbeck. As his biographer delicately notes, she 'made him happy by relieving his boredom and frustration'. That was enough to commend her to most anxious hosts, without the added advantages of her own vivacity, cleverness, and good looks.[36]

Nonetheless, the Countess of Warwick, who had preceded Mrs Keppel as a recipient of Edward's favours and who was an expert in discreet flirtations, regarded shooting and fishing parties as 'intolerably boring'. When possible she would excuse herself and let her husband go to them alone. 'I preferred to remain among my own pursuits at Easton.'[37] But good manners and social custom often made this difficult, especially as her husband was:

> such a crack shot that we were asked everywhere, Blenheim, Chatsworth, and all the great places. . . . We began the day by breakfasting at ten o'clock. . . . The men went out shooting after breakfast and then came the emptiness of the long morning from which I suffered silently. I can remember the groups of women sitting discussing their neighbours or writing letters at impossible little ornamental tables. . . . We were not all women. There were a few unsporting men asked – 'darlings'. These men of witty and amusing conversation were always asked as extras everywhere to help to entertain the women; otherwise we should have been left high and dry.[38]

As luncheon approached the females prepared to join the guns. They changed into tweeds 'and trying to look as sportsmanlike as the clothes of the day allowed, we went out together to some rendezvous of the shooters. A woman who was very bloodthirsty and sporting might go and cower behind some man and watch his prowess among the pheasants. But there were very few . . . of those brave ones.'[39] Perhaps their caution was justified. Apart from the discomfort of standing for long periods in the cold and the damp of a winter's day, the noise from the guns was appalling. There was also a danger, when thousands of birds were being killed, that an unwary spectator might be hit by a falling pheasant. When this happened to Lady Ailesbury she took three months to get over it, and the Dowager Lady Westmorland had a similar unfortunate experience at a shoot at Crichel.[40]

According to Lady Warwick, therefore, once the female members of the party had consumed a large luncheon, they would wend their way back to the house. There they spent the intervening time until the men returned for tea by changing into elaborate tea-gowns:

Lord Granard takes aim at a pheasant at a shooting party at Warter Priory, home of the Wilsons. His American-born wife apparently did not appreciate the noise of the guns! (January 1911.) (British Library Newspaper Library)

> Conversation at tea was slumberous. Nobody woke up to be witty until dinner time with its accompanying good wines. The men discussed the bags of the day and the women did the admiring. With the coming of bridge in later years the hours between tea and dinner were relieved of their tedium. It used often to be sheer boredom until seven when we went off to dress for dinner.[41]

Nor did the flirtations always go well. On one occasion Lord Charles Beresford, who had a well-publicized affair with Lady Brooke in the late 1880s, made an embarrassing navigational error when seeking a lady-love in the darkness of an unfamiliar house. In an exuberant effort to surprise her he entered an unlit bedroom and jumped on the bed, shouting 'cock-a-doodle-do'. Unfortunately the bed was occupied by the Bishop of Chester and his wife, and they were distinctly unamused at his sudden appearance.[42]

It was doubtless from similar motives of not wishing to disturb the wrong people that the young 2nd Duke of Westminster advised those engaged in nocturnal adventures 'to walk on the outside of the staircase, as it creaked less, and never to touch the bannisters as one surreptitiously crept upstairs'. But even the notorious womaniser, Wilfred Scawen-Blunt, received a rebuff on at least one occasion when he attempted to enter the bedroom of Emily Lytton. Although she was infatuated with him and had allowed him to hold her hand under the table while they played 'the letter game in the evening', she was not prepared to 'yield to him in every way. Happily I locked my bedroom door, as I heard someone trying to open it some time during the night.'[43] Doubtless he looked around for a more co-operative victim at his next country-house party.

Apart from the leisure aspects of these hunting, shooting and fishing parties, they had their economic implications, too, as some hard-hit landlords sought to combat the effects of falling agricultural incomes by renting – or selling – sporting rights to wealthy enthusiasts. Often these were members of the thrusting *nouveaux riches*, who valued the status which the purchase or renting of an estate could bestow, or who needed the dignity of landed property to support their aspirations to a peerage. By the early 1890s it was claimed that in some parts of the country the letting of land for sporting purposes was more profitable than letting it for cultivation. One man ironically commented that 'the partridge had been the salvation of Norfolk farming.'[44] Often, too, when estates were offered for sale during these years, more emphasis was laid on their sporting advantages than upon their agrarian possibilities. Hence the advertisement in *Country Life* for 21 January, 1911, of an estate of 7,100 acres in East Anglia. It included first-rate stabling for sixteen horses, a cricket ground, and:

> excellent partridge shooting. Over 3,000 partridges have been shot in one season. From 7,000 to 8,000 pheasants are reared annually. Eight-and-a-half miles of good trout fishing.

The Tatler also drew attention to the remunerative possibilities of renting out salmon rivers. In one case a stretch of river had been hired for a single season at £1,000, and with the tenant limited to a catch of ninety fish – which made each one worth over £10! Nor was this exceptional. There were several instances 'of men paying £1,000 and £1,500 for fishing rights and catching fish the total value of which did not amount to £30'.[45]

At the beginning of November 1911, the magazine estimated national expenditure on the most popular male sports, differentiating between the capital investment they required and their annual running costs:[46]

	Capital Investment	*Annual Expenditure*
	£	£
Shooting	4,067,000	8,182,000
Fishing	550,000	589,000
Racing	8,320,000	10,593,000
Yachting	5,600,000	3,032,000
Coursing	520,000	317,400
Coaching	290,250	237,700

	Capital Investment £	Annual Expenditure £
Polo	87,000	110,000
Fox-hunting	over 15,000,000	over 8,000,000

Some enthusiastic shooters, including the Prince of Wales, also went on big-game expeditions overseas. In 1882, for example, the Duke of Portland went on a shooting trip to India with Lord de Grey, Lord Charles Beresford, and other friends. During six 'very happy and interesting weeks' in Nepal they bagged, 'beside other game', fourteen tigers and eight rhinoceros. They then joined a shooting party arranged by the Maharajah of Durbungah, where the game 'simply swarmed' and their bag comprised 3 tigers, 28 buffaloes, 273 pigs, 435 deer, 48 hares, 6 floriken, 499 partridges, 11 quails, 90 snipe and 119 ducks.[47] Early in the twentieth century British East Africa, notably Kenya, also became a favourite resort of big-game hunters. Even in the late 1890s men like Lord Cranworth and Lord Delamere were making regular trips to slaughter elephants, lions and giraffe, and by the First World War Nairobi had become Africa's principal safari centre. Some of the visitors, including Lord Cranworth, subsequently settled in Kenya, prompted by 'love of sport . . . and shortage of cash'. The tract of land which Cranworth purchased faced Mount Kenya, and behind it 'rolled plains on which herds of game fed'.[48]

Meanwhile, in England itself country-house parties held during the summer months inevitably centred around other sports than hunting and shooting. At Lady Warwick's Easton Lodge the annual cricket week was a popular event. 'We used to put up at least two teams in the house, spread a big luncheon tent, and invite the County to see the play', she recalled. 'Various teams of the Guards, the I Zingari, and other well-known elevens would play on the ground.'[49] Her half-brother, the Earl of Rosslyn, brought 'many noted batters and bowlers, and my son Guy was a promising player'.[50] George Cornwallis-West, too, delighted in informal house parties held at the end of the Season at country houses which boasted a private cricket ground in the park. A particular favourite was Frampton Court in Dorset.

> The parties lasted a week, and the relaxed atmosphere, the long hours of outdoor activity, the good talk and laughter at the end of the day, provided a setting in which he was at his happiest. When cricket was over, the trout-fishermen would rush to the river for the evening rise until dinner, after which there would be dancing.[51]

Tennis, croquet, golf, boating and yachting also had their devotees, while even table-tennis seems to have attracted some. Maggie Wyndham, staying at Aberlady in Scotland for a Saturday to Monday party, confessed that on the first day 'every available minute . . . was taken up with golf & ping pong. Sunday morning we drove to Church at N. Berwick, in the afternoon [we] took a walk & ping pong immediately after tea. It was a very pleasant . . . party.'[52]

Golf at Ranelagh c. 1900. The game became an increasingly popular leisure activity for the upper classes in the Edwardian years. (The author)

However, a few days earlier, when Maggie had been staying with her maternal uncle, the Earl of Rosebery, at his Scottish estate, Dalmeny, near Edinburgh, her social encounters had been rather more complicated. That was especially the case when Lady Warwick arrived, shortly before she and Lord Rosebery were due to catch the evening express to London from Edinburgh.

> That evening she sent down to beg that we should go into dinner without her, which was as well we did as she came down ¾ hour late! We expected to see her in her travelling dress; far from it, a pale pink gauze [gown] cut very low, roses and diamonds in her hair, a large diamond bow & a string of priceless pearls, and pursued into the dining-room by a huge colley dog.
>
> You can imagine Uncle Archie's feelings (they were to start in an hour!) He begged the dog at least might be sent out of the room but Lady W. said this was impossible . . . Ten minutes before the carriage was ordered Lady W. went upstairs to change her dress and sauntered down . . . in a quarter of an hour just as Uncle Archie was going without her. And then not only was Lady Warwick to get into the Victoria but the colley, a large bandbox, containing the pink gauze, and a large handbag! It was really the vilest manners I have ever seen as she really drove Uncle Archie almost to frenzy and if he hadn't possessed his extraordinary sense of humour it might really have been disagreeable.[53]

Many socialites were attracted by the major race-meetings at Newmarket, Ascot, Sandown, Goodwood, Doncaster and Epsom, and house parties were frequently arranged to coincide with these. The Eton and Harrow cricket match and Henley regatta

Lady Warwick with her son, Maynard,
c. 1902. (The author)

likewise had their enthusiastic supporters. At Henley, as an American visitor, Richard Harding Davis, shrewdly observed, racing was only a minor part of the proceedings.

> Henley is a great water picnic, not a sporting event; it is the out-of-door life, the sight of the thousands of boats and thousands of people in white and colours, all on pleasure bent, and . . . beautiful flowers of the house-boats, and the coloured lanterns at night and the fireworks, which make Henley an institution . . . Some [house-boats] were pink and white, with rows of pink carnations, or white and gold, with hanging vines of green, or brilliantly blue, with solid banks of red geraniums . . . and all had gorgeously striped awnings and Chinese umbrellas and soft Persian rugs everywhere, and silk flags of the owners' own design flapping overhead. It is only a step along the gang-plank to the lawn, and so on down the line to the next open space, where some club has a bit of lawn reserved for it, and has erected a marquee, and brilliant standards proclaiming its name, and guiding the thirsty and hungry member to its luncheon table.[54]

Davis was less favourably impressed by Ascot. He regarded it as a 'tame affair after the rowdy good nature and vast extent of the Derby'. 'The smart people, to whom Ascot primarily and solely belongs, have all the best places and the best time; but even the best

Spectators at Henley Royal Regatta, *c*. 1898. (The author)

time does not seem to be a very good time.' The ladies were afraid of disarranging their elaborate outfits, and the young men looked, walked and dressed alike, 'even to the yellow leather field-glass over the right shoulder, which never comes out of its case'. All the well-known regiments had their luncheon tents erected, with soldier-servants in front, and many of the London clubs similarly offered hospitality to members and their friends. But what Davis found most surprising, as an American, were the strict social divisions associated with the royal enclosure and the 'celebrities' who frequented it:

> it is interesting to hear the present bearer of a very great name fuss and fret because there are two and not three lumps in his tea, and to find that the very much made up lady is *the* professional beauty, and *not* the young and very beautiful one who is laughing so heartily at a song of a coloured comedian on the other side of the rail . . . It is also curious to consider that 'only a brandy bottle' stands between a shy little man and a title which is written up in bronze from Hyde Park corner to Westminster Bridge, and that the 'black man,' who is not at all black, in the ill-fitting gray frock-coat, is a prince of half of India, and that the very much bored young man who is sitting down while three women are standing and talking to him is a manufacturer's son who is worth a million pounds sterling. It is also interesting to hear the policemen tell the crowd outside the fence that they must not even 'touch the railing.' It makes you think you are at a circus, and listening to the keeper warning the group in front of the lion's cage.[55]

Davis was, of course, an outsider and his acid comments doubtless reflected this fact. But they also underline the snobbishness which events like Ascot engendered. Certainly George Cornwallis-West, who was one of the 'insiders', frankly admitted he preferred the exclusive atmosphere of the pre-war years to the situation which applied after 1918. 'If one was jostled it was at least by one's own friends,' he wrote, 'and not by the curious people that are now met with.'[56] However, his 'chief recollection of racing in Edwardian days [was] wondering how I could pay the bookies on Monday morning.' In those days of heavy betting many members of the 'smart' set shared his predicament. Lord Rosslyn, who in 1890 inherited securities worth £50,000 and an annual income of £17,000 from the collieries and estate at Dysart bequeathed by his father, was declared a bankrupt on his own petition seven years later. Most of the money had gone on betting, gambling and running a string of racehorses. Although the bankruptcy was annulled in 1902 and he made a successful third marriage six years later, he 'never quite succeeded in giving up gambling, were it on a horse or a card'.[57]

According to Lord Alfred Douglas, his father, the eccentric 8th Marquess of Queensberry, and his brother, the 9th Marquess, were two others who speculated on a massive scale. Between them they dissipated more than £700,000 on various ventures.[58] However, Lord Alfred himself, as an inveterate gambler on horses and at the casino, was rapidly to run through the £16,000 he inherited on the death of his father.[59]

It was, indeed, racing and gambling – although not gambling on horses – which combined in the early 1890s to create one of the greatest crises in the life of the Prince of Wales himself. The Prince's enthusiasm for horse-racing was long-established. Already in the 1860s Queen Victoria had repeatedly urged him to cut down on the number of race meetings he attended, but without avail. Later he acquired his own stable and although at first this enjoyed little success, in 1896 his luck changed. In that year he won the Derby with *Persimmon*. It was a feat he was to repeat with two other horses in 1900 and 1909, respectively. In all, between 1886, when he began racing, and 1910, when he died, he earned £269,495 from his stallions in stud fees, and £146,345 in stake money from his horses' victories.[60] Racing was one of his most absorbing interests and a critic commented sourly that in 1890 he attended twenty-eight race meetings, which was almost three times as many as the days he attended in the House of Lords.[61]

One of the meetings which Edward particularly relished was that at Doncaster for the St. Leger. For many years he stayed at Brantingham Thorpe with Christopher Sykes, the second son of a large Yorkshire landowner. The tall, slender, mournfully elegant Sykes spared no expense to please his royal guest. As a descendant ruefully recalled, if the Prince wished to gamble,

> there were the very newest and best counters, cards, tables, and what-nots; did he wish to dance, there was the best of orchestras; and did he wish for some innocent royal horse-play, that was also to hand.

Sykes's solemn deference to the Prince's wishes made him the butt of many juvenile practical jokes. Bottles of brandy were poured down the back of his neck, he was pushed underneath the billiard-table, while the Prince and his entourage prevented his escape by spearing at him with billiard-cues, and his bed was damped by watering cans brought into his bedroom for the purpose. 'His hat would be knocked off . . . [and] soda-water pumped over his head, and he would incline, and murmur: "As Your Royal Highness pleases."'[62] So highly did he value the Prince's friendship that he was prepared to accept it all, and also the heavy drain on his resources which this lavish entertaining entailed. Then, at the beginning of the 1890s the inevitable crash came. Sykes's income had fallen to below half its original figure, his debts were enormous, and the creditors closed in. Only his formidable sister-in-law saved him from bankruptcy. She approached the Prince and bluntly told him of Christopher's plight, and indicated the part he had played in this. As a result, the main part of Sykes's debts were settled, but most of his capital had vanished and his large house in London, as well as Brantingham Thorpe in Yorkshire, had passed out of his possession for ever. His connection with the Prince continued, but now the once great host was destined to be an eternal guest. He died in 1898 after suffering several years of poor health.[63]

It was because of Sykes's financial difficulties that in September 1890 Edward and his friends accepted an invitation to spend Doncaster race week with the shipowner, Arthur Wilson, at his home, Tranby Croft. Wilson was not a member of the Prince's regular circle, and the party began badly when his current favourite, Lady Brooke, was prevented from attending by the sudden death of her step-father. Initially the evening of the first day, 8 September, was spent in conversation and music, but it was then decided to play baccarat, a gambling game of which the Prince was very fond. Indeed, as early as July 1889 his enthusiasm for the game had brought him into conflict with the peppery Duke of Richmond with whom he was staying for Goodwood. According to Sir Edward Hamilton, the Duke objected to baccarat being played in his house, but,

> contrary to his wishes, implied if not directly expressed, the Royal Party would not refrain from indulging in the game. Though they called it by some other name, he was not to be taken in; & he came down upon the Prince not without some loss of temper, expressing surprise that H.R.H. should have had the bad taste to resort to gambling in his House. The Prince was extremely annoyed at being pulled up by the Duke and declared he would never set foot in the House again. However, on the morrow when the party broke up, both parties cooled down, the Duke apologizing for any excess of warmth he had displayed and the Prince admitting that he had been in the wrong.[64]

In January of the following year, Winifred Sturt, a daughter of Lord Alington, similarly complained to her fiancé of the way in which baccarat was played at Sandringham into the early hours. 'I think it is a shocking affair,' she wrote, 'for the Royal Family to play an illegal game every night. They have a real table, and rakes, and everything like the rooms at Monte Carlo.'[65]

It seems that Arthur Wilson shared these reservations about baccarat and a year before the arrival of the royal party he had banned it at Tranby Croft. However, in deference to Edward's wishes an impromptu table was rigged up and the game began, with the Prince acting as banker. While it was in progress, the Wilsons' son detected one of the guests, Sir William Gordon-Cumming, cheating by surreptitiously increasing his stake after he had seen his cards. Sir William, a lieutenant-colonel in the Scots Guards, was a large

144

The Prince and Princess of Wales in the royal box at Goodwood, *c*. 1900. (The author)

Scottish landowner and a close friend of the Prince of Wales. Hence when young Wilson confessed his suspicions to his family and a friend they were incredulous. However, the following evening watch was kept on Sir William and others detected him in what they believed to be dishonest play. The next morning it was decided that two older fellow-guests, Lord Coventry and Lieutenant-General Owen Williams, should confront Gordon-Cumming with the accusation made against him. The baronet denied hotly that he had cheated but eventually agreed, with much reluctance, to sign a paper promising never to play cards again. He did this in the knowledge that if he were publicly convicted of cheating not only would his army career be at an end, but he would have to leave his clubs and be doomed to what *The Times* called 'social extinction'.[66] In return, ten of those staying at Tranby Croft, including the host, his son and son-in-law, and the Prince of Wales, agreed to preserve silence over the accusation. In this way scandal would be avoided and the Prince's addiction to baccarat would remain out of the public eye.

Unfortunately, the vow of silence proved impossible to keep. Someone gossiped, and as the news spread, Gordon-Cumming decided to bring an action for seditious libel against his host's wife, son, daughter, son-in-law and a subaltern in his own regiment, Mr Berkeley Levett, who was also a member of the Tranby Croft house-party. The trial began on 1 June 1891 and lasted for over a week. In the course of it the Prince of Wales had to give evidence, and through his testimony and that of other witnesses the sordid details of the whole affair were brought to light. In the end the jury found for the defendants and Gordon-Cumming was, by implication, deemed guilty of cheating at cards. *The Times*, in stern mood, declared: 'He has committed a mortal offence; society can know him no more.'[67] And this, indeed, did prove to be the end of his involvement in the social world. Although he married an American heiress immediately after the trial and she attempted to give house-parties in their huge, gloomy Scottish mansion, Gordonstoun, her efforts failed. She turned for consolation to religion, and he responded by bringing two girls to stay at Gordonstoun as his mistresses.[68] For some time after the trial there was persistent gossip in High Society that Tranby Croft was not Gordon-Cumming's first fall from grace. Indeed, according to Sir Edward Hamilton, cheating at cards had become 'undoubtedly a mania'.[69]

Nor was the baronet the only victim of press and public condemnation as a result of the Tranby Croft case. The Prince of Wales was also heavily criticized. *The Times* regretted that he should have been involved not only in the legal proceedings 'but in the social circumstances which prepared the way for it', including the fact that the game of baccarat had been played to please him and with his counters, which had been specially taken to Tranby Croft for the purpose. Sir William had been made to sign a declaration that he 'would never touch a card again'. 'We almost wish, for the sake of English society in general, that we could learn that the result of this most unhappy case has been that the PRINCE OF WALES had signed a similar declaration,' the paper pronounced in a leading article.[70]

It seems that the Tranby Croft case did lead to the Prince abandoning baccarat and turning instead to bridge, although as late as 1907 one courtier recounted an occasion when baccarat was played in his presence, apparently at the request of Queen Alexandra. He did not take part.[71] But he certainly did not give up gambling. At the beginning of the 1900s George Cornwallis-West described a train journey he made with Edward soon after the death of Queen Victoria. The King played bridge to pass the time and when Cornwallis-West won some money from him he produced 'an enormous roll of notes from his pocket from which to pay me. I had always understood that kings never carried money, which shows how mistaken one can be.'[72]

Not all of the pleasures and pastimes of the late Victorians and Edwardians were of this raffish nature. For the women, needlework, painting, writing letters, music, walking and gardening occupied a good deal of time. Others, like Lady Craven, Lady Evelyn Cottrell, and Lady Howe, devoted attention to the raising of prize poultry, while Lady Edith Villiers was the owner of prize dogs.[73] At a more intellectual level, even spinsters could arrange occasional theatre parties, as Maggie Wyndham, the widowed Lady Leconfield's youngest daughter, pointed out. 'Celia & Capt. Coates & Eric Villiers dine here tonight & we go & see "Milestones". . . . The play parties are most successful, as getting a couple & one man is not difficult,' she told her mother while staying at the family home in Great Stanhope Street, London.[74]

The men had their more thoughtful diversions, too. The Duke of York, later George V, was an enthusiastic philatelist; and a few members of noble families, including Bertrand Russell and the Hon. Charles S. Shelley-Rolls, a co-founder of Rolls-Royce, took up the tradition of aristocrat-scientist. Even those, like Lord Walsingham, who were keen sportsmen, had their more academic pursuits. Walsingham was an enthusiastic and well-informed ornithologist and in this sphere, too, he used his skill with the gun. All the humming-birds in the Natural History Museum were reputedly killed by him,

LE MONDE OÙ L'ON S'AMUSE.

Ethel. " I HOPE BICYCLING WILL GO OUT OF FASHION BEFORE NEXT SEASON, I *do* HATE BICYCLING SO !"
Maud. " SO DO I ! BUT ONE *must*, YOU KNOW !"

Cycling became a widespread – if not always enjoyable – female activity. (*Punch*, 1911)

using powder shot in order to preserve them from unnecessary damage. He was likewise a member of the exclusive Literary Society, as well as a director of the British Museum and a founder member of the Castle Museum at Norwich.[75]

Many men found companionship while they were in London through membership of a club; for only a few catered for women. By 1911, when there were estimated to be over two hundred clubs in the capital, around half of them had been founded during the previous thirty or so years. On the eve of the First World War club membership in London was put at over 200,000.[76] Some, like Brooks's, the Carlton, and the Reform had a distinctly political slant; others, including the Turf, the Marlborough, White's and the Bachelors' were primarily social. The Marlborough had been founded by the Prince of Wales himself in 1869 when the committee at White's had refused to relax what he considered their excessive restrictions on smoking. Members were only admitted with his approval, and apart from such customary facilities as a billiard room it also had a skittle-alley.[77] Its light-hearted atmosphere was very different from that at Brooks's, where the general air of solid comfort was described by one member as 'like dining in a Duke's house with the Duke lying dead upstairs'.[78] Another member complained of being served refreshments in its 'dreary coffee room' and of the snobbishness of some younger members:

> Algernon West & Ribblesdale dining in the corner – Ag. West I always thought a kindly ass – Ribblesdale has stuck up manners. So many young men are spoilt by

147

Ladies' Day at the Constitutional Club, *c*. 1902. (The author)

being lords when they are young. My greetings with Ribblesdale are therefore of the coldest nature.[79]

The Athenaeum was even more solemn, being the haunt of bishops and judges and 'a terror of the frivolous'. The Turf Club was the most fashionable of the clubs connected with sport – or as Sir Edward Hamilton put it, when he joined in February 1887: 'it is the Club where almost everybody one meets is either a person one knows or . . . knows about, which is what a Club ought to be.'[80] Then there was the St. James's, which attracted diplomatists of every nationality.[81]

According to Sir Wemyss Reid, men went to clubs:

> not to indulge in sumptuous feastings, but to lunch modestly and cheaply, to read the evening newspapers, and, above all, to drink an afternoon cup of tea. . . . Lawyers and men of business, whose work is over for the day, delight to go to their clubs to discuss the news with their friends over the homely tea-cups. Members of Parliament look in on their way down to the House, whilst men about town, having nothing better to do, feel that the club is a 'sure draw' of an afternoon if they are in search of an acquaintance.[82]

Many men were members of more than one club. Earl Granville, a leading light at Brooks's, belonged to no less then seven at the time of his death in 1891. Prospective entrants were carefully vetted and those deemed unsuitable were black-balled. In the case of the most popular or prestigious clubs applicants might have to wait several years to be admitted.[83]

But club life had its darker side. Gambling and childish horse-play characterized many of them. At the Turf Club there was heavy betting on the results of billiards matches, as the Earl of Rosslyn discovered to his cost, while at White's even in the early twentieth century George Cornwallis-West remembered games of chance being played for very high stakes.

> One or two rich men used to take the bank, and others, who were called 'the Villagers' used to punt against them. Many thousand pounds changed hands in a week . . . Providentially, it died a natural death, as what was going on got to the ears of King Edward, who, it was said, made some very trenchant remarks to the chairman of the committee.[84]

Then there was the Pelican Club, first founded in 1887 and reorganized two years later. Its concentration on sport attracted the more raffish elements of the aristocracy as well as actors, journalists, dubious businessmen and moneylenders. Its committee included the 8th Marquess of Queensberry, who had earlier helped to reform boxing by persuading Britain and the United States of America to agree to the 'Queensberry rules'. The future Duke of Manchester, George Edwards, manager of the Gaiety Theatre, and a number of other 'bright young men about town' were other committee members, while the 5th Earl of Lonsdale was chairman of its boxing committee. In the Pelican, patrons were for the first time able to enjoy boxing contests in relative comfort and with reasonable certainty that the large number of aristocrats in the audience would provide protection against police interference in a sport whch was still regarded as of doubtful legality.[85] The Pelican particularly appealed to Hugh Lonsdale and his friends because of its lack of ceremony and its conversation, which concentrated largely on horses and boxing. Its atmosphere was described by one commentator as 'more reminiscent of a rag in a public-school common room than anything else.'[86] The Pelican faded away in 1892, when it was replaced by the National Sporting Club, with Lord Lonsdale as its first president.

Even dignified Brooks's had occasional wagers, as in July 1888 when Lord Moreton bet Mr Buller '£3 to £1 that a certain couple they have in their eye will not have any children before Jany. 1 1891'; and on 20 July, 1908, a Mr Marsh unwisely bet Mr Somerset ten guineas 'that there will not be war between any two great European powers within 20 years'.[87]

Contrary to the accepted image of club life, which suggests that these august institutions were staffed by aged retainers, many of those employed by them were extremely young. In 1891, for example, the Marlborough had a resident staff of seventeen, of whom nine were under the age of twenty (including a 17-year-old billiard marker and four pages); the 38-year-old steward was the only staff member over thirty. Similarly at prestigious White's, which was the oldest club in London, a third of the staff of eighteen were under the age of twenty and only the housekeeper was over thirty. However, Brooks's, as befitted its more stately atmosphere, defied this cult of youth.

Only two of its resident servants in 1891 were under the age of twenty – a page and a kitchenmaid – and a quarter were over the age of forty, including the steward and the housekeeper.[88] The recruitment of so many young people to work in the clubs must have added to the air of light-heartedness which characterized institutions like the Marlborough, where the Prince of Wales and his friends engaged in gambling and noisy practical jokes. It was doubtless this uneasy mixture which caused Lady Augustus Hervey to note anxiously in January 1885 that her eldest son had been invited by the Prince to 'put his name down for the Marlborough Club! . . . I hate it – they are all blackguards & it *costs* a lot.'[89] It is not clear whether he accepted the invitation but, in such circles, refusal would have been difficult.

At the United Service Club another kind of embarrassment arose in 1880 when one of the housemaids gave birth to a baby on the premises. As she could not be moved, the Club had to pay a five-guinea fee to a doctor for attending her.[90] The event was all the more shocking because the Club at that time was dominated by staid older members, who each had their particular chairs and clearly resented younger members sitting in them. 'The library was . . . peopled only by a few recumbent forms and enlivened only by snores.'[91]

Finally there were those dubious amusements which High Society preferred to keep from the public gaze. These included notorious extra-marital affairs like that involving

The smoking room at the Marlborough Club. *c.* 1900. (The author)

the Earl of Lonsdale and an attractive young actress named Violet Cameron. When Violet became pregnant the affair was so widely publicized that Queen Victoria intervened to make it known that she expected the Earl to leave the country until the scandal had blown over.[92] As a consequence in February 1888 Lonsdale sailed for Canada where he spent more than a year collecting specimens for the Scottish Naturalist Society. On his return, Violet was not allowed to re-enter his life, and he took care to conduct future affairs with more discretion.

On occasion these unwise associations with actresses could also prove very costly. Harry Vane Millbank's father paid Mabel Grey, a star at the Holborn Casino, £10,000 to give up the idea of marrying his son.[93] But even this was insignificant compared to the penalty paid by Earl Compton, later the Marquess of Northampton. In 1912, Compton met Daisy Markham, a leading actress at the Globe Theatre. At the time he was senior subaltern of the Royal Horse Guards and a well-known 'man about town'. Soon he announced his intention of marrying Daisy, and this led to an immediate clash with his father.[94] The old Marquess steadfastly refused to entertain such a union and reluctantly Compton wrote to Daisy to tell her that the affair must end. But she was not prepared to abandon the prospect of becoming the Marchioness of Northampton so easily. She had in her possession letters from the Earl promising marriage and she decided to sue for breach of promise. During the course of the subsequent negotiations the old Marquess died, and Compton decided to settle the matter out of court. The sum offered was the then unprecedented figure of £50,000, plus all her legal costs. In modern terms that would amount to more than half a million pounds. According to one newspaper:

> A gasp of astonishment ran through the crowded court when the amount that Miss Markham was to receive was . . . disclosed. At first people could scarcely believe it. Such a sum was the largest that had ever been granted by way of damages. It set up a record.[95]

However, the gossip engendered by scandals like those concerning Violet Cameron and Daisy Markham was relatively innocuous when compared to cases involving homosexuality. That was especially true after the passage of the 1885 Criminal Law Amendment Act had provided that any male who committed 'an act of gross indecency with another male person' was liable to two years' imprisonment, with or without hard labour.[96] Even before this there had been concern about the rising incidence of homosexuality in the upper ranks of society. Most men, like Reginald Brett, the future 2nd Lord Esher, were able to keep their relationships out of public view, but already in the late 1870s there had been one unpleasant scandal. That had involved Lord Henry Somerset (nicknamed 'Penna' by his family). He was the second son of the 8th Duke of Beaufort and in 1873 he married Isabella, the heiress daughter of the last Earl Somers. In May 1874 they had a son but soon Isabella found her husband's homosexual tendencies intolerable and she left him, taking the child with her. The Duchess of Beaufort wrote sadly to her daughter-in-law at the time: 'We have nothing whatever to say in defence of Penna and unless he is mad cannot understand his behaviour.' The Duke was more forthright, telling Lord Henry that his 'conduct and language' were not those of a gentleman.[97]

A year or two later Lady Henry obtained a judicial separation from her husband and in the course of the legal proceedings made clear the reason for her application, thereby bringing the issue of homosexuality into the open. She did not seek a divorce because of religious scruples, but her frankness concerning the grounds for the separation shocked her social circle and she was ostracized. She found consolation during the remainder of her life in performing good works.[98]

In the meantime, Lord Henry began a long drawn out battle to try to gain custody of his young son. The case began in 1877 and ended a year later with his wife being awarded custody of the child subject to the father having reasonable access.[99] At this point Lord Henry decided to leave the country. Initially he settled in Monaco before moving on to Florence, which was then a popular resort for expatriate homosexuals. There he earned a reputation as a writer of sentimental songs for Victorian drawing-rooms. He published a book of poems called *Songs of Adieu* which was allegedly inspired by a young man named Henry Smith, who had been the cause of the break-up of his marriage, and who eventually emigrated to New Zealand.[100]

Just over a decade after Lord Henry's affair the Duke and Duchess of Beaufort were to receive a still greater blow, when their third son, Lord Arthur Somerset, was accused of involvement in the notorious Cleveland Street scandal, concerning a male brothel. At the time the affair became public in 1889, Lord Arthur was an officer in the Blues, an equerry to the Prince of Wales, and superintendent of the Prince's stables. For this latter role he had an office in Marlborough House and Edward was said to rely greatly on his judgement in purchasing horses for racing and breeding.[101]

The case arose during police investigations into the running of the Cleveland Street brothel. Its owner, a professional prostitute named Charles Hammond, fled abroad on hearing of the police's involvement, but a bogus clergyman who had lived with him and another, younger, confederate were arrested and committed for trial. Meanwhile rumours circulated that 'men in high positions' had frequented the brothel, and it was in this connection that Lord Arthur's name was mentioned. During the course of the subsequent police inquiries three boys who had worked at Cleveland Street positively identified Lord Arthur as a client. At first the Home Secretary refused to prosecute, considering the evidence against him too weak.[102] So in August 1889, Lord Arthur decided to go to Bad Homburg, ostensibly to take a 'cure' but really in the hope that in his absence the matter would fade away. There he met the Prince of Wales and carried on a normal social life. But by September he was back in England, preparing to attend the autumn horse sales at Newmarket.

In mid-September the two defendants in the Cleveland Street case came before the Central Criminal Court. Both were found guilty of committing homosexual offences and were sentenced to nine months' and four months' imprisonment, respectively, with hard labour.[103] Lord Arthur and his solicitor feared that he would be next on the list for arrest and prosecution. In the middle of the Newmarket sales, therefore, he fled in a panic to Dieppe. Once there, he realized that the rumours of his imminent arrest were false – or at least premature – and he decided to return to England after three days. He landed at Newhaven and, carefully skirting London, made his way to the family estate at Badminton. While still in France he had sent a telegram to the Prince of Wales excusing his precipitate departure for Dieppe on the grounds of 'urgent private affairs'. The Prince had expressed regret at his absence but had otherwise accepted the excuse at its face value.[104]

On 9 October Somerset briefly visited London, where he learnt from his solicitor that despite the Home Secretary's reluctance, the police and the Director of Public Prosecutions were determined to proceed against him. As late as 17 October he appeared ready to stay and fight any charges levelled against him, but the following day, worn out by the nervous strain of the whole sorry business he fled to France once more. In practice the government delayed taking any action until Somerset had had time to resign his army commission and that resignation had been gazetted. Otherwise, if a warrant for his arrest had been issued he would almost certainly have been discharged from the service with ignominy.[105] The warrant was at last issued on 12 November, charging him with offences of gross indecency with several boys.

Meanwhile, when the Prince of Wales first heard in mid-October of Somerset's involvement in the Cleveland Street case he refused to believe it, declaring it was as incredible as 'if they had accused the Archbishop of Canterbury'. Just over a week later, however, as the truth emerged, he wrote to Lord Salisbury, the Prime Minister, expressing anxiety that no warrant should be issued 'against the "unfortunate Lunatic" (I can call him nothing else), as, for the sake of the Family and Society, the less one hears of such a filthy scandal the better'.[106] But his appeal was in vain, and about three weeks later the warrant was issued.

As a fugitive from justice, Lord Arthur's exile from England was permanent. He never returned for even the briefest visit, and after various abortive attempts to obtain employment in Turkey and Hungary, he settled down in France, moving eventually to Hyères on the French Riviera. There he and an English male companion occupied a villa, with a French cook and servants to attend them. Somerset died on 26 May, 1926, and was interred in the English section of the town cemetery under a headstone recording his name and paternity, the dates of his birth and death, and a brief text, 'The Memory of the Just is Blessed.'[107]

Yet, even Lord Arthur's unfortunate fate was but a pale shadow of the humiliation which awaited the leading dramatist and literary figure, Oscar Wilde, when he became a victim of homosexual scandal. Wilde was at the peak of his theatrical fame when his connection with Lord Alfred Douglas, third son of the 8th Marquess of Queensberry, came under scrutiny. The two men had first met in the summer of 1891, but it was not until the spring of the following year that their relationship developed. It grew at a time when Lord Alfred was being blackmailed for sexual affairs involving boys whilst he was an undergraduate at Oxford University. Wilde helped him out of that difficulty and they had a brief affair. This was resumed in the summer of 1892 when Lord Alfred came down from Oxford for the vacation. Soon it intensified, with Oscar praising one of the younger man's poems in extravagant terms:

> Your sonnet is quite lovely, and it is a marvel that those red rose-leaf lips of yours should have been made no less for music of song than for madness of kisses. Your slim gilt soul walks between passion and poetry. I know Hyacinthus, whom Apollo loved so madly, was you in Greek days.[108]

He signed the letter, 'Always, with undying love, yours OSCAR.'

By the spring of 1894 the liaison had become the subject of widespread gossip. It was in these circumstances, after seeing Lord Alfred and Wilde at the Café Royal, that the Marquess of Queensberry wrote to his son on 1 April, threatening to disown him and to stop his allowance unless the connection were ended immediately:

> I am not going to try and analyse this intimacy . . . With my own eyes I saw you both in the most loathsome and disgusting relationship as expressed by your manner and expression. . . . No wonder people are talking as they are. Also I now hear on good authority . . . that his wife is petitioning to divorce him for sodomy and other crimes. . . . If I thought the actual thing was true, and it became public property, I should be quite justified in shooting him at sight.[109]

He signed the letter, 'Your disgusted so-called father.'

Lord Alfred's reaction was speedy and intemperate. Without telling Wilde, he sent a telegram to his father on 2 April, declaring defiantly, 'WHAT A FUNNY LITTLE MAN YOU ARE.'[110] This impudent rejoinder aroused Queensberry's ire still further, and on 3 April, he wrote threatening to thrash his son if any more such telegrams were sent. 'Your only excuse is that you must be crazy. . . . If I catch you again with that man I will make a public scandal in a way you little dream of.'[111] He was as good as his word, as Lord Alfred and Wilde were to discover to their cost.

Throughout the following months Queensberry made known his angry disapproval of the affair throughout clubland, and on 14 February, 1895, the first night of *The Importance of Being Earnest*, he even tried to enter the theatre in order to create a disturbance. This was thwarted by the management but his fury was doubtless increased by the play's great success. Four days later he left a card at Wilde's club, the Albemarle, bearing the inscription, 'For Oscar Wilde posing as a somdomite [sic].' This was given to Wilde when he went to the club ten days later. Thereupon, with Lord Alfred's encouragement, although against the advice of most of his other friends, he decided to charge Queensberry with criminal libel. A warrant for the Marquess's arrest was issued on 1 March and this gave him the opportunity he had been seeking. In a Plea of Justification entered just before the trial commenced he accused Wilde of soliciting more than twelve boys (ten of whom were named) to commit sodomy. When the trial commenced on 3 April damaging details of Wilde's private life quickly emerged. The case collapsed on the morning of the third day with Sir Edward Clarke, Wilde's counsel, telling him that no jury would convict 'of a criminal offence a father who was endeavouring to save his son from what he believed to be an evil companionship.'[112] Clarke then conferred with Queensberry's counsel and the prosecution was withdrawn.

Within hours of the trial's end a warrant was issued for Wilde's arrest on a charge of committing indecent acts. He was arrested later that day and after various delays was eventually convicted on 25 May of committing 'acts of gross indecency' with two named men and 'certain persons whose names were unknown'. Throughout the trial Lord Alfred's name was not mentioned – a fact which the foreman of the jury raised with the judge, only to be informed testily that 'they had nothing to do with that. The question which the jury had to decide was whether Wilde was guilty of the charge made against him.'[113] When the guilty verdict was announced, Oscar was sentenced to two years' imprisonment with hard labour, the judge declaring that 'it had never been his lot to try a case of this kind so bad.' About a month earlier, on 24 April, a bankruptcy sale of his effects had taken place, enforced by Queensberry, who demanded payment of the £600 costs awarded to him at the close of the criminal libel trial, and by other creditors.[114] Wilde was now a broken and bitter man, his reputation in ruins and his literary career at an end. After his release from prison in May 1897 he went to France, where he died on 30 November, 1900.

Lord Alfred Douglas, meanwhile, had left for France on 24 April, 1895. He found it expedient to spend several years in exile, and other homosexuals shared his reactions. According to the testimony of Frank Harris, a dubious journalist friend of Oscar's, after the Wilde conviction:

> Every train to Dover was crowded, every steamer in Calais thronged with members of the aristocratic and leisured classes . . . Never was Paris so crowded with members of the English governing classes; here was to be seen a famous ex-Minister; there the fine face of a president of a Royal society; . . . The wind of terror which had swept them across the Channel opposed their return and they scattered over the Continent from Naples to Monte Carlo and from Palermo to Seville under all sorts of pretexts.[115]

Most members of English High Society, fortunately, were able to seek their pleasures in less controversial ways than these. Hunting, shooting, and fishing, despite their frequent overtones of mass slaughter of defenceless wild life, were safe and respectable occupations when compared to the unconventional activities of Lord Alfred and his friends.

CHAPTER SEVEN

Power, Politics and War

Burning questions in those days divided London society, and 'Home Rule' was a most disturbing element. I had made many friends in the Home Rule party, while others among my Sunday afternoon friends regarded the Irish leaders as their natural enemies. . . . The Home Rule question absolutely divided London society into two factions, and the cleavage was distinct.

LADY ST HELIER, *Memories of Fifty Years* (1909), 183 and 243.

Despite the increasing importance of industrialists and financiers in the economic life of the nation and, to a lesser degree, within its social leadership, for most of the Victorian period parliamentary power remained in the hands of its traditional rulers. At the general election of 1885 men from a business background for the first time outnumbered those from the landed sector in the House of Commons. But as late as 1910 around two-fifths of MPs were still either landowners or the sons of landowners.[1] And it was not until the Liberal cabinet of 1906 that the aristocracy and gentry ceased to form a majority at the highest level of government. Perhaps significantly, it was in that year that Edward VII's private secretary, Sir Francis Knollys, commented gloomily: 'the . . . idea that the House of Commons was an assemblage of "gentlemen" has quite passed away.'[2] A year or two later another representative of the old order considered the Lower House to be 'a veritable temple of untidiness' after one August evening debate, adding sourly:

> Some Members in evening clothes, some in grey & some in black hats, some in white or grey summer suits, some still faultless in frockcoat & waistcoat. In fact a general medley of conventions & oddities, who on a hot night appear far from personable.[3]

Prior to this, however, the heads of the great landed families of Cecil, Cavendish, Percy, Stanley, and a few others had believed unquestioningly in their 'prescriptive right to rule the country, as they ruled their estates'.[4] They had the leisure, the confidence, the experience and the status to govern and they expected to continue to do so. In the Countess of Warwick's view, they regarded England:

[as] their domain . . . and if they administered it with integrity of purpose, nothing more was required of them . . . Down to the time of the [First World] War, there were houses whose heads regarded themselves as second to none in the kingdom, though they revelled in going through all the forms and ceremonies of homage to their sovereign.[5]

This attitude led to a spirit of élitism which caused them to resent the intervention of 'outsiders' in the affairs of government, and which was accompanied, on occasion, by an unfortunate covert anti-semitism. Hence the claim by Lord Balcarres that Sir Alexander Acland-Hood, the Conservative chief whip in the Commons between 1902 and 1911, was furious at the wish of some county constituencies to select Jewish candidates to contest seats,

in preference to good old-fashioned Tory country gentlemen. . . . Our party will suffer severely through this cosmopolitan type of candidate, not to mention the prospects of corruption which are involved. Thus Van Raalte, now standing for Dorsetshire speaks English as broken and foreign as is that of Strauss or Gustav Wolff. The number of Jews in Parliament is considerable, but as a rule they represent towns which does not signify so much.[6]

A year or two earlier, when attending a large party invited by Alfred de Rothschild and the Earl of Rosebery to meet the Prince of Wales, Balcarres confessed to having studied 'the anti-semite question with some attention, always hoping to stem an ignoble movement: but when confronted by the herd of Ickleheimers and Puppenbergs, Raphaels, Sassoons, and the rest of the breed, my emotions gain the better of logic and justice'.[7] He was certainly not alone in his prejudices, although they were not shared by Edward himself. On one occasion he even chided his nephew, Tzar Nicholas II, for his anti-semitic policies.[8]

Many of the major magnates owned estates which were spread across several counties and, in some cases, lay on both sides of the Irish Sea. At both local and national level their political influence was too great to be ignored, while in Parliament the colleagues they met, debated and intrigued with were, often enough, relatives and friends. As late as 1914 the heirs to the Atholl, Lansdowne, Londonderry, Zetland, Dartmouth, and Halifax titles were members of the Commons, as were younger sons of the Duke of Norfolk, the Marquess of Bute and the Marquess of Bath, and close relatives of the Duke of Portland, the Marquess of Salisbury, and the Earl of Derby. In 1895 when Richard Greville Verney, later Lord Willoughby de Broke, entered the Commons as MP for the Rugby Division of Warwickshire he discovered the Conservative benches were filled with:

men of substance and broad acres . . . ; Masters of Foxhounds past and present . . . ; owners of racehorses . . . and many others who knew each other intimately quite apart from Westminster. . . . On the Liberal side, too, there were sportsmen and cricketers with whom we shared tastes in common, such as Jack Pease, who beat us all across country in a point-to-point steeplechase at Buckingham.[9]

It was this sense of a shared inheritance and of common values which intensified the

Tea on the Terrace at the Houses of Parliament, *c*. 1900. (The author)

feelings of bitterness and betrayal which arose between the Parties in the 1880s and beyond when disputes arose over the issue of Home Rule for Ireland or the need for reform of the House of Lords. The private correspondence of some of the more intemperate protagonists was freely larded with accusations of duplicity levelled at fellow parliamentarians who adopted a different stance from their own. In August 1911, for example, Sir Henry Howorth, a former Tory MP, wrote angrily after the passage of the Liberals' controversial Parliament Bill, which reduced the power of the Upper House:

> It will be very disappointing to many of our people . . . if . . . steps are not taken to mark the disapproval of all right thinking people for the treachery of the [Conservative] Peers who voted with the Government. I think a public meeting devoted to them would be a good thing or still better if we could turn the gang out of the Carlton [Club]. Except Camperdown and 2 or 3 more they are a worthless lot, and their leader St. Aldwyn . . . I was in the H. of C. 15 years with him and it seemed to me his politics were always dictated by personal considerations.[10]

Three years later Lord Colville was even more outspoken:

> When gentlemen associate themselves with the enemies of their Country & class, and, whilst professing loyal devotion to their Sovereign & receiving honours & titles from him, are instrumental in placing him in a quagmire of difficulty, one is inclined to classify them with Judas.[11]

It was in these circumstances that Margot Asquith, the wife of the Liberal Prime Minister and herself a leading socialite, wrote bitterly to a non-Liberal friend of her ostracism by the 'Derbys, Wolvertons, Ilchesters, Londonderrys, Farquahars (unless they have the King & Queen) . . . etc. etc. I shall survive but I confess if my own real friends intend taking the same line then I shall know to a hair exactly how much their love is worth to me. . . . I dont want to see any man, woman or child whose affection for me is so flimsy & capricious.'[12]

In the years ahead she became aware just how strongly former members of her social circle disliked the policies the Liberals were pursuing. In 1914, when she brought out her seventeen-year-old daughter, Elizabeth, not only did they receive fewer invitations than expected but, as she confessed angrily in her autobiography, 'every donkey in London was cutting or trying to cut us . . . My presence at a ball with Elizabeth . . . was considered not only provocative to others but a danger to myself.'[13] Perhaps most hurtful of all was the reaction of George Curzon, who had once been one of Margot's closest friends but who was now a leading member of the Conservative opposition. In May 1914 he gave a magnificent ball of a kind not seen since the death of Edward VII. King George and Queen Mary and 'everyone who was anyone' were invited and Elizabeth had looked forward to attending. However, as the time for the ball drew near the Asquiths had still received no invitation. Margot asked Mrs Keppel why this was and was astounded to discover that Curzon was so angry at her husband's determination to carry through Irish Home Rule that he would not have them inside the house.

> Frantic with rage, Margot remembered all the many kindnesses George Curzon had received both from her parents . . . and from Henry and herself . . . But most of all Margot minded the unkindness to Elizabeth.[14]

The wives of leading political figures were, of course, expected to play their part in the parliamentary round by entertaining for their husband's benefit and that of his chosen party. Molly Trevelyan remembered wryly that their home in Great College Street was so close to the Commons that a division bell was put in. In this way her husband could be away from the House and yet able to get there to vote. 'The ring of the Division Bell,' she recalled, 'used sometimes to devastate our dinner parties; all, or nearly all, the men would vanish, and return within ten minutes, as soon as the division was over.'[15]

The drawing-rooms of the leading hostesses became the rendezvous of younger men anxious to advance their careers, as well as of established leaders who found them a useful meeting ground. Austen Chamberlain maintained that he could assess the 'state of his own political fortunes by the number of fingers, ranging from two to ten' which Lady Londonderry extended to him when they met.[16] At country-house weekends, also, parliamentarians were able to meet and discuss their future campaigns away from the overheated atmosphere of Westminster. Lady Warwick remembered the amazement of guests at Chatsworth when they discovered that Austen's father, Joseph Chamberlain, who had made a reputation as a Radical in Birmingham during the 1870s, was to stay from Friday to Monday:

> one of the outer barbarians, to storm the ducal door! I recall someone asking me if I thought he would know how to conduct himself with outward decency . . . That evening Mr Chamberlain must have reassured the doubting one. His calm appraisement of the company, his dignified appreciation of the atmosphere, established him immediately as someone with whom even great hostesses would have to reckon.[17]

In the mid-1880s Chamberlain was to leave the Liberal Party over the Home Rule issue. Indeed, his resignation from Gladstone's government in May 1886 precipitated the collapse of that government.

The major political hostesses at the end of the nineteenth century were Theresa, Lady Londonderry, the Duchess of Devonshire, Lady Lansdowne, the Marchioness of Salisbury, the Duchess of Buccleuch, and Lady Ellesmere, for the Conservatives, and Lady Spencer and Lady Tweedmouth among the Liberals. The Duchess of Buccleuch and Lady Londonderry adopted a particularly exclusive stance, with the latter refusing to entertain any who did not share her political opinions. At first she regarded Bonar Law, a middle-class businessman who became the Conservative Party leader in 1911, with hostility because of his non-landed origins and refused to entertain him. Only when persuaded by Henry Chaplin, a Lincolnshire landowner and leading Tory politician, that this would damage the party did she become more friendly.[18] 'As is often the case with those who are born to rule,' wrote Lady Warwick drily, 'her temper was what you might call brief, and she made a host of enemies. . . . She refused to acknowledge such a thing as Radicalism.'[19] Her husband was a major Ulster landlord and she was an implacable opponent of the Liberals' Home Rule policy. Lady Warwick regarded her as 'the "strong man" of her family', and it was under her influence that Londonderry House became a centre of Unionist hostility to constitutional change in the 1912–14 struggles over the Irish question.[20] So powerful was the hostility engendered over Ireland that on one occasion Lord Londonderry refused an invitation to dinner to meet the King because Lord Crewe, a leading Liberal, was also to be present.[21]

Nevertheless, despite the continuing importance of these grandees, the economic difficulties faced by many of them as a result of agricultural depression and the erosion of some of their political dominance through various reform measures introduced between 1880 and 1914, helped to dent their self-confidence. In many respects the history of these years is that of a powerful élite waging a vigorous and largely successful rearguard action against those who wished to deprive them of their power. At the same time, they displayed growing frustration at the course of political events and, especially between 1909 and 1914, at the failure of the Conservative Party to regain power. Some of the strongest opponents of Liberal policies were peers who were also actively involved in various military pressure groups. Among them were the Duke of Somerset, who presided over the Navy League for several years, and Lord Willoughby de Broke, who headed the Imperial Maritime League, set up in 1907.[22]

In the sphere of local government, meanwhile, the aristocracy and gentry continued to retain much of their political power, at least in England. In Wales, the situation was rather different. Consequently despite the fact that the 1888 Local Government Act, setting up county councils, had been designed to inaugurate a system of 'representative democracy' in rural areas to replace the old system of Quarter Sessions, it had little effect. Most of the new authorities were dominated by the same sort of people as those who had controlled the previous non-elective régime. Just before 1914 well over a third of the chairmen of county councils in England and Wales were either peers or baronets.[23]

This continuity was illustrated in Wiltshire, where the 4th Marquess of Bath, who had previously been chairman of Quarter Sessions, became chairman of Wiltshire County

Lord and Lady Lansdowne with the Earl of Derby at the wedding of Lord Valletort to Lady Edith Villiers. Lord Lansdowne was the leader of the Conservative opposition in the Upper House during the difficult 1909–14 period and Lady Lansdowne was a major 'political' hostess. (*The Tatler*, 24 May, 1911.) (British Library Newspaper Library)

Council. He served between 1889 and 1896 and was then succeeded by his Quarter Sessions vice-chairman, Lord Edmond Fitzmaurice. In West Sussex, the Duke of Richmond, whilst admitting his dislike of the new policy, nonetheless was determined to show that 'landowners are quite as good men of business as the class below them.' He, too, became council chairman.[24]

Often the larger magnates also played a major part in the selection of candidates. In Bedfordshire, where the Duke of Bedford was chairman of the county council, a relative, Lord Ampthill, and his agent-in-chief, Rowland Prothero, both became councillors. In Woburn itself the Duke's influence was considered decisive.[25] Lord Plymouth's Worcestershire land agent likewise became a county councillor, while his principal Glamorgan agent not only served as a JP but as chairman of various local bodies, including the Cardiff Rural Sanitary Authority, the Llandaff Highway Board, and the Llandaff and Dinas Powis Rural District Council. He, too, was a county councillor.[26] In many of these cases, land agents were expected to oversee not merely their employer's agricultural and commercial concerns but his political interests as well.

Only in parts of Wales, where there were large numbers of small peasant farmers and where religious nonconformity was strong, was the anti-landlord, anti-Tory feeling sufficiently influential to bring about substantial change. When the first county council elections were held in the principality in 1889, the Liberals won control of every county except one. 'No cry was more vigorous at the polls than that of "Down with the magistrates," and none produced more startling results,' was one assessment of the outcome.[27]

In rural England, meanwhile, the existing power structure at local level was reinforced on the Conservative side by the activities of the Primrose League. This was set up in 1883 to enhance the party's electoral appeal and became all the more important when the franchise was extended in 1884 to cover all male householders living in country districts. The League placed much emphasis on the need for patriotism, religion, and imperialism, but it was anxious to secure unpaid volunteers to act as canvassers and election organizers as well.

The League began to recruit females in 1884 and in the following year a Ladies' Grand Council was formed with the Duchess of Marlborough as its first President. Soon after Lady Salisbury came in to share that role.[28] Lady Randolph Churchill, whose husband had done much to initiate the League, was another activist. She claimed subsequently that despite its deliberate use of much medieval flummery, with members known as Dames and Knights and branches given the name of habitations, the League played a major part in keeping the Conservative Party in power for most of the twenty years between 1886 and 1906.[29]

Where branches were established, they frequently enjoyed the support of neighbouring landowners. In Gloucestershire, Lady Hicks-Beach formed a habitation for the purpose of ensuring that voters were registered and carriages loaned at election times to take them to the polls. Likewise in Durham, the Marquess of Londonderry was actively involved, and it was claimed in 1890 that his return from Ireland 'had stimulated a doubling in the membership at Seaham,' which was part of the Londonderry estate. Around Eye in Suffolk, the initiative in promoting the Primrose League was taken by

Lord Henniker of Thornham Hall. His daughter, Mary, sponsored nine habitations within the Eye constituency, all of them bearing her name, as well as nine more in other parts of Suffolk.[30] For many aristocratic wives and daughters, the Primrose League offered a welcome opportunity to develop both their organizational skills and their political awareness at a time when they were excluded, on gender grounds, from participating in parliamentary elections directly.

In 1887 the Liberal party responded to this female activity among the Tories by forming a Women's Federation of its own. But with 10,000 members in 1888 and 60,000 in 1904, it was unable to match the large-scale appeal of the Primrose League. By 1910 this boasted over two million supporters, divided among a network of 2,645 habitations.[31]

Molly Trevelyan was one of those involved in the Women's Liberal Federation. Just over a year after her marriage she was congratulated on a speech she had made by Lady Aberdeen, herself an experienced political wife: 'It was charmingly done and very much to the point'.[32] Molly was also strongly in favour of votes for women, although she disliked the militant campaigning of Mrs Pankhurst and the suffragettes. Once when she was attending an evening party a suffragette suddenly broke into the conversation by beginning to read a speech aloud. 'The hostess sounded a whistle, and the speaker was promptly collared and removed by plain clothes policemen, who were sent to attend all parties where such a thing might happen.'[33]

Molly's reaction was typical of most members of High Society to the female suffrage issue, even among those who favoured votes for women. Only a few, like Lady Constance Lytton, advocated direct action to achieve their aims. Lady Constance and others who broke ranks on the issue were regarded with annoyance by friends and relatives. Lord Balcarres, staying with Arthur Balfour at his Northumbrian estate, Whittingehame, confessed to groaning 'under the feminist propaganda with which the unfortunate guest is bombarded'. This emanated from Arthur's two sisters-in-law, Lady Frances and Lady Betty Balfour, who were both enthusiasts in the female cause, the latter being Constance Lytton's elder sister.[34]

Even Buckingham Palace itself was not immune to these issues. Early in June 1914, at the third royal Drawing-Room, Miss Mary Blomfield, who was being presented, suddenly fell on both knees 'when passing the Royal presence and cried in a loud shrill voice, which could be heard throughout the Throne Room, "Your Majesty, won't you stop torturing women?"' In another version of the same incident she allegedly also shouted, 'We have no King but thank God we have a Mrs Pankhurst', and then tried to spit at King George.[35] She was speedily removed before she could complete her protest, and the King and Queen continued with the ceremony as if nothing had happened. But Queen Mary admitted in her diary that it had all been 'very unpleasant'.[36]

Throughout the period it was regarded as perfectly proper for social leaders to exercise political influence in the areas where they lived. As late as 1910, when a trial was held into a disputed parliamentary election in the East Dorset constituency, the judge declared of the landed Wimborne family, whose third son, Captain Guest, was the MP at the centre of the controversy, that it would be 'a poor thing for this country if those possessing wealth, position, and so forth, should not exercise some influence upon those who are . . . subject to their influence'.[37] In this case the Wimbornes, once enthusiastic Tories and Primrose Leaguers, changed their allegiance to the Liberals. They seem to have expected their tenants to follow their example and when some resisted soon made their displeasure clear. There were allegations that one Conservative sympathizer lost his post as an estate worker after twenty-five years' service, ostensibly because of inefficiency, and another pro-Tory – a small tenant farmer – was threatened with the loss of his holding. In the end the judge conducting the 1910 inquiry dismissed these charges as unproven; he also rejected claims of bribery which were raised, although he did comment 'severely on . . . the action of the agent of one of the Wimborne estates in standing before a polling station with a notebook', presumably to record the names of those voting.[38] However, Captain Guest was unseated because he had exceeded his legitimate election expenses.[39]

Voters in country areas often expected to be rewarded for giving their franchise to a particular candidate despite the restrictions of the 1883 Corrupt Practices Act, which was designed to outlaw such practices. Sometimes they were content with quite trivial marks of favour. In January 1906, when Frederick Hervey was elected MP for Bury St. Edmunds, his position as nephew and heir of the 3rd Marquess of Bristol at nearby Ickworth was well understood. One canvasser who offered his congratulations expressed gratitude at the way the Marquess had allowed him and a young nephew to fish in the lake at Ickworth Park while the boy was on his school holiday:

> his Lordship wrote me a letter himself granting us two days fishing for two weeks, when I went round to Canvass for you, I carried that letter to show waverers so that they could see what sort of an English Gentleman the Noble Marquis is that done it, almost every one that seen that letter said I'll vote for Hervey.[40]

Prior to the election Frederick had also received demands for financial support from various local organizations. In September 1905, for example, the honorary secretary of the Billiards Committee of the Constitutional Club asked him to give a prize for a 'Billiard Handicap', the suggested sum being £2 2s.[41] When he refused a political sympathizer wrote to warn of the possible electoral consequences.

> Personally I do not wonder at anyone refusing to subscribe to such an object – but electioneering has its own way & . . . votes have to be got. Sir Walter Green [the retiring Member] used to subscribe £5 to this Handicap, consequently his not now doing so and your not is a blow which might lose some votes.[42]

Requests for gifts of game and fruit for a Conservative dinner and a demand for cash to provide prizes for a tenants' garden show for the local allotments association were just two of the many other appeals with which he was inundated. Small wonder in these circumstances that another aristocratic MP, Lord Balcarres, should regard parliamentary contests with distaste: 'I . . . abominate this forthcoming election,' he wrote in December 1909, 'with its waste of time, trouble and money, with all the virulence and vulgarity from which there can be no escape.'[43] To grandees like Hervey and Balcarres these indignities were penalties which had to be endured in order to maintain the political standing of their class.

In the late nineteenth century electioneering also involved much travelling to attend meetings in farflung rural constituencies, especially as most had to be reached by horse-drawn vehicles. Not until the general elections of 1906 and 1910 did motor vehicles come into widespread use. Yet once the franchise had been widened in 1884, it was impossible for MPs to neglect village meetings. As J.W. Lowther confessed wearily in November 1884, 'every petty hamlet expects its member . . . to pay annual visits in person as well as contribute to its local charities.'[44] Walter Long, a local landowner who contested the East Wiltshire constituency as a Conservative in 1885, remembered driving forty to fifty miles a day to attend four or five meetings in the afternoon and evening. Often he left home at 2 p.m. and did not return until one or two o'clock on the following morning. He eventually scraped in with a majority of 97 votes.[45]

In the early twentieth century it became increasingly common for wives to share in the electioneering. In January 1910, Molly Trevelyan not only addressed overflow meetings while her husband spoke to the main gathering but she went on ahead to keep meetings alive when he was delayed elsewhere. Often she would rush off to start the next one as soon as he arrived.[46] May Harcourt reluctantly played a similarly supportive role. 'I *loathe* the rôle of a Public Woman striding on Platforms "saying a few words",' she told her step-mother-in-law.[47]

But if these were the day-to-day experiences associated with the political life of the social élite, there were also more discordant elements at work. Of these the first and, in many ways the most dangerous, developed over the issue of Irish Home Rule. It was to create a deep split in the ranks of High Society.

In the early spring of 1886 the Liberal Prime Minister, William Gladstone made public his conversion to the Home Rule cause, believing that only so could the violence and strife within Ireland be ended. The decision aroused immediate Conservative fury, with many condemning it as an attack upon the integrity of the Empire and an abandonment of Ulster loyalists – as well as a threat to the landed estates which many of them held in Ireland. But more seriously from Gladstone's point of view, it divided the Liberal Party. Most of the party's remaining landed patricians, headed by Lord Hartington, later the Duke of Devonshire, left at this point, as did a group of Radical imperialists led by Joseph Chamberlain. With the defection of Hartington and his supporters, the House of Lords became overwhelmingly dominated by the Conservative and Unionist element, as did landed society generally. This political dominance of the Upper House by one political grouping was to have profound constitutional implications during the next three decades.

The defections also created a financial crisis for the Liberal Party and led in 1891 to Mr Gladstone reluctantly agreeing to 'sell' two peerages in return for substantial contributions to party funds. The contributors were Sydney Stern, a Jewish banker, who later became Lord Wandsworth, and James Williamson, a nondescript Lancashire manufacturer and Liberal MP, who became Lord Ashton.[48] From the mid-1890s the Conservatives, too, began to accept large sums from men whose prime object was to become a baronet or a peer. As a consequence the party became indebted to people like W.H.A.F. Watson-Armstrong, who had inherited an engineering business and in 1903 was created Lord Armstrong. Although such transactions were not quite the same as 'selling' peerages, they became very like it. Hence while peers were created at an average rate of just over five a year between 1837 and 1881, after 1885 the process was so changed that in their seventeen years of office from the mid-1880s to 1905 the Conservatives bestowed 146 titles at an average of 8.5 per annum. The Liberals, during their nine and a half years in government between 1885 and 1911, responded with an annual average of 10.5 peerages. Small wonder that H.J. Hanham has concluded that by 1912 the practice of exchanging cash for honours which 'Mr Gladstone had accepted as a temporary expedient, had come to be recognized as a normal incident of political life'.[49] But this was to be a long-term result of the Home Rule divisions between the parties. Many other problems arose in the short run.

Gladstone's Home Rule Bill was defeated on its second reading in the Commons during the early summer of 1886, by 434 votes to 313, 93 Liberals voting against it. At the general election held in July the Conservatives were returned to power, with the support of the breakaway Liberal Unionist faction. But the whole affair engendered much bitterness between many erstwhile friends and political colleagues. 'Nothing divided society like the Home Rule question,' wrote Lady St Helier. 'The years between 1880 and 1890 represented one of the most stirring and deeply interesting epochs of English political life.'[50]

One victim of this strife was Earl Spencer. He continued to support Gladstone and found himself ostracized by both the court and fellow peers for his pains. Former friends ignored him in the street. 'I hear Lord Fitzwilliam cut him . . . the other day and that the Listowels declined to be guests at Bagshot Park during Ascot week if the Spencers were to be there. Such behaviour is hardly conceivable,' wrote Sir Edward Hamilton.[51] Still more extreme was the verdict of Sir Dighton Probyn, comptroller and treasurer of the Prince of Wales's Household. He observed acidly that he was 'worried over Lord Spencer. I have always looked upon him as . . . an honest Englishman, and a Gentleman . . . But he has fallen into the traitor's clutches.' Even the Queen ceased to invite him to Windsor, while Lord Hartington, his second cousin and a former political ally, waited twelve months before asking the Spencers to stay at Chatsworth once more.[52]

Family circles were also divided. According to Alfred Pease, 'father and sons ceased to speak to each other, and brothers were at daggers drawn.' Hence while the Marquess of Lansdowne rejected Gladstone, his younger brother, Lord Edmond Fitzmaurice, remained loyal. Similarly, the Duke of Bedford became a Unionist but his cousin, G.W.E. Russell, stayed a Liberal. Wilfrid Scawen Blunt too, was condemned by his Tory family for his 'treason' in supporting Irish independence. In his case he gradually withdrew from active participation in militant Home Rule politics to concentrate on more agreeable diversions.[53]

Many of the Unionists blamed Gladstone for 'inciting the masses against the Classes', and the Duke of Westminster, a former close friend of the Liberal leader, was so displeased with him that he decided to sell his Millais portrait of Gladstone. Sir Edward Hamilton, a Gladstonian loyalist, considered it was 'almost inconceivable that a man should part with such an historic picture short of his being very hard up'. The fact that the Duke was prepared to do so showed 'how strong is the political animus of the "classes" against Mr G. . . . He forgets what he owes to Mr G. – a Garter, & a peerage, a Lord Lieutenancy, . . . &c. and this is all forgotten.'[54]

Even London club life was disrupted. The Devonshire and Reform Clubs, both Liberal in origin, were riven by disputes, although the majority of members followed Gladstone. Even the prestigious Brooks's Club was split, though there the Liberal Unionists formed a majority. Lord Edmond Fitzmaurice, with some poetic licence, described the mutual blackballing which occurred at Brooks's over Home Rule as a 'circle of carnage'. In fact four candidates for entry seem to have been the victims of this 'most detestable of all methods of political fighting'.[55] But the festering ill-feeling between the two factions was only brought to an end in April, 1887, when a long-established member, the 2nd Earl Granville, was persuaded to intervene. Shortly before balloting to admit a fresh batch of entrants was due to take place, he appealed to members to remember the Club's antiquity and the party divisions it had already survived. He hoped 'that there [would] be at least one place left in London where a truce might be allowed . . . and friends might still be allowed to meet one another on the same terms as of old'.[56] His plea succeeded, and although in the years which lay ahead the split between Liberals and Liberal Unionists widened, Brooks's remained a club to which both sides could belong. Indeed, Henry Asquith, the Liberal Prime Minister during the difficult years before the First World War, was an active member, as were several of his Cabinet colleagues. Despite the acrimony between the Liberals and the Unionists between 1909 and 1914, there was only one revival of the blackballing phenomenon. It occurred in 1914 and was rapidly followed by a truce.[57]

Gladstone's second attempt to deal with Home Rule came in 1893, following the Liberals' return to office the previous year. This time the Bill passed the Commons but was rejected decisively in the Lords by 419 votes to 41. As before, opponents were concerned not only with the threat to the integrity of the Empire and their dislike of the Nationalists' violent anti-landlord agrarian campaigns, but with the challenge to their own economic self-interest where they held land in Ireland. Already some were considering the use of force, should the Government seek to impose its will over the issue. In 1892 Lady Monkswell was much impressed by the declaration made, 'with flashing eyes', by Edward Ponsonby (later Lord Bessborough) that Irish Unionists would fight rather than accept Home Rule.[58]

Landed hostility towards the Liberal government was increased further in 1894 when the Chancellor of the Exchequer, Sir William Harcourt, sharply raised death duties up to a maximum of 8 per cent on estates of a million pounds or more, with rentals of well above £40,000.[59] Although the top rate affected a very few members of the social élite only, the fact that the measure was enacted during a period of agricultural depression and by a radical Chancellor, created a major outcry. The immensely wealthy Duke of Devonshire argued that with 'the clouds of increased taxation . . . gathering' he might have to close three of his residences – Hardwick Hall in Derbyshire, Bolton Abbey in Yorkshire, and Lismore Castle in Ireland. The Earl of Ancaster sounded a similarly alarmist note, claiming that it would be impossible for his son to keep the buildings on his estates 'even in a tenantable state of repair', so great would the death duty burden be that he would have to shoulder when he inherited them from his father.[60]

Following the resignation of the Liberal Government in 1895 and the return of a Conservative and Unionist administration under Lord Salisbury, most of the landed élite's fears about further punitive taxation disappeared. Even the Irish question became less acute, aided as it was by the passage of further ameliorative land tenancy measures in the 1890s. However, at the end of that decade a new cause for concern was to manifest itself with the outbreak of the Boer War.

Already many male members of High Society had strong military links dating back to Army service in their youth or to membership of a local yeomanry or other reserve force in the vicinity of their estates. For several weeks each year they would turn their attention to military manoeuvres and would allow their parklands to be used for drills and the holding of summer camps. Some enthusiasts established firing ranges on their property, and a high proportion took part in the activities themselves. The Duke of Westminster, for example, commanded the Cheshire Yeomanry between 1870 and 1891 as well as serving as president of the county Rifle Association. And when military manoeuvres took place at Hatfield in September 1909, Lord Salisbury noted that the family's conversation was 'entirely about flank movements and extended lines'.[61]

With the outbreak of the South African war in the autumn of 1899 large numbers of younger men seized the opportunity to take up their military duties in earnest. Some, like the Duke of Marlborough, served with the Imperial Yeomanry. In 1902, Marlborough became assistant military secretary to Lord Roberts, the commander-in-chief. Others took private initiatives, including Lord Lovat, who organized a troop of scouts known as Lovat's Scouts from volunteers from the Scottish highlands, and Lord Leith of

Irate Major. "WHERE THE DEUCE ARE YOU GOING TO?"   *Gallant Yeoman (faintly).* "THE 'ORSE COMES FROM 'UNTINGDON, SIR!"
Punch is mocking the amateurish military manoeuvres of the yeomanry. (17 July, 1912)

Fyvie, who fitted out and maintained at his own cost two companies of the scouts.[62]

In all, between 1899 and 1902 131 peers and their heirs served in the Boer War and of those, nine were killed or died as a result of wounds.[63] If the brothers and younger sons of peers were included, the total would be far higher.

Years later Lady Randolph Churchill recalled the misplaced optimism with which the outbreak of hostilities was greeted:

> England thought and looked upon it practically in the nature of a punitive expedition. 'Those wretched Boers must be taught a lesson, their arrogance was not to be tolerated.' London Society was quite gay over it – soldiers were tumbling over each other to get out to the Front and 'see the fun,' the only fear they had was to be too late. Those 'darlings of the gods,' our sporting Guardsmen, looked upon it as a big-game expedition, and all thought the war 'such as it was' would be over in a couple of months. It was nearly four years before the last shot was fired![64]

Among the enthusiasts was Geoffrey Gathorne-Hardy, then an undergraduate at Oxford. At Christmas 1899 he confessed his desire to enlist. 'My best talent, rifle shooting, seems wasted if I don't go. I have achieved all the success, certainly all the Oxford success I am ever likely to, and though I am decidedly wanting in courage that surely would keep me in my place,' he confided in his diary. At first his family refused to agree to his abandoning his studies and embarking on such an unplanned military adventure. Anxious parental conclaves followed until at last on 8 January, 'after a hard fight father capitulated unconvinced, and gave his permission to me to volunteer!!! Hurrah!!!'[65]

The next day he went to join up, although his father seemed so 'down and sad that at times I almost regret my victory'.[66] After waiting for some time he was accepted by the 13th Regiment of Imperial Yeomanry and began to receive riding lessons, with, at first, a humiliating lack of success. A few weeks later he embarked for South Africa, where he arrived in March. Two months after that he found himself in Bloemfontein, but almost as soon as he went into action he was wounded. His injury was sufficiently serious for him to be sent home to Britain. By this time his brief encounter with the harsh realities of warfare had clearly dampened his ardour. 'If I had a chance of going on and fighting a more glorious fight with the rest of my battalion it might be different, but I frankly do not want to fight again, drafted into a lot of men I don't know with the chance of being in hospital without knowing a soul,' he told his father. 'The general opinion among the wounded here is that army regulations would consider a man with a finger off a cripple, and in any case they seem at this stage of the proceedings to be casting almost anyone.'[67]

Geoffrey's short and inglorious military career was more than outweighed by that of many other enthusiasts, like Lord Brooke, the Countess of Warwick's eldest son. He joined up from Eton, selling his fur coat, some jewellery and his guns in order to raise the necessary funds, and determining to make his own way out to South Africa. Before his departure, he visited Sir Evelyn Wrench, a Warwickshire neighbour and an adjutant at the War Office. Wrench persuaded the youngster to undergo preliminary training at Aldershot, and Brooke finally sailed for the front with his regiment at the age of seventeen. His parents used their influence to ensure that he had a safe posting, and on his arrival in South Africa he became a galloper to Sir John French, a general whom they knew.[68]

Meanwhile, the high spirits evinced at the outbreak of war began to evaporate as disease and the stubborn resistance of the Boer farmers started to take their toll. As early as 5 November, 1899, Lady Warwick wrote to a friend confessing that 'one can think of nothing but the developments of this tragedy in the Transvaal.'[69] Lady Cranborne, too, described the anxieties of a friend who was feeling 'wretchedly ill' during her pregnancy as a result of worry over a favourite brother who was besieged at Ladysmith. 'I never remember anything like this war; there is not a single person one meets, who has not someone there; Nelly has *8* brothers now out.'[70]

The young Susan Grosvenor, in bed with influenza, likewise remembered the deep unhappiness which overhung the whole household during one week of serious British reverses:

> The generals were blamed, the War Office was anathematized for inefficiency, and the war was the major topic discussed by our elders.
>   We young people felt bewildered and uncertain. Our history books had played down our failures, so that our past seemed one long success story. . . . we felt the world had altered and we could not understand the significance of our defeats in South Africa.[71]

The popular reaction to military successes, like the relieving of the long-besieged garrison at Ladysmith in late February 1900, or of that at Mafeking on 17 May in the same year, was even more exaggerated. Lady Cranborne wrote of the 'wild delirium of joy' which greeted the latter event. It had been:

> something quite outside all known demonstrations; with its parading crowds & flying flags; not in London only but all over the Country; . . . even at Hatfield on the Friday night at ½ past 11, a howling crowd with lamps & flags came & paraded in front of the house.'[72]

During these difficult months social life in London continued, with the usual Drawing-Rooms and presentations at court taking place. But the shortage of young men and the anxieties over the conflict cast a dark shadow over everything, and the entertainments chiefly took the form of charitable bazaars for the provision of soldiers' comforts.[73] 'Sometimes I feel as if it is impossible that this strange life should ever end,' admitted Lady Cranborne, 'or that we should ever go back to those old days only a year ago, which seem like another world.'[74] She was to have a particular cause to grieve, for her brother-in-law, the Earl of Airlie, was killed in action early in June 1900.

Many society women decided to follow their menfolk out to South Africa, as Lady Airlie had done. Sometimes they helped with the nursing of the sick and wounded. Mabell Airlie, for example, took an ambulance class before she set off. But often they were merely concerned to experience the thrills of day-to-day life. 'Every boat came out crammed with men and women who wanted to be "in" all the excitement,' wrote Lady Edward Cecil (later Violet Milner), disapprovingly. 'Especially women. Nobody in those free and spacious days objected to women who came out to see their husbands and brothers, but there were plenty of others, some of whom were even mischievous.'[75]

Among the more frivolous was Lady Sophie Scott. When War broke out she was on holiday in Ceylon with her recently reconciled husband, from whom she had briefly eloped with a hunting friend. Sir Samuel Scott was recalled to his regiment in South Africa and they sailed to Durban in their luxury yacht, *The Golden Eagle*. While her husband went off to his military duties, Lady Sophie stayed on the yacht, using it to give hospitality to wounded officers and even bringing her butler out from England to help. For the rest, as she told her brother, Edward, her mornings were spent writing letters or completing any business she had to transact, and then she read or played cards or went for a sail. In the afternoons she went on shore for shopping expeditions and to ride. She also attended race-meetings: 'there is quite a nice little race-course, the races are really not half bad, ponies and galloways . . . ; unfortunately they are all flat races, no jumps.'[76] When the evacuation of the men from the relieved garrison at Ladysmith began she made it her business to go and see them brought off the hospital train: 'I can't *tell* you how *ghastly* the sights are,' she wrote ghoulishly. During the siege 563 members of the garrison had died, 393 of them from the effects of typhoid, and as soon as she could make arrangements, she and a friend went to Ladysmith to inspect the devastation. Later she paid a brief visit to Cape Town but by June 1900, as the War began to wind down and the climate to pall, she decided to return home by liner, leaving her yacht to be brought back to England by the crew.[77] One of her brothers, who was serving in South Africa, accompanied her for part of the journey.

It was sensation-seeking visitors like Lady Sophie, particularly those flooding into Cape Town, that eventually caused Queen Victoria to intervene. At her command a telegram was sent expressing regret at the 'large number of ladies now visiting and remaining in South Africa, often without imperative reasons, and [she] strongly disapproves of the hysterical spirit which seems to have influenced some of them to go where they are not wanted'.[78] The Prince of Wales shared his mother's feelings. He expressed blunt annoyance at the 'silly Society women' who were going out ostensibly to nurse but in reality only to make themselves 'conspicuous for their general incapacity and for dressing up in Cape Town as if they were at Ascot or Monte Carlo.'[79] In the face of this royal condemnation a number of the unwanted visitors were speedily ordered home again.

But the Boer War, with its initial military reverses, had revealed deficiencies in British army tactics which were to serve as a warning of the still greater tests which lay just over a decade away, with the outbreak of the First World War in 1914. For many aristocratic families, nonetheless, the South African campaign was a crucial experience. Among the men who served between 1899 and 1902 were many whose political, military and imperial attitudes were significantly influenced by what they had encountered in those years of service.

Moreover the cessation of hostilities in South Africa did not signal a return to peaceful politics in England. Almost immediately it had ended the Conservative Party was split by Joseph Chamberlain's call, in May 1903, for tariff reform, including the imposition of import duties on food. He advocated this partly from a desire to protect British industry and agriculture from increasing foreign competition but also, and most crucially, because of his belief that the Empire must be bound more closely together if Britain were to retain its position in the world. The best way to achieve this, he argued, was through tariff reform and imperial preference.[80] Many of his colleagues disagreed and some, like Winston Churchill, left the Party to join the Liberals, who still espoused Free Trade.

Internal party feuding over the tariff issue as well as the electorate's fear of dearer food were significant factors in the Conservatives' defeat at the 1906 general election. In Warwickshire, Lord Willoughby de Broke, as a committed Tory, described the sense of shock felt by the landed classes when the election result was announced. The Liberals had been returned with 429 seats, compared to the 158 achieved by the Conservatives; they thus had a substantial overall majority in the Commons independent of the support of their allies, the Irish Nationalists and the fledgling Labour Party. In Willoughby de Broke's view the Conservative Party now 'had nothing to fall back upon except the House of Lords'.[81] He and those peers who shared his views were determined to frustrate those aspects of the Liberal Government's programme they disliked. They were also committed to a defence of the hereditary system of leadership represented in the Upper House. 'I have been brought up in the midst of stock-breeding of all kinds all my life,' wrote Willoughby de Broke, 'and I am prepared to defend the hereditary principle . . . whether the principle is applied to Peers or . . . to foxhounds.'[82] These hunting analogies were to occur in many of his pronouncements during this period, as politics became almost a kind of field sport in his eyes.

With the overwhelming Conservative and Unionist dominance of the House of Lords, it was clear that the peers could veto Liberal legislation at will. One measure to which they turned their attention was a Bill to reform the licensing laws. Willoughby de Broke recalled that a number of 'backwoodsmen' who had 'never spoken in the House of Lords, and who had never been consulted about anything outside [their] own counties, met each other fresh from the hunting-field'. Despite an excellent speech in favour of the Bill by Lord Lytton, 'the backwoodsmen, who had mostly breakfasted at cock-crow in order to catch the early train to London, were in no mood to listen to any tampering with the liquor traffic.'[83] The measure was rejected. Its fate was indicative of the more serious Lords versus Commons clashes which lay ahead and which were to divide High Society more deeply than the Home Rule skirmishes of the 1880s. Budgetary questions and land taxation; the veto powers of the House of Lords; the Irish question – all were to surface in an atmosphere of rancour and bitterness between 1909 and 1914.

Symptomatic of the heightened tensions was the reaction of the strongly Conservative Lord Elcho to the news that his daughter, Cynthia, wished to marry Herbert Asquith, son of the Liberal Prime Minister. Not only did he refuse to countenance the match but every effort was made to keep the young couple apart, including the despatch of Cynthia to Canada for a whole winter. When these tactics failed and reluctant acquiescence to the marriage was given, the ceremony was conducted amid what she herself called 'a kind of Montagu and Capulet feeling'. So deep were the animosities that 'one of my friends was actually forbidden by her father to be my

The landowner in politics. The mayor of Oxford announcing the return of Lord Valentia, the Conservative candidate, at the general election of 1906. Despite his success, the election proved a landslide victory for the Liberals. (The author)

bridesmaid! . . . So crackling with party politics was the atmosphere of July 1910 that I told the ushers to substitute for the usual query "Bride or Bridegroom?" the words, "Conservative or Liberal?"[84]

Another commentator described how 'the passions and prejudices of the hustings' affected ordinary social relationships during this period,

> even in those circles which held that strong emotions should be left outside the drawing-room door. A conversation which drifted on to politics could ruin an evening party. The most frivolous of hostesses knitted their brows over their dinner-lists and painstakingly rearranged their tables. New friendships withered and old ones were broken. Even families quarrelled – or feared doing so. Lord Londonderry, whose sister, Lady Allendale, was a near neighbour of his in London, wrote to her at the height of the crisis that in the present state of feeling between the parties he thought it would be better if she ceased calling at Londonderry House – her husband was one of the Liberal Party Whips in the House of Lords.[85]

Liberal anger at the wrecking tactics of the Upper House reached a climax in the spring of 1909, with the announcement of the Budget. Faced with the need to raise additional revenue to pay for its new social legislation, as well as an increased naval building programme, the government decided to raise death duties to unprecedented levels and to impose a new supertax on all incomes above £5,000 per annum. Duties on alcohol, tobacco, motor vehicles and petrol were raised. But most controversial from the viewpoint of the social élite was a series of new imposts on land, including a 20 per cent levy on the increased value of land each time it was sold, a capital tax on the value of undeveloped lands and minerals, and a 10 per cent reversion duty on the 'benefits to lessors of the termination of leases'. These latter burdens were aimed at large urban landlords like the Dukes of Bedford, Westminster and Norfolk. Purely agricultural land was exempted from them, but not from a land survey and valuation for which the Budget also provided. This valuation and the implications of the new taxes aroused fury in landed circles. In the early summer a Budget Protest League was set up, headed by the Wiltshire landowner and leading Tory MP, Walter Long, and talk of rejection of the Budget by the Lords began to spread, even though such a move was unprecedented in modern times. The Marquess of Lansdowne, the Unionist leader in the Lords, described the Finance Bill as 'a monument of reckless and improvident finance', and major landowners not only complained of their new-found poverty but made clear that others would share the penalties they anticipated. Lord Sherborne announced that he would be cutting his estate expenditure because 'super-taxation' necessitated 'super-economy'. Lord Onslow informed his tenants that he would have to dismiss all directly

The fiery Welsh orator, David Lloyd George, who served as Chancellor of the Exchequer from 1908–15. A political opponent described him as 'adroit, unscrupulous, [he] . . . well knows how to surrender a small point with outward reluctance while maintaining the essentials of his policy.' He was the scourge of the landed classes and in 1910 at Mile End, London, he described the aristocracy as 'like cheese, the older it is, the higher it becomes!' (The author)

employed labourers and put work out to contract instead. And the dukes 'made a series of speeches that were especially imprudent. Beaufort wanted the Liberal politicians put in "the middle of twenty couple of dog hounds". Rutland condemned them as "piratical tatter-demalions". And Buccleuch announced that he would be cancelling his annual subscription of one guinea' to a local football club.[86] Lord Balcarres, then a Conservative whip in the Commons, considered this 'tactless intervention' by the peers had injured the Tory cause. 'Their threats and peevishness have wrought incalculable damage to the party,' he confessed in his diary.[87]

The Liberal Chancellor of the Exchequer, David Lloyd George, responded in kind. In a provocative speech at Newcastle-on-Tyne on 9 October, he declared that since the Budget was introduced,

> Only one stock has gone down badly – there has been a great slump in dukes . . . a fully-equipped duke costs as much to keep up as two Dreadnoughts – and they are just as great a terror – and they last longer.[88]

In the same speech, he asked his audience rhetorically who had ordained 'that a few should have the land of Britain as a perquisite? Who made ten thousand people owners of the soil, and the rest of us trespassers in the land of our birth?'[89]

Such statements infuriated the peers and angered the King. It was, therefore, in this fevered atmosphere that the Lords rejected the Finance Bill on 30 November, 1909, by 350 votes to 75, after a debate lasting six days.[90] Unable to carry its Budget, the Government resigned. Parliament was dissolved on 3 December and a general election was held in the following January.

Although the Liberals were unable to repeat their 1906 landslide, they were returned to power with the support of the Labour Party and the Irish Nationalists. Ironically the Budget – the original cause of the dispute – passed the Commons on 27 April and the following day was approved by the Lords without a division, as Lansdowne had promised would be the case before the general election. But the Liberals were now determined on more fundamental changes. They resolved not only to end the power of the Upper House to interfere with Money Bills but to ensure that other measures which passed the Commons in three successive sessions of a Parliament would become law despite the opposition of the Lords. This latter reform was particularly significant in connection with the Irish Home Rule issue, as many peers recognized.

Whilst these proposals were being drawn up, Edward VII died on 6 May, 1910, and in an effort to protect the new King from immediate controversy, a constitutional conference was held to try to resolve the differences between the warring parties. But feelings were too embittered for this and it was obvious that the Parliament Bill, with its aim of restricting the powers of the Upper House, would never be passed unless extreme action was taken. The bi-partisan talks broke down on 10 November and Asquith then asked George V for a dissolution. The King refused until the Lords had voted on the Bill and only when they rejected it was Parliament dissolved. The second general election of 1910 was held in December and it showed little overall change from that of the previous January. The final struggle between Lords and Commons was about to begin.

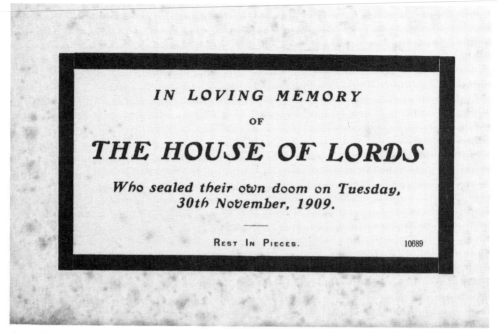

A mock mourning card produced in 1909, when the House of Lords rejected the Liberal budget and precipitated a general election. (The author)

Immediately prior to the December election George V had reluctantly given a secret pledge to create sufficient new peers to carry through the Parliament Bill if there were no other way of guaranteeing its passage. Not until July 1911 did Asquith formally reveal that the pledge had been made. In the interim the peers apparently gambled on the Liberals retreating rather taking such a drastic action. Feelings in the Upper House, influenced by diehards like Lord Willoughby de Broke and the former Conservative Lord Chancellor, Lord Halsbury, were meanwhile hardening. Typical of the attitude of some of the militants was the Duke of Abercorn, who wrote to a fellow peer on 26 June:

> If we do not now fight to the uttermost we shall be done and beaten for ever. I think we should shew a firm front to the Nation, and they will respect and support us at the proper time. If we exhibit what is commonly called 'funk', or any sign of meeting the Government half-way, this will be looked upon as weakness on our part.[91]

Views from the shires seemed to confirm this. One Welsh landowner stressed that the 'Veto Bill ought to be fought to the last ditch. . . . I have no idea what will be settled but my idea is – fight it out. There seems to be a want of pluck on our side, and we had better be killed than commit suicide.'[92]

The diehards' suspicions about the temporizing attitude of their official leaders, the Marquess of Lansdowne in the Lords and A.J. Balfour in the Commons, were confirmed when in July Asquith advised Balfour of the King's pledge to use his prerogative for a mass creation of new peers. In the face of this threat to swamp the Upper House, the

The elegant and erudite Arthur James Balfour, nephew of the Marquess of Salisbury and Conservative Prime Minister in succession to his uncle 1902–5. He subsequently became leader of the Conservative opposition in the House of Commons. On his resignation in 1911 he was replaced by Andrew Bonar Law. (The author)

Unionist leaders drew back. Lansdowne advised his followers to abstain in the vote on the Parliament Bill rather than allow such a constitutional catastrophe to take place. The vast majority accepted that view, even if, as in the case of the Marquess of Hertford, it was with reluctance and merely to prevent the appearance of hundreds of 'Bogus Radical Peers whereby the entire command of [the] House (as well as the Commons) would be in the hands of the Radical party for years to come'.[93]

However, Willoughby de Broke and his friends determined on a policy of 'No Surrender'. One of them, the Duke of Somerset, bluntly told Lansdowne:

> I feel that not only the honor (sic) of the Peers as a body but my own as an English gentleman is concerned in this crisis and that if I were to do anything to make easy the passing of this revolutionary measure I should deserve the execration of every loyal and patriotic Englishman.[94]

Lord Ampthill, another opponent of the Bill, described it as a 'crime' and 'the gravest political outrage that has ever been perpetrated short of bloodshed . . . we regard the objects of the Bill as utterly corrupt'.[95]

The seriousness of this revolt stemmed from the fact that if the diehards persisted they would outnumber the Liberal peers, even if Lansdowne and his allies abstained. Once more a mass creation of peers seemed to threaten. Only the energetic action of Lord Curzon, himself a former diehard, and the negotiating skills of Lord Crewe and Lord Cromer averted the danger. On 10 August the Government won the division by the narrow margin of seventeen votes.[96] In order to do this, thirty-seven Conservative peers were persuaded to enter the Government lobby, to the undisguised fury of the Bill's diehard opponents. After the division, feelings ran so high that the wife of the diehard leader, Lord Halsbury, refused to shake hands with Lord Lansdowne when she and her husband met him as they left the House. The following day Lady Halsbury wrote to Lord Willoughby de Broke asking if there were a list of Unionist associations and clubs that had supported the 'No Surrender' cause to which she could send a card 'printed with the names of the traitor Peers. . . . One can hardly believe Englishmen could do such a dastardly thing and in such an underhand way.'[97] There was even organized hissing of some of the peers at the Carlton Club.[98]

Many of the diehards blamed the indecisive leadership of Lansdowne and Balfour for the débâcle rather than their own intransigence. To the Duke of Somerset it was impossible that any Conservatives or Unionists could ever support the two leaders again:

> they have by their miserable folly & dishonesty done their best to wreck the party. . . . Curzon is if possible the worst of the set – he went round getting Unionists to vote with the govt. to what they called spare the King's face – wh. was disgraceful. If the King after swearing to maintain the Constitution at his Coronation is such a coward & fool as to destroy it & get Curzon to help him he is no King for me.[99]

The 'traitor' peers were likewise condemned in the Tory press, the *Globe* expressing the hope that 'no honest man will take any of them by the hand again, that their friends will disown them, their clubs expel them, and that alike in politics and social life they will be made to feel the bitter shame they have brought upon us all.'[100]

With the Parliament Act on the statute book, however, the way was now clear to overcome the Upper House's opposition to Home Rule, since any Bill which received Commons approval during three successive sessions would automatically become law whatever the attitude of the Lords. Against this background the Government of Ireland Bill began its parliamentary life in 1912, and the diehards and their Ulster Unionist allies made ready to oppose it with all the force at their command.

As early as January 1907 some of the more committed anti-Home Rule Conservatives had set up a Union Defence League (UDL) to carry out propaganda work. Among its active supporters were Walter Long, a leading member of the Tory opposition in the Commons, the Earl of Harrowby, the Earl of Westmeath, and Lord Balcarres. In 1913 the UDL was to be joined by the British League for the Support of Ulster and the Union, formed under the chairmanship of Lord Willoughby de Broke and dedicated to resisting Home Rule by force if necessary. Its promoters included the Duke of Bedford, Lord Castlereagh, heir to the Marquess of Londonderry, and Lord Lewisham. In a letter to the Conservative *Morning Post* of 18 November, 1913, these peers appealed for the holding of another general election before Home Rule was granted, for:

we are well within sight of civil war. The Government have it in their power to save our King and our country from this supreme calamity by advising his Majesty to dissolve Parliament. . . . But if they do proceed . . . to the last extremity, then we call on all our able-bodied fellow-countrymen who think that the Ulstermen are arming in a righteous cause to enrol themselves and prepare to reinforce the ranks of the men who are going to risk their lives for the integrity of the Empire as well as for their own civil and religious liberty secured to them by the British Constitution. . . .

We want men who have been trained to bear arms, and who have been accustomed both to command and to obey.[101]

By the beginning of 1914 the League had enrolled around four hundred agents and ten thousand members.

In Ulster itself, meanwhile, resistance was strengthening, under the determined leadership of Sir Edward Carson. On 28 September 1912 there was a mass signing of a Covenant opposing Home Rule and this move was accompanied by the setting up of a private army, the Ulster Volunteer Force, which proceeded to secure weapons for itself on a major scale. In this, several Ulster landlords played a major part. In 1913, both Lord Farnham and Lord Leitrim ran guns from England to Donegal for the Volunteers, the latter using his own steam boat and employing his London-born chauffeur to pick up the weapons. In the 1870s Lord Leitrim's grandfather had been murdered in an agrarian outrage.[102]

Although the importation of weapons was banned during December 1913, a core of determined landowners ensured that it continued. In April 1914, Lords Masserene and Templetown were involved in a major operation to bring in eleven thousand rifles at Larne in South Antrim – an action which required a cordon to be thrown round the whole district. English magnates also gave support to direct action, and in January 1914 the Duchess of Somerset assured Carson that the 'day that the first shot is fired in Ireland . . . the Duke and I will both come over to give all the help we can.'[103] Not surprisingly, this activity on the part of the Unionists encouraged the Nationalists to set up their own private army. They, too, started amassing arms.[104]

In England the Union Defence League began to organize a British Covenant to support Ulster during the early months of 1914. It was under the direction of Lord Milner and by the outbreak of the First World War claimed to have obtained the support, and the signatures, of over a million men and around three-quarters of a million women.[105] More clandestinely, Milner began raising funds to support resistance in Ulster. Among the subscribers were Waldorf Astor, Lord Rothschild, Lord Iveagh, and the Duke of Bedford, the three last giving £10,000 apiece and Astor £30,000, 'subject to certain conditions'. Other contributors included the Duke of Portland, who gave £5,000 and Sir Ernest Cassel, who provided £4,500. In all, £134,500 was collected in this way, excluding 'many contributions of £1,000' from unnamed donors. It is almost certain that some of this money was used to purchase rifles for the gun-running operations.[106]

During the spring of 1914, therefore, the social and political tensions over the Irish question became ever more intense among the nation's élite as the Home Rule Bill came before Parliament for the third time. In order to allay the fears of the Ulstermen, Asquith offered them the opportunity to remain outside an independent Ireland for six years, should they so elect. But to committed Unionists this temporary respite was unacceptable and, in any case, it left out of consideration Union supporters who were living elsewhere in Ireland. Yet the Irish Nationalists, upon whom the Liberals relied for support, resisted any more permanent concessions. Conflict and civil war seemed to loom ever nearer.

Meanwhile some of the more determined English diehards, emulating the Somersets, were volunteering to fight in Ireland on Ulster's side, should the Government seek to impose its will by military force. On 21 March, 1914, Lord Willoughby de Broke wrote to the commanding officer of the Ulster Volunteer Force in Belfast offering to 'serve in the ranks, or do any duty you wish. I am a retired Yeomanry Officer, aged 45. I can ride and shoot, and have commanded a Squadron of Yeomanry.'[107] The offer was tactfully refused, it being suggested that Willoughby de Broke would be of greater value to the cause if he remained in England to head the British League.[108]

Even the Primrose League began to prepare for civil war. In 1913 it agreed to assume responsibility for the refugee women and children who were expected to flee from Ulster should hostilities break out. Under the auspices of a 'Help the Ulster Women' Committee the League obtained promises to provide accommodation for eight thousand people and by August 1914 had secured donations of £17,000.[109]

But perhaps the most dramatic confirmation of the feverish temper of the times was the action of fifty-eight army officers in the 3rd Cavalry Brigade serving at the Curragh near Dublin in declaring that they would rather be dismissed from the service than go north to put down political protest against Home Rule. This refusal to become involved in what was called the 'coercion of Ulster' aroused immediate consternation in Government circles. Hasty consultations were held and it was then declared that the whole dispute had arisen from a misunderstanding; there had been no intention to use the British army in the way suggested.[110]

Similar hostile feelings were widespread among officers elsewhere in the Army. Anthony Eden's eldest brother, Jack, threatened to refuse orders to act against the Ulster Volunteers and instead to resign from the army. His father, an eccentric old-style Conservative, was furious at such a suggestion and threatened to disinherit him totally should he do so.[111] And Lord Stanhope referred irreverently to 'that ass H.M.' when he learnt of George V's anger at the behaviour of the officers involved in the Curragh 'incident'. He added gleefully that the men had 'extracted terms from the Govt.' and certainly all were reinstated.[112] Even Asquith himself admitted to a friend in late March 1914 that if the Government were to order 'a march upon Ulster . . . about half the officers of the Army – the Navy is more uncertain – would strike'.[113]

Within the Commons itself, meanwhile, there were hysterical scenes during the autumn and winter of 1913–14 whenever the Irish question was under discussion. Cries of 'traitor' were levelled at Government ministers from the Conservative benches, and there was much rowdy conduct. In the Ladies' Gallery Mrs Asquith and Lady Londonderry nearly came to blows.[114]

The constitutional struggle over Ireland between 1912 and 1914 showed how far some of the diehards were prepared to go in order to thwart the lawfully elected government. The then Conservative leader, Bonar Law, when speaking of the threat of revolt stated

The Liberal Prime Minister, Herbert Henry Asquith, attending the Ridley-Benckendorff wedding in the spring of 1911. Asquith was highly intelligent but there were claims that he was drinking heavily. One of his nicknames was 'P.J.', that is Perrier Jouet, after a well-known brand of champagne. (*The Tatler*, 3 May 1911.) (British Library Newspaper Library)

that he could imagine 'no length of resistance to which Ulster will go which I shall not be ready to support'.[115] Several peers anticipated the outbreak of civil war if the Liberals sought to implement their legislation.

But not all diehards were prepared to countenance violence in order to get their way. The Duke of Northumberland, a former Conservative Party conference president, was not willing to approve the organization of armed resistance in Ulster:

> I believe that those who are preparing it are hatching a brood of chickens which will some day – and probably at no distant date – come very awkwardly home to roost in England.[116]

The Earl of Selborne, too, had reservations, although in his case based largely on self-interest:

> the last party in the world that ought to turn to arms . . . or go outside legal and constitutional forms is the Conservative and Unionist Party. If they did so lightly, it is likely that it would mean the breaking up of Society and the end of the Nation, for it would remove all restrictions on Radicals and Socialists who are blinded to the value of tradition and authority.[117]

Selborne's brother-in-law, Lord Robert Cecil, frankly admitted to having a 'profound horror of civil war'.[118]

Yet while these deep and dangerous divisions existed in High Society, there was still much outward gaiety as the last Season of the pre-war world went on its way. Elizabeth, wife of the diehard Irish peer, the Earl of Fingall, considered the Season of 1914 to be the most magnificent London had ever seen.

> To me there was something terrible about it . . . The wild extravagance, the entertaining, the money spending. There were two or three parties every night . . . It was quite common for people to go to . . . one after another, leaving a party which they found dull for better amusement elsewhere . . . I went as a dutiful mother, with my daughters, and shook hands with people I had never seen before, and ate their wonderful food, in their own houses, or at the Ritz, and sat on the bench with other dowagers, watching my daughters dance.[119]

Lady Desborough (whose husband had been an early signatory of the British Covenant in support of Ulster) also remembered that last summer as a happy time marked by much hot weather. On 25 July she held her final Saturday-to-Monday party of the Season at her Taplow home and recalled how the guests were 'absorbed in the subject of the Dublin Riots; but the first murmurs about graver causes of anxiety had begun'.[120] Just over a week later Britain and Germany were at war.

Such were the strange contrasts of those final months of peace. On the one hand, the social round of the élite continued much as usual, with parties, plays, and pleasures of all kinds; on the other, the male members of some of the families were plotting armed resistance to the lawful Government of the day. And although the diehards never amounted to more than about a sixth of the peerage, yet, as Gregory Phillips has written:

> Those who opposed Home Rule at any cost . . . were not merely bluffing . . . Private correspondence reveals that diehard peers (along with others) were prepared to spill blood to achieve their goals. This was the ultimate extension of the diehards' alienation from the political trends of the last three decades . . . The outbreak of the Great War, in which [they] participated with courage and much sacrifice, diverted this potential revolutionary outburst from many of Britain's oldest and supposedly most conservative families.[121]

In that bitter conflict many of the diehard families were to suffer grievously. Over a quarter of them lost a successor, either a son or a brother; some were themselves killed.[122] Yet by this means they were at least able to avoid the tragedy of civil conflict which in the summer of 1914 had seemed dangerously near.

When the War ended the old world of High Society had been irrevocably destroyed. Despite the frivolities and pleasure-seeking of the inter-war period, the balance of economic and political power in the nation had shifted farther away from its pre-1914 leaders. It was an experience with which they had slowly and painfully to come to terms, particularly after the major sales of country estates in the immediate post-war years, when perhaps a quarter of the land of England changed hands.[123]

'When I first lived at Welbeck the great neighbouring houses, such as Clumber, Thoresby and Rufford, were all inhabited by their owners, who . . . employed large staffs,' wrote the 6th Duke of Portland in 1937. 'Now, not one of them is so occupied,

SEMI-DETACHMENT.

GAMEKEEPER (*to poacher*). "WHAT ARE YOU DOING HERE?"
MR. LLOYD GEORGE (*innocently*). "I MUST REFER YOU, SIR, TO THE FERRET, WHO IS ACTING INDEPENDENTLY."

David Lloyd George, the Chancellor of the Exchequer, cast in the role of a poacher with a ferret because of the provisions in his 1909/10 Budget to institute an inquiry into the ownership of land. To most members of High Society this was the precursor of heavier taxation. (*Punch*, 1912) except for a very few days in the year, and the shooting attached to them is either let or abandoned . . . Whether or no this is for the general good I leave for others to judge. It is certainly the fact.'[124] Portland's lament was for a way of life which, as he himself recognized, had disappeared – for ever. It was echoed by Lord Crawford, as he gloomily contemplated his own difficult financial position and the possible sale of some of his pictures. 'Who knows how long our precious possessions will remain with us – possessions which give us the only position worth having, the status of thoughtful and cultivated people,' he wrote in his diary, in an attempt to come to terms with his changed standing in the world, and that of his friends.[125]

Yet, despite the anxieties and the diminished political role of the former leaders of Britain's landed élite after 1918, it must be remembered that even with land sales and other difficulties many of the largest magnates remained major estate owners. As late as 1976 one estimate suggested that a mere 1,500 families still owned about thirty per cent of the rural land of England and Wales, while in Scotland the Duke of Buccleuch, with an estate of 220,000 acres, and Lord Seafield, with 213,000 acres, owned the two largest estates in Great Britain.[126] (See Appendix C also). What was different was that in the 1970s they no longer belonged to an exclusive and plutocratic world of High Society, in the way their grandfather's and great-grandfather's generation had done.

APPENDIX A

High Society Through American Eyes

[Extracts from a letter written by Lelia (Belle) Wilson to her mother in New York, concerning a stay in Cowes during August, 1886. Belle was the second daughter of Richard T. Wilson, who served in the Confederate Army during the American Civil War, before moving to New York, where he made a fortune in banking and railroad promotion. Belle's elder sister, May, had married Ogden Goelet, a member of one of New York's most exclusive families in 1877, and in 1888 she herself married the Hon. Michael (later Sir Michael) Herbert, a brother of the 13th and 14th Earls of Pembroke. In 1902, Sir Michael became British Ambassador in Washington. He died the following year. Belle and Mr and Mrs Goelet were at Cowes on board the yacht 'Norseman'.]
[In F.4/74 at Wilton House.]

DIEPPE.

SATURDAY, Aug. 14, 1886.

Darling Mother,

There are such endless and delightful things to tell you about our Cowes week that I scarcely know where to begin. . . . I have not had such a good time or enjoyed that pleasing sensation of being interested in everything to the degree that I was there since I came out, and consequently I came away with the brightest and most pleasing reminiscence of English hospitality under the especial patronage of the Prince of Wales. I have always had a great desire as you know to 'do' a London season and if my success in that immense crowd of people were only a third to what ours was in the small portion of English society represented at Cowes, I am sure I should enjoy it, for I was very much amused, and at all the dances had delightful evenings and lots of partners . . . at one of the parties I was asked to go into supper by *four* people . . .

The fact is . . . the Prince's kindness to us *made* our visit to Cowes. Without it, for so short a time as a week, of course we would have had no foothold and would have had no time to make one for ourselves. Of course, his kindness to us was greatly owing to his last 'mash' (excuse vulgarity) Mr Poker, and also his desire to see new things and in consequence curiosity about The 'Norseman'. . . . I am very much indebted to her for

185

having aided me in my desire to have a little peep at English ways and customs even though Cowes is only a small part of a large society.

I arrived at Cowes at seven o'clock Thursday afternoon and went directly on board the yacht . . . After dinner about 9.30 we went above to see the *fireworks* from the Gardens of the Castle (Club House) and there it was . . . that I met Lord Cork . . . He's the kindest dearest old gentleman ever lived. There was just going to be a dance that evening, an informal affair at an eccentric old individual's called Mrs Cust, and just as Mr Poker and sister were talking together the Prince of Wales and all his suite came out so he came up to us and we were re-presented to him and while all his attendants stood and waited he talked to us for about fifteen minutes and told us we must just take off our hats and go on to the dance, that he would send our names in! Fancy! we hadn't dressed our hair all day and were in simple little white yachting dresses. Then he and his people went on to the dance – we told Lord Cork we could *not* go like that & that we would be back in fifteen minutes. He said he would wait for us outside the door but as the yacht was at least half a mile out, our quarter of an hour must have been three-quarters. . . . We put on little black lace dresses which we had on board and got back to find Jemima Poker coming down to the yacht landing to look after us – sent by the Prince who wanted to know what had become of us – and it is not etiquette to be so late you know . . .

Later on in the evening a Quadrille was danced and I was asked by Lord Clonmell, a funny old Irish earl and a guest of the Prince's on board the Osborne. I refused to dance at first as I really did *not* know how and I heard afterwards that refusing to dance in the set with the Prince of Wales was a dreadful breach of etiquette and scandalized all the English maidens. To make matters worse when I got into the set H.R.H. motioned me to stand opposite to him, which being a command I had to do. However I got through with it pretty well – only turning my back on His Royal Highness once!! Of course everyone was criticizing us that night and I heard next day that some English women had said 'Very peculiar that Miss Wilson refused to dance the Quadrille, very peculiar that she did not know it – she will see that the Prince will not pay her any more attention!' However this little prediction was not true, as at every dance we went to he danced once or oftener with either me or sister . . . The last one on Tuesday night he danced a Lancers with sister, asked her to be his vis-à-vis in a Quadrille and a delightful valse with me, and I had a nice polka with him. I don't however think he has taken any particular fancy to us personally as he says we do not look like American women and I am sure we did not amuse him. I think he liked the novelty and was showing us hospitality and extending civilities, much, as I said before, owing to Mr Poker. . . .

We were tired out the next day but had to get up early as Ld. Cork had said he was coming on board. He brought two such nice men with him, one elderly gentleman, Ld. Dorchester, who was nice to me during all my stay at Cowes . . .

Mr & Mrs Poker came to lunch that day and at four o'clk. the Prince with Col. Paget, Ld. Clonmell and a pretty English woman . . . came for [us] and took us off in his little steam launch to see those races and sports which before we witnessed from the window of the Hotel. It *was rather* more amusing this time! Then, if you please, before we returned he simply said he would come aboard the 'Norseman' on our return to tea! This was rather trying for sister as Peters & Theodore are not connoisseurs in the *arts* of

English five o'clock tea. However there was nothing to be done but let him come and it did not turn out so badly and he was so enthusiastic about the yacht. The harbour that afternoon was a beautiful sight, all the two hundred yachts were decked out in flags in honor of the Duke of Edinburg (sic) whose birthday it was, and the little launches and bright sunlight made it very gay & pleasant. The ball that evening was quite a large affair given at a big old house with long halls and great large ball room. . . . My *shadow* that evening was a man called Lord Greenock. It was very convenient to have someone ready to dance all the spare dances and be particularly polite even though he is what they call 'very odd' . . .

Saturday evening we went to a supper party – given to the Prince of Wales. The host of the said supper party is a very shy young man and they said he had been so nervous all day that he was nearly ill.

Sunday was the day appointed by the Prince to lunch on board the 'Norseman'; and though he had sent word that he wished to sail on the 'Norseman' on Tuesday we were so tired that we tried to get off on Monday by saying that Robert was not well, however it would not do – H.R.H. was very quiet and rather cross during the first part of the luncheon until sister said she would remain and send a telegram to see if 'the boy' was better. After which he was charming. He has the *best* manners and more tact than any man I have ever met. . . .

I expect you will be wondering if we were not just a little bit uneasy about the ceremonious part of entertaining royalty, but when one is put to one's test and a fact has to be faced I find that the obstacles are never so grave as the imagination presents them. After attending to everything as best we could, and ordering as nice a luncheon as Ogden's cooks knew how to prepare there was nothing to do but to receive His Royal Highness and treat him much as one would do any other honored guest. The only peculiarity of the luncheon on account of royalty being present was that no one had any finger-bowl except the Prince! Mr Poker remembered this just in time and told us, and it was very fortunate as neither Ogden or any of the rest of us knew of this habit. It would have been a most shocking piece of ignorance to see us all at the table comfortably dipping our finger tips into our bowls! Only the Prince is permitted to have one – not even the Princess and it is a strictly observed remnant of the old Feudal custom which happily we found out just in time. Otherwise the luncheon was much as other luncheons. The table looked very pretty dressed in red geraniums in some silver vases and bowls which sister got in Paris. There were twelve people and the Prince and Ogden sat at the respective heads of the table. He was very charming and quite amusing. At the end of the luncheon came a note to Mr Poker from the Duke of Connaught saying if quite convenient to Mr & Mrs Goelet they would be delighted to take tea on board the 'Norseman' that afternoon. Of course they must come and as 'tea' in England means a complete meal of bread & butter, jams, eggs etc. you can understand that *Sunday* was *not* a 'Day of Rest' as the hymn tells us it is! After luncheon the Prince proposed being photographed on board, so we made a group and John took us, and also a Frenchman . . . who was visiting the Prince on board the 'Osborne' . . . We had hoped that the Prince of Wales would leave before the Duke & Duchess [of Connaught] came as he knew they were to do at five. But not at all! He stayed on purposely they say as he likes to annoy his royal brother in this way. You see one has to use great diplomacy when one has two royalties together! When the Duke of Connaught visits one alone one can make one's lowest curtsies to him, one can say 'Sir' & 'Your Royal Highness' in the most flattering manner and insinuate that he is very near the throne of England. But when his big brother is there his big brother *likes* to make him aware that *he* is future King and in consequence one has to be full of tact to please both these personages!

However we found the Duke too delightful and the Duchess such a lovely kind young German. He is easier to talk to than the Prince of Wales and is so good looking. . . . The Prince expressed himself much pleased with his luncheon and I think we behaved with proper respect – in fact I fear he thinks us rather stupid and quite unlike our compatriotes (sic) and I am afraid this is rather a disadvantage as he is so fond of the peculiarities of our nationality. However he set the following Tuesday to come and sail in the 'Norseman' and named the people he wished invited – About this we were really a little nervous, especially Ogden – as he considered it such a responsibility to have him on board . . . Ogden had a beautiful revenge on the secretary of the yacht club who, you remember, was so insolent and impolite to him when here before. . . . Ogden had the satisfaction of simply walking up to him and saying that H.R.H. had ordered him to send a pilot & tug to the 'Norseman'! He was most servile and subservient. . . .

Monday night Mr Mackay gave a very pretty dance, and I wore a *lovely* grey tulle ball dress which I had all beautifully packed to send home. – It was immensely admired and I don't suppose I will ever have the chance to wear it in *more* distinguished company and it was so lucky that I had pretty dresses as everyone talked so much about our clothes. . . . Sister had no ball dresses with her and had to wear one of mine! I let her have my new white one . . . She wore it twice so she says she is going to buy it from me. Our Cowes week was most disastrous on our clothes, every thing that we wore there is nearly ruined so that I am afraid it will be rather hard on papa's purse. Ask him if he is willing to *pay* for my having had such a good time, for I *did* enjoy it so much and don't believe I should have found it so amusing if I had not worn my best clothes and been conscious that we were *decidedly* the best dressed women there. But it is worse on clothes than Newport [the most prestigious American yachting resort] and hard on the health I should think as *every one* walks in the gardens after dancing. However I felt so well there – that I am thankful for! Or at all events – I had no time to think *how* I felt – so I had a fine week!

. . . Tuesday morning dawned in thick fog and a dead calm at nine o'clock made us think there would be no sailing that day but by twelve, the time appointed by the Prince to come aboard, the wind had sprung up, and though it was pouring rain he sent word he would like to sail. He has a wonderful personality and the minute he came aboard seemed to set things bright and make it pleasant for every body – even the weather itself for by lunch time (two o'clk.) the clouds had all dispersed and the sun was shining brightly after which we had the most heavenly sail . . . He interested himself in seeing the yacht sail, talking to Mr Poker and the usual little incidents of a sailing party. He brought with him a bundle of photographs of himself and gave sister & myself two large ones . . . He also brought with him a pretty little silver box with a commodore's yacht flag on it which he gave to sister as a souvenir of Cowes. All this I think shows that he could not have been more hospitable or shown us more civilities if we had been his own guests . . .

Then for five o'clock tea we had hot 'baker-cakes' which he found delicious – we told him they were entirely a southern dish and he ate them with relish.

The next and most flattering part of our visit has yet to be told you. When Mrs Poker came on board she told us we were to be asked to dinner that night on the 'Osborne' to meet the Princess of Wales! This is considered a tremendous honor – no one is ever asked to dine with the Princess of Wales until they have either been presented or met her somewhere and we had not yet made her acquaintance. Was it not nice, – so when the Prince came he told sister that we were to come to dinner on board the 'Osborne' at half past eight. We had no time to think; as the party did not leave the 'Norseman' until half past seven we had very little time to dress. We wore short dinner dresses . . . very pretty and Mrs Poker gave us a few 'points' chiefly about when to leave! It is etiquette for the guests not to make the move to go home but wait until the Princess makes the sign, or something of the kind. . . .

We went on the 'Osborne' at the proper hour and were ushered from one servant to the other until we reached the large sitting room or cabin which is below the upper deck and also *below* the dining-room. We found about seven gentlemen there or more and one lady waiting to receive us – Miss Knollys who is lady in waiting to the Princess. She was very pleasant and begged us to sit down 'as we would have plenty of standing to do later'. Then a Miss Stonor, a girl about my age who is also maid of honor to the Princess came in and presently Her Royal Highness herself with her daughter, looking even more lovely than her photos and far lovelier than she does in her bonnet. She entered very silently and gracefully bowing her head as she passed the people and coming up quietly – shaking hands with sister and myself who of course made her our prettiest 'reverence'. . . . Soon after the Princess came in the Prince appeared and directly dinner was served. The Prince took sister in, the Princess went in with Comte de St. Priest and others followed in precedence, I going in with Sir Allen Young and Ogden taking in Miss Knollys. I was surprised to find myself on the other side of the Prince so that you see every distinction and civility was paid us. The table and service were exceedingly pretty and the dinner served like lightning by some twelve enormous good looking footmen & butlers . . . Though there were a great many courses the dinner was really no time in being got through – One's plates were whisked off before they were scarcely in front of one, and what struck me as strange while one person was eating one thing another would be eating something else – the next course for instance. Otherwise I find that we are quite royal in our entertaining and differ very little in our habits. After dinner the Princess presented us to Princess Louise, her daughter. She seemed a nice girl. – All through dinner it amused me *very* much to see her staring at me and watching me somewhat as one watches the antics of a young savage! She is shy herself, but seemed so simple and kindly disposed to me and wanted to be *amiable* and make me feel at my ease. I really liked this young Princess.

The Princess of Wales was also charming and did the honors of her house by showing us photographs and trying to interest us. To tell you the truth I am afraid we were woefully dull and appeared somewhat stupid. It is exceedingly difficult to draw that fine line which separates *respect* and dullness – and it was difficult to find a subject in common; still it was very nice . . .

After the men came in we all talked together for about three-quarters of an hour, the Princess I think waited for a sign from the Prince and then got up and said that perhaps we would like to be going as we were going to a dance. We said good night to her and thanked her for her kindness. The Prince asked us to wait for him a moment and we would all go over together in his launch. So outside we put on our wraps and waited until H.R.H. put on another coat, one less *smart* and with less braid and then saying goodnight again to the Princess who had come on deck we all stepped into the launch and had a very jolly time going ashore. . . .

The dance we went to the last evening was at the same house as the one of the first night of our arrival, a certain Mrs Cust, a hateful old woman who no one seems to like but the Prince *uses* her and makes her entertain at Cowes though I believe she goes nowhere in London. The last night we were *none* of us invited, he simply *took* us to her house. Sister said, 'Sir I don't think she likes Americans,' and he said – 'I *know* she doesn't' and thought it a great *joke*! She is noted for saying horrid things about everyone and is a perfect old character, half crazy. I must tell you how she greeted me the first night I went to her house. She said 'she thought America must be a dreadul place, she had heard no one had any servants there.' I told her one or two families *had*. Then she said, 'Oh she thought no one had a lady's maid and she would hate to be without a lady's maid.' I begged her pardon and said I knew someone who had a lady's maid. 'I thought Americans did not like to be servants' she replied. 'They don't' I answered '*all our working class are English*!!!' That finished her and I was so amused as she was so polite afterwards. Don't you think I 'scored one'?

It seems luck was on our side at Cowes as we had the most heavenly weather while we were there and Ogden kept so well . . . Of course the nicest & most flattering thing was meeting the Princess and dining with them, as that always disarms the public when they say the Prince goes with everyone. All the world acknowledges that the Princess *does not* so it is well to keep this in mind. . . .

BELLE.

[Quoted by kind permission of the Earl of Pembroke.]

APPENDIX B

A 'Man-about-Town' in the 1880s

[Extracts from the 1887 diary of Sir Edward W. Hamilton (1847–1908). Hamilton was the eldest son of the Bishop of Salisbury and was educated at Eton and Christ Church, Oxford. He entered the Treasury in 1870 and served as a private secretary to Mr Gladstone in 1873–74 and 1880–85. He became Joint Permanent Secretary to the Treasury in 1902 and was a member of Brooks's the Marlborough, and the Turf Clubs. The diary is at the British Library, Add.MSS. 48, 646.]

1887

Tuesday, 10 May. Dined tonight at F. Rothschild's – a small & pleasant little gathering of men. One can never take part in such a dinner without reflecting how times have in one sense improved of late years. Twenty years ago eight or ten men could not have met at dinner together without making questionable stories their staple of conversation. Now men are content to discuss the political & social topics of the day. . . .

Wednesday, 18 May. The season is becoming more brisk. There are lots of dinners & a certain number of Balls; young ladies' balls & married women's Balls. I am only now suited for the latter, & only go to them as a means of coming across one's friends. The first Queen's Ball was last night. It is always an interesting & pretty sight; but last night's Ball was generally considered dull. The supper arrangements were worse than usual: it was really a fight to get near a table at all. They are really a disgrace; but there will be no change in the present reign. Foreigners must be a good deal surprised at such a prandial bear-garden. There is an absurd remnant privilege which is kept up. Cabs are still excluded from the Palace gates; so anyone like oneself has to walk in with one's white legs or have a brougham if it is a wet night. Another indefensible remnant of privilege is the reservation to a select few of the use of Constitution Hill. One wonders how long this reservation will be maintained. I have rather a hankering for selling Buckingham Palace & its site & building up one really fine Palace on the site of St. James' Palace; or (if the demolition of that Palace were considered too much of a sacrilege) on the sites of Marlborough House and the War Office. . . .

Monday, 23 May. . . . Social engagements are now at their height. Certainly dinner-giving, & dinner-giving without running to banquets, has much increased of late years. The exception is not to have a dinner provided for one now-a-days. Balls on the other hand are somewhat less in favour; & they get later & later every year. Nobody now dares to go to a House much before midnight. . . .

Tuesday, 24 May. Dined last night at the George Bentincks – a well arranged dinner of 24 at two tables – afterwards to a ball given by Mrs Oppenheim, whose entertainments are always most pleasant & well done. The Prince of Wales was there (one might add, as usual); for there is hardly a Ball now with any pretentions (sic) to smartness which he not only attends but at which he remains till a very late hour. This is scarcely dignified at his age. His capacity for amusing himself is extraordinary; he is able to get on with hardly any sleep, some 4 or 5 hours appear to suffice for him. This morning he was on Parade at 10 o'clock punctually for the trooping of the colours in celebration of the Queen's Birthday which is for the first time for many years being kept on the real day this year: (in my recollection the Queen's Birthday has always been kept on a Saturday). . . .

Tonight dined at Goschen's* Ministerial dinner. He gave it in his house in Portland Place. Six months ago his house is one of the least likely of all places at which I should have expected to eat my 'Queen's Birthday' dinner. The unexpected has certainly happened with a vengeance.

After dinner which was very successful, went on to the F[oreign] O[ffice], where there was the usual crowd. As might be expected Lady Salisbury's arrangements were hardly up to the arrangements of the Roseberys last year. I saw Lord Acton there, who retains his influence with Mr G[ladstone]. He had just come over from abroad, & was to go down to Dollis Hill [the Gladstones' London residence] tomorrow . . .

Thursday, 26 May. The Derby won yesterday by Merry Hampton, the first favourite 'The Baron' being second . . .

Went last night to dine with the Jeunes to meet Dilke & his wife. It was the first time I had seen him since the trial.** He seemed in good spirits & to find plenty of occupation with his pen-article writing &c. . . . Had a good deal of talk after dinner with Lady Dilke. She must certainly be a woman of great pluck. She is moreover clever & agreeable. She is a very fair authoress herself & can address a meeting from a platform. She busies herself with political affairs in Chelsea. She finds socialism much on the increase, among the masses, & an anti-monarchical feeling spreading. It is difficult to get a hearing given to 'God Save the Queen'. There is nothing personal about it; but it is one of the ways in which socialism finds expression. Besides the Dilkes, there was the Greek Minister, Mrs Oscar Wilde (a shapeless woman with a pretty face – just what one would

---

* The Rt. Hon. George J. Goschen, 1st Viscount Goschen (1831–1907) unexpectedly became Chancellor of the Exchequer in January 1887 when the former Chancellor, Lord Randolph Churchill, resigned at short notice from the Marquess of Salisbury's second administration.

** The Rt. Hon. Sir Charles Wentworth Dilke (1843–1911) was President of the Local Government Board from 1882 to 1885. His promising political career was destroyed in the latter year when he was cited as co-respondent in a divorce case brought by Donald Campbell, a Scottish lawyer and Liberal candidate, against his twenty-two-year-old wife. During the lengthy trial sensational allegations were made about Dilke's private life. In 1885 he married Emilia Pattison, widow of Mark Pattison, the former rector of Lincoln College, Oxford. She was his second wife, his first having died in 1874.

have expected to find the wife of such a man), Justin McCarthy & his daughter, a nice bright girl with whom I had a good deal of conversation at dinner . . .

From Mrs Jeune's, on to Great Stanhope St. where the Duchess of Manchester had her 'Derby' entertainment for the Princess of Wales & the young Princesses – one room with baccara[t] (gambling always delights H.R.H.]; the other room the Hungarian band & dancing, most pleasant & jolly. . . .

Saturday, 2 July. On Wednesday the Queen gave a great Garden Party at Buckingham Palace. Six thousand people are supposed to have been asked. I had never seen the gardens before. They are very extensive, & perfectly useless. There was no crowd in spite of numbers. The Queen looked beaming. She walked about; & wherever she walked a line was formed. There was comparatively little interest taken in the Foreign Royalties. She left the Palace about 7.15, in order to return to Windsor. She seems to prefer any amount of additional exertion to passing a single night in London. The party was extremely well arranged. There were three entrances, one at the top of Constitution Hill, another at the bottom of Grosvenor Place, in addition to the ordinary entrance through the Palace; so ingress and egress were made easy. Dined later with the Campbells of Craigie.

On Thursday there was a Royal fête at the Crystal Palace. I drove down in the afternoon with the Arthur Sassoons. The Duchess of Manchester had with her usual energy got up a party, which included R. Churchill and Chamberlain – 'Masher Joe' as he may well be called now. They both made themselves very pleasant. We first attended a Concert and after a little walk in the garden proceeded to a scrambling dinner. We were given excellent places in the gallery next to the Royal box from which we saw the fireworks. It was a gorgeous display; especially the shells which now supersede the old rocket, and the cascade of fire. After the fireworks we were taken to see an open-air ballet – a new & special diversion for the evening; and then drove back to London. Clifden gave us supper in Chesterfield Gardens. . . .

Yesterday afternoon I went and experimented on the new Lawn Tennis Club at West Kensington – the Queen's Club. It is a splendid flat piece of ground; & the Courts are of the very best. If the Club were a little less distant, it would be a great success. Curzon & myself got up a small party together. Dined afterwards most pleasantly at the A. Sassoons; & afterwards for a short time to a Ball at the Adrian Hopes.

The visit of the two young Princes – Prince Eddie & Prince George – to Ireland appears to have been a considerable success. They got a good welcome in Dublin despite the offensive & illjudged decision of the Parnellites*** to hold aloof from all Jubilee festivities. I don't believe there is any real widespread feeling in Ireland against the Sovereign and her children; though Ireland has been distinctly slighted by the Queen. The real hostility of the Irishmen is confined to the British *Government*. . . .

*** The supporters of Charles Stewart Parnell (1846–1891), the Irish political leader who headed the Home Rule Party from 1879 until shortly before his death in October 1891. His political career was undermined in November 1890 when Captain William O'Shea, a former member of the Home Rule Party, obtained a divorce from his wife, Katharine, naming Parnell as the co-respondent.

APPENDIX C

Twenty-five Major Landowners in England and Wales (Excluding London): 1876 and 1976

[In 1876, the *Spectator* published a list of the largest landowners in England and Wales. Fifty-four of them owned more than 30,000 acres – some, as in the case of Lord Leconfield and the Duke of Bedford, spread over three counties; others, as with the Earl of Pembroke and the Earl of Lisburne, concentrated largely in one. A century later the *Spectator* obtained details of the ownership position of the descendants of thirty-three of these men and below are statistics relating to twenty-five of the largest of them. Scottish and Irish owners were excluded from the original survey, apparently because although many of them owned massive estates – the Duke of Sutherland was the largest landlord in the country – much of their land, especially in the highlands, was of relatively low value.]

Landowner	1876 acreage	1976 acreage	gross rental in 1876 (£)
The Duke of Northumberland	186,397	105,000	176,044
The Duke of Devonshire	132,996	56,000	140,403
Sir Watkin Williams-Wynn	91,021	26,000	47,425
The Duke of Bedford	87,508	11,000	140,547
The Earl of Carlisle	78,541	3,000	49,602
The Duke of Rutland	70,019	18,000	89,945
The Earl of Ancaster	67,638	22,680	n.a.
The Earl of Lonsdale	67,457	72,000	69,960
The Earl of Powis	61,008	19,000	63,306
Lord Leconfield	58,460	13,000	57,271
Earl Brownlow	57,798	10,000	85,076

Landowner	1876 acreage	1976 acreage	gross rental in 1876 (£)
The Earl of Derby	56,597	22,000	163,326
The Earl of Yarborough	55,272	30,000	76,226
The Duke of Portland	53,771	17,000	68,935
The Marquess of Ailesbury	53,362	5,500	58,030
The Earl of Londesborough	52,656	none (estate split among relatives)	67,878
The Earl of Cawdor	51,517	26,000	34,987
The Duke of Beaufort	45,848	52,000	48,245
The Earl of Leicester	43,024	27,000	49,009
The Earl of Lisburne	42,666	3,230	10,579
The Marquess of Bath	41,690	10,000	47,768
The Earl of Pembroke	40,447	14,000	41,781
The Duke of Norfolk	40,176	25,000 (in trust for family)	264,564
The Earl of Feversham	39,312	12,500	34,328
The Earl of Middleton	34,701	13,500	47,016

Source: *The Spectator*, 16 Feb., 4 March and 18 March, 1876 and 1 January, 1977.

N.B. In 1976 Lord Cawdor, Lord Ancaster and the Duke of Portland also held land in Scotland, as did a number of their 1876 predecessors. These acreages are excluded.

The high value of the Duke of Norfolk's 1876 land holding is due to the fact that many of his 40,176 acres included mines and urban property.

Notes

CHAPTER ONE

1   Jennifer Ellis ed., *Thatched with Gold. The Memoirs of Mabell Countess of Airlie* (1962), 106.

2   Lady St Helier, *Memories of Fifty Years* (1909), 182.

3   George Cornwallis-West, *Edwardian Hey-Days, or A Little about a Lot of Things* (1930), 131.

4   David Cannadine, *The Decline and Fall of the British Aristocracy* (1990), 346.

5   *Etiquette for Ladies and Gentlemen* (n.d. [*c.* 1894]), 54.

6   Leonore Davidoff, *The Best Circles* (1986 edn.), 25.

7   Diary of Sir Edward Hamilton in the British Library, Add. MSS. 48,646, entry for 24 May, 1887.

8   Frances Countess of Warwick, *Life's Ebb and Flow* (1929 edn.), 36.

9   Nancy W. Ellenberger, 'The Souls and London "Society" at the end of the Nineteenth Century' in *Victorian Studies*, Vol. 25, No. 2 (Winter 1982), 146–8, 151. Angela Lambert, *Unquiet Souls: The Indian Summer of the British Aristocracy, 1880–1918* (1985 edn.), 8.

10 Frances Countess of Warwick, op. cit., 77.

11 Consuelo Vanderbilt Balsan, *The Glitter and the Gold* (1973 edn.), 58–9. Quentin Crewe, *The Frontiers of Privilege: A Century of Social Conflict as reflected in The Queen* (1961), 64.

12 Lady Dorothy Nevill, *Under Five Reigns* (ed. Ralph Nevill) (1910), 140.

13 Lady Dorothy Nevill, op. cit., 147.

14 Ralph Nevill ed., *The Reminiscences of Lady Dorothy Nevill* (n.d. [*c.* 1906]), 128.

15 Ralph E. Pumphrey, 'The Introduction of Industrialists into the British Peerage: A Study in Adaptation of a Social Institution' in *American Historical Review*, Vol. LXV, No. 1 (October, 1959), 11.

16 David Cannadine, op. cit., 200. F.M.L. Thompson, *English Landed Society in the Nineteenth Century* (1963), 296.

17 Mark Bence-Jones and Hugh Montgomery-Massingberd, *The British Aristocracy* (1979), 96 and 98.

18 Y. Cassis, 'Bankers in English Society in the Late Nineteenth Century' in *Economic History Review*, 2nd Series, Vol. XXXVIII, No. 2 (May, 1985), 218 and 223. David Cannadine, op. cit., 347.

19 Raleigh Trevelyan, *Grand Dukes and Diamonds. The Wernhers of Luton Hoo* (1991), xxi, 177 and 231.

20 Susan Tweedsmuir, *The Lilac and the Rose* (1952), 82.

21 Barbara Drake and Margaret I. Cole ed., *Our Partnership* by Beatrice Webb (1948), 347.

22 F.M.L. Thompson, op. cit., 314.

23 F.M.L. Thompson, op. cit., 304–5.

24 Peter Gordon ed., *The Red Earl. The Papers of the Fifth Earl Spencer 1835–1910*, Vol. II (Northamptonshire Record Society, Vol. XXXIV, 1986), 37, 194, 200 and 237.

25 Susan Tweedsmuir, *The Edwardian Lady* (1966), 17. F.M.L. Thompson, op. cit., 299. W.D. Rubinstein, *Men of Property* (1981), 60–1.

26 John Van der Kiste, *Edward VII's Children* (1989), 28–9 and 49.

27 'The Enlargement of Society' in the *Saturday Review*, 5 May, 1900, 553.

28 'The Enlargement of Society' loc. cit., 553.

29 Consuelo Vanderbilt Balsan, op. cit., 45.

30 Lady Jeune, 'The Future of Society' in *Lady's Realm* (Jan. 1902), 365.

31 David Cannadine, op. cit., 345.

32 Raleigh Trevelyan, op. cit., 98. Peter Gordon, op. cit., 36.

33 List of Properties included in the Long MSS. at Wiltshire Record Office, 947/1924.

34 *Etiquette for Ladies and Gentlemen*, 38. David Cannadine, op. cit., 345.

35 Hugh E.M. Stutfield, *The Sovranty (sic) of Society* (1909), 16.

36 Consuelo Vanderbilt Balsan, op. cit., 81–2.

37 Jennifer Ellis ed., op. cit., 158.

38 Draft report of the Committee appointed to safeguard the status of the holders of Baronetcies in Pembroke MSS. at Wiltshire County Record Office, 2057/F3/1.

39 Frances Countess of Warwick, *Afterthoughts* (1931), 49.

40 David Cannadine, op. cit., 349.

41 *Lady's Realm* (Aug. 1897), 464–5. Mrs George Cornwallis-West, *The Reminiscences of Lady Randolph Churchill* (1908), 301–2.

42 *The Tatler*, 3 Feb., 1910, 122. 'Open Letter to the Duchess of Norfolk.'

43 Angus Wilson, *The Naughty Nineties* (1976 edn.), 8.

44 Hervey MSS. at Suffolk Record Office, Bury St. Edmunds, 941/71/1.

45 Hervey MSS. 941/71/1, letter dated 18 March, 1885.

46 Marie Corelli in Marie Corelli, Lady Jeune, Flora Annie Steel, Susan, Countess of Malmesbury, *The Modern Marriage Market* (1898), 31 and 38.

47 Leonore Davidoff, op. cit., 56.

48 *Lady's Realm* (July 1901), 359.

49 Mrs George Cornwallis-West, op. cit., 39–40.

50 The Duke of Portland, *Men Women and Things* (1937), 142. Mrs George Cornwallis-West, op. cit., 41–5.

51 Mrs George Cornwallis-West, op. cit., 42–5.

52 Diary of Mary Elizabeth Lucy consulted by kind permission of Sir Edmund Fairfax-Lucy, Bart.

53 Cynthia Asquith, *Remember and Be Glad* (1952), 64.

54 Beatrice Webb, *My Apprenticeship*, 2nd edn. (n.d.), 39–41.

55 Beatrice Webb, op. cit., 42.

56 The Viscountess Rhondda, *This was my World* (1933), 83.

57 The Viscountess Rhondda, op. cit., 93–4.

58 Hervey MSS. Mrs Hodnett to Frederick Hervey, 27 May, 1885 and Lady Augustus Hervey to Frederick Hervey, 16 June, 1885 in 941/71/1.

59 Quoted in Pat Jalland, *Women, Marriage and Politics 1860–1914* (1988 ed.), 276.

60 Pat Jalland, op. cit., 276–7.

61 Pat Jalland, op. cit., 278.

62 Nancy W. Ellenberger, op. cit., 157.

63 Consuelo Vanderbilt Balsan, op. cit., 76–7.

64 Quoted in Angela Lambert, op. cit., 92.

65 Gail MacColl and Carol McD. Wallace, *To Marry an English Lord: The Victorian and Edwardian Experience* (1989), 82.

66 *Lady's Realm* (March 1902), 654. It added sourly: 'in the matter of looks she cannot rival her companions, our three countrywomen, the Duchesses of Montrose, Portland, and Sutherland.'

67 E.F. Benson, *As We Were* (1930), 101–2.

68 The Hon. Vicary Gibbs ed., *The Complete Peerage*, Vol. I (1910), 65–6. Mark Bence-Jones and Hugh Montgomery-Massingberd, op. cit., 84. *The Times*, 11 April, 1894. Christopher Simon Sykes, *Black Sheep* (1982), 206–10.

69 F.M.L. Thompson, op. cit., 314.

70 Jennifer Ellis ed., op. cit., 106.

71 Angus Wilson, op. cit., 7.

72 Nigel Nicholson, *Mary Curzon* (1977), 145–6.

73 *Lady's Realm* (May 1909), 73–4. For Lord Balcarres's comments see John Vincent ed., *The Crawford Papers* (1984), 67.

74 Consuelo Vanderbilt Balsan, op. cit., 84–5.

75 C.F.G. Masterman, *The Condition of England*, 6th edn. (1911), 45–6.

CHAPTER TWO

1 Gregory D. Phillips, *The Diehards. Aristocratic Society and Politics in Edwardian England* (1979), 13.

2 George Cornwallis-West, *Edwardian Hey-Days or A Little about a Lot of Things* (1930), 132.

3 Ralph Nevill, *London Clubs: Their History and Treasures* (1911), 156–7.

4 Angela Lambert, *Unquiet Souls: The Indian summer of the British aristocracy* (1985 edn.), 5 and 6.

5 Diary of Sir Edward Hamilton for 1891 at the British Library, Add. MSS. 48,656, entry for 16 July.

6 Leonore Davidoff, *The Best Circles* (1986 edn.), 24.

7 W.H. Mallock, *Memoirs of Life and Literature* (1920), 103–4.

8 Quoted in Gregory D. Phillips, op. cit., 15.

9 Raleigh Trevelyan, *Grand Dukes and Diamonds. The Wernhers of Luton Hoo* (1991), 177–178. At Oxford, Derrick became involved in various other dubious financial practices and in 1912 he was declared bankrupt, his father having refused to meet any more of his debts. Raleigh Trevelyan, op. cit., 247.

10 James Lees-Milne, *The Enigmatic Edwardian. The Life of Reginald 2nd Viscount Esher* (1986 edn.), 10–11 and 110–11.

11 Lady Selborne to Roundell Viscount Wolmer, later the 3rd Earl of Selborne in MS.Eng.hist. d.444, f.21 [n.d. 1902], in the Bodleian Library, Oxford.

12 C.B. Otley, 'The Educational Background of British Army Officers' in *Sociology* (May 1973), Vol. 7, No. 2, 193 and 194.

13 Basil Tozier, 'The Unemployed Gentleman' in *The National Review*, Vol. 49, (June 1907), 595.

14 Gervas Huxley, *Victorian Duke. The Life of Hugh Lupus Grosvenor, First Duke of Westminster* (1967), 137. The Eaton light railway was completed in 1896. Pamela Horn, *The Changing Countryside in Victorian and Edwardian England and Wales* (1984), 36.

15 Gervas Huxley, op. cit., 145–7.

16 Gregory D. Phillips, op. cit., 18.

17 Richard Greville Verney Lord Willoughby de Broke, *The Passing Years* (1924), 152.

18 Richard Greville Verney, op. cit., 193.

19 George Cornwallis-West, op. cit., 38.

20 Eileen Quelch, *Perfect Darling. The Life and Times of George Cornwallis-West* (1972), 42.

21 George Cornwallis-West, op. cit., 47–9.

22 Quoted in Hugh E.M. Stutfield, *The Sovranty of Society* (1909), 135.

23 Lord Ernest Hamilton, *Forty Years On* (n.d. [c. 1922]), 159.

24 Lord Ernest Hamilton, op. cit., 172 and 177–80.

25 David Cannadine, *The Decline and Fall of the British Aristocracy* (1990), 272.

26 Eileen Quelch, op. cit., 21 and 29. George Cornwallis-West, op. cit., 178.

27 Peter Gordon ed., *The Red Earl. The Papers of the Fifth Earl Spencer, Vol. II 1885–1910* (Northamptonshire Record Society, Vol. XXXIV, 1986), 237, letter from Lord Spencer, 30 January, 1894. As early as August, 1886, Lord Spencer was reporting to his half-brother and heir that he had 'given notice to all Servants not needed to take care of House, excepting Under Butler. We shall begin afresh on a small scale after a time.' Peter Gordon ed., op. cit., 134.

28 Quoted in Pamela Horn, op. cit., 33–4.

29 Quoted in David Cannadine, op. cit., 99 and 110. F.M.L. Thompson, 'Presidential Address: English Landed Society in the Twentieth Century: I, Property: Collapse and Survival' in *Transactions of the Royal Historical Society*, 5th Series, Vol. 40 (1990), 13.

30 F.M.L. Thompson, *English Landed Society in the Nineteenth Century* (1963), 315.

31 C.B. Otley, 'The Social Origins of British Army Officers' in *Sociological Review*, Vol. 18, No. 2 (1970), 214.

32 Quoted in David Cannadine, op. cit., 253.

33 David Cannadine, op. cit., 252.

34 David Cannadine, op. cit., 260.

35 David Cannadine, op. cit., 257.

36 Kenneth Rose, *Curzon: A Most Superior Person* (1985 edn.), 16–17.

37 David Cannadine, op. cit., 257–58.

38 David Cannadine, op. cit., 240, 241 and 243. Henry Roseveare, *The Treasury. The Evolution of a British Institution* (1969), 174.

39 Henry Roseveare, op. cit., 178.

40 David Cannadine, op. cit., 240. Hamilton was an enthusiastic musician and a friend of Arthur Sullivan. Henry Roseveare, op. cit., 218.

41 Sir Edward Hamilton's diary for 1889 at the British Library, Add. MSS.48,651.

42 Sir Edward Hamilton's diary for 1891, loc. cit., entry for 12 July, 1891, Add.MSS. 48,656.

43 Sir Edward Hamilton's diary for 1891, entry for 19 July, 1891.

44 Michaela Reid, *Ask Sir James* (1987), 39.

45 James Lees-Milne, op. cit., 100.

46 James Lees-Milne, op. cit., 108–9.

47 James Lees-Milne, op. cit., 133.

48 Lord Ormathwaite, *When I Was at Court* (1937), 108.

49 Lord Ormathwaite, op. cit., 127.

50 T.H.S. Escott, *England: Its People, Polity and Pursuits* (1885), 558.

51 T.H.S. Escott, op. cit., 315.

52 Major-General W. Feilding, 'What Shall I do with my Son?' in *Nineteenth Century*, Vol. XIII (1883), 578.

53 W.D. Rubinstein, 'Education and the Social Origins of British Élites 1880–1970' in *Past and Present*, No. 112 (August 1986), 169.

54 F.M.L. Thompson, *English Landed Society*, 317.

55 Gregory D. Phillips, op. cit., 33–4. Randolph S. Churchill, *Lord Derby 'King of Lancashire'. The Official Life of Edward, Seventeenth Earl of Derby 1865–1948* (1959), 95.

56 Hon. Vicary Gibbs and H.A. Doubleday eds., *The Complete Peerage*, Vol. V, (1926), Appendix C, 780–3.

57 Gregory D. Phillips, op. cit., 39.

58 F.M.L. Thompson, *English Landed Society*, 305–6.

59 Quoted in Gregory D. Phillips, op. cit., 39.

60 *The Tatler*, 7 February, 1906. According to *The Complete Peerage*, Lord Cottesloe had been a director of five companies in 1896.

61 Diary of Sir Edward Hamilton for 1891, entry for 19 July.

62 Quoted in Eileen Quelch, op. cit., 81. Anita Leslie, *Jennie* (1992 edn.), 254.

63 George Cornwallis-West, op. cit., 124 and 159–60.

64 George Cornwallis-West, op. cit., 162, 166–8 and 169.

65 Quoted in David Cannadine, op. cit., 413.

66 Sir Frederick Milner, Bart. to 5th Earl Cadogan, 30 October, 1893 in CAD/593 at House of Lords Record Office. See also Sir Frederick Milner to Lord Willoughby de Broke, 8 August, 1912, in which he noted: 'It about broke my heart when I was driven from my dear old Home, for good alas! . . . I have never been the same man since.' In Political Papers of the 19th Lord Willoughby de Broke at House of Lords Record Office, WB.5/3.

67 Ralph Nevill, ed., *The Reminiscences of Lady Dorothy Nevill* (n.d. [*c*. 1906]), 125–6.

68 Ralph Nevill ed., op. cit., 124–5.

69 Raleigh Trevelyan, op. cit., 128–9, 146, 165 and 173–4. Beatrice Webb, who stayed at Luton Hoo in 1906, commented acidly about living 'in close contact with an expenditure of thirty thousand a year on a country house alone'. Raleigh Trevelyan, op. cit., 174.

70 M.J. Daunton, '"Gentlemanly Capitalism" and British Industry 1820–1914' in *Past and Present*, No. 112 (Aug. 1991), 179–80.

71 T.H.S. Escott, op. cit., 26.

72 T.H.S. Escott, op. cit., 25.

73 P. Blackwell, ' "An Undoubted Jewel": a case study of five Sussex country houses, 1880–1914' in *Southern History*, Vol. 3 (1981), 194. Petworth House Archives at West Sussex Record Office, PHA.2885, ff. 53, 325, 360 and 398.

74 Richard Greville Verney, op. cit., 48.

75 P. Blackwell, op. cit., 194.

76 Diary of Lady Frederica Loraine of Bramford Hall, Suffolk for 1891 at Suffolk County Record Office, Ipswich, HA.61/436/448. Sir Charles Petrie, *Scenes of Edwardian Life* (1975 edn.), 40. Michaela Reid, op. cit., 223.

77 See, for example, Leslie Field, *Bendor. The Golden Duke of Westminster* (1986 edn.), 101 and 103 for one father who spent little time with his young son. The same was true of Sir George Sitwell and his children. Victoria Glendinning, *Edith Sitwell. A Unicorn Among Lions* (1986 edn.), 22 and 24–5.

78 Anthony Glyn, *Elinor Glyn* (1968 edn.), 72.

79 James Lees-Milne, op. cit., 110–11 and 136.

80 Quoted in Adeline Hartcup, *Children of the Great Country Houses* (1986 edn.), 22.

81 Adeline Hartcup, op. cit., 17–18.

82 Quoted in P. Blackwell, op. cit., 190.

83 Diary of Lord Carrington for 1893 at the Bodleian Library, Oxford, MS.Film 1102, entry for 4 April and also 14 June.

84 Diary of Lady Carrington for 1894 at the Bodleian Library, Oxford, MS.Film 1100, entry for 1 April.

85 Diary of Lady Carrington for 1892 at the Bodleian Library, Oxford, MS.Film 1100, entries between 24 August and 21 September, and 30 September.

86 Quoted in Douglas Sutherland, *The Yellow Earl. The Life of Hugh Lowther 5th Earl of Lonsdale 1857–1944* (1965), 81.

87 Douglas Sutherland, op. cit., 132.

88 George Cornwallis-West, op. cit., 131–2.

CHAPTER THREE

1 Consuelo Vanderbilt Balsan, *The Glitter and the Gold* (1973 edn.), 104.

2 Margaret Blunden, *The Countess of Warwick* (1967), 76–8 and 126–8.

3 Margaret Blunden, op. cit., 202–5 and 238–9.

4 Frances Countess of Warwick, *Afterthoughts* (1931), 161–2 and 165.

5 Jessica Anne Gerard, 'Family and Servants in the Country-House Community in England and Wales 1815–1914' (University of London Ph.D. thesis, 1982), 194.

6 Jessica Anne Gerard, op. cit., 215 and 233.

7 Emily Lutyens, *A Blessed Girl. Memoirs of a Victorian Girlhood* (1989 edn.), 251.

8 Randolph S. Churchill, *Lord Derby 'King of Lancashire'. The Official Life of Edward, Seventeenth Earl of Derby 1865–1948* (1959), 95 and 101.

9 'A Member of the Aristocracy', *Manners and Rules of Good Society or Solecisms to be Avoided* (32nd edn.) (1910), 5.

10 *Etiquette for Ladies. A Complete Guide to the Rules and Observances of Good Society* (1900), 15.

11 Frances Countess of Warwick, *Afterthoughts*, 168.

12 Lucy Masterman ed., *Mary Gladstone: Her Diaries and Letters* (1930), 201–2.

13 Emily Lutyens, op. cit., 245 and 251.

14 Mary Lady Trevelyan, *The Number of my Days* (Unpublished autobiography, c. 1964 in University of Newcastle Library), 24.

15 Lady Augustus Hervey to Frederick Hervey at Suffolk County Record Office, Bury St. Edmunds, 941/71/1, 18 and 24 March, 1885.

16 Randolph S. Churchill, op. cit., 107.

17 Randolph S. Churchill, op. cit., 103 and 104.

18 P. Blackwell, '"An Undoubted Jewel": a case study of five Sussex country houses, 1880–1914' in *Southern History*, Vol. 3 (1981), 191. Jessica Gerard, op. cit., 216.

19 G.H. Fleming, *Victorian 'Sex Goddess'; Lady Colin Campbell and the sensational divorce case of 1886* (1990), 78. Lady Greville, *The Gentlewoman in Society* (1892), 172.

20 Mary Lady Curzon's Dinner Invitation Book 1895–1897 at the India Office Library, London, MSS. Eur.F.112/788.

21 Cyril Heber Percy, *Us Four* (1963), 31–2.

22 Jessica Gerard, op. cit., 216.

23 Simon Blow, *Broken Blood. The Rise and Fall of the Tennant Family* (1987), 122–4 and 129.

24 Osbert Sitwell, *Left Hand Right Hand!* Vol. 1 (1947), 99–100.

25 Lady Constance Malleson, *After Ten Years* (1931), 14.

26 Lady Constance Malleson, op. cit., 18.

27 Quoted in Leonore Davidoff, *The Best Circles* (1986 edn.), 53–4.

28 Emily Lutyens, op. cit., 8.

29 The Earl of Carnarvon, *No Regrets* (1976), 6.

30 The Earl of Carnarvon, op. cit., 15.

31 The Earl of Carnarvon, op. cit., 15.

32 Frances Countess of Warwick, *Afterthoughts*, 41.

33 Mary Lady Trevelyan, op. cit., 4 and 19.

34 Pauline Dower, *Living at Wallington* (1984), 30.

35 Consuelo Vanderbilt Balsan, op. cit., 141–2.

36 See, for example, entries in her diary for 10, 16, 18 and 20 June, 1892 at the Bodleian Library, Oxford, in MS. Film 1100.

37 Lady Carrington's diary, loc. cit.

38 Cynthia Asquith, *Remember and Be Glad* (1952), 4–6. Lady Diana Cooper, who visited Stanway at around this time, remembered it as 'short on comfort, "luke-warm water, blankets that are no prison to one's wayward toes, and every horizontal object wears a coat of dust, like a chinchilla".' Philip Ziegler, *Diana Cooper* (1983 edn.), 55.

39 Entry in Lady Carrington's diary for 14 October, 1894, in MS. Film 1100.

40 May Harcourt to Lady Harcourt in MS.Harcourt dep. 647 at the Bodleian Library, letter dated 22 July, 1906, f.215.

41 Consuelo Vanderbilt Balsan, op. cit., 92–3 and 119–20.

42 Consuelo Vanderbilt Balsan, op. cit., 83–4.

43 Lady Augusta Fane, *Chit-Chat* (1926), 261–2. Elinor Glyn, *Romantic Adventure* (1936), 66.

44 Elinor Glyn, op. cit., 69–70.

45 Elinor Glyn, op. cit., 66 and 74.

46 Nancy Cunard, *GM. Memories of George Moore* (1956), 32–3. Anne Chisholm, *Nancy Cunard* (1981 edn.), 32–4 and 45.

47 Nancy Cunard, op. cit., 23.

48 Susan Mary Alsop, *Lady Sackville* (1978), 100.

49 Consuelo Vanderbilt Balsan, op. cit., 96–7.

50 May Harcourt to Lady Harcourt in MS. Harcourt dep. 647, 30 October, 1901.

51 Philip Ziegler, op. cit., 26.

52 Lady Greville, op. cit., 32–3.

53 Susan Mary Alsop, op. cit., 106 and 139.

54 Lady Greville, op. cit., 33.

55 Dorothy Henley, *Rosalind Howard. Countess of Carlisle* (1958), 85–6.

56 Violet Powell, *Margaret Countess of Jersey* (1978), 156 and 161.

57 Christopher Simon Sykes, *Black Sheep* (1982), 14. *The Manners of the Aristocracy* by One of Themselves (n.d. [c. 1882]), 25.

58 Lady Constance Malleson, op. cit., 14.

59 Lady Helena Brabazon to Frederick Hervey in 941/71/1 at Suffolk Record Office, Bury St. Edmunds, 22 October, 1898.

60 May Harcourt to Lady Harcourt in MS. Harcourt dep. 647, 16 October, 1905, f.187.

61 Sylvia Brooke, *Queen of the Head Hunters* (1972 edn.), 11–13.

62 Susan Tweedsmuir, *The Edwardian Lady* (1966), 15.

63 Consuelo Vanderbilt Balsan, op. cit., 25.

64 Mary Lady Trevelyan, op. cit., 23.

65 Mary Lady Trevelyan, op. cit., 23.

66 Emily Lutyens, op. cit., 238.

67 Lady Constance Lytton, *Prisons and Prisoners: Experiences of a Suffragette* (1976 edn.), 1.

68 Pamela Horn, *Ladies of the Manor* (1991), 174.

69 Patricia Marks, *Bicycles, Bangs, and Bloomers. The New Woman in the Popular Press* (1990), 181.

70 Patricia Marks, op. cit., 7–8.

71 Patricia Marks, op. cit., 166. Alice Fairfax-Lucy ed., *Mistress of Charlecote. The Memoirs of Mary Elizabeth Lucy* (1990 edn.), 170.

72 Birthday Book of Mary Elizabeth Lucy, entry for 15 July, 1882, at Charlecote Park, consulted by kind permission of Sir Edmund Fairfax-Lucy, Bart.

73 Lady Harcourt to Sir William Harcourt in MS. Harcourt dep. 634, ff. 20–2, n.d. [1902], at the Bodleian Library, Oxford.

74 Lady Greville, op. cit., 131.

75 Lady Greville, op. cit., 142.

76 The Marchioness of Londonderry, *Retrospect* (1938), 23.

77 Susan Tweedsmuir, op. cit., 71–2. Joan Morgan and Alison Richards, *A Paradise out of a Common Field. The Pleasures and Plenty of the Victorian Garden* (1990), 226.

78 *Lady's Realm* (April 1902), 745.

79 Alice Fairfax-Lucy, op. cit., 170.

80 G.H. Fleming, op. cit., 242–4.

81 Susan Mary Alsop, op. cit., 150–5. Nigel Nicolson, *Portrait of a Marriage* (1990 edn.), 55 and 58.

82 Foreword by Charles Graves to Elinor Glyn, *Three Weeks* (n.d. 'Digit Books' edn.), 5.

83 Anthony Glyn, *Elinor Glyn* (1968 edn.), 163–7.

84 *Lady's Realm* (August 1909), 403.

85 *The Tatler*, 24 May, 1911.

86 *Lady's Realm* (December 1896), 216.

87 *The Tatler*, 28 June, 1911, 'Society Borrowers', xvi.

88 Lady Augustus Hervey to Frederick Hervey in 941/71/1 at Suffolk Record Office, Bury St. Edmunds, 16 June, 1885.

89 Lady Augustus Hervey to her son, Frederick, now 4th Marquess of Bristol, in 941/71/2 at Suffolk Record Office, 6 December, 1908.

90 Consuelo Vanderbilt Balsan, op. cit., 29–30. Gail MacColl and Carol McD. Wallace. *To Marry an English Lord. The Victorian and Edwardian Experience* (1989), 89.

91 Leonore Davidoff, op. cit., 63.

92 John Pearson, *Façades. Edith, Osbert and Sacheverell Sitwell* (1978), 65.

93 John Pearson, op. cit., 66.

94 John Pearson, op. cit., 93–4. Victoria Glendinning, *Edith Sitwell. A Unicorn Among Lions* (1983 edn.), 41–3.

95 Michaela Reid, *Ask Sir James* (1987), 176.

96 Jennifer Ellis ed., *Thatched with Gold. The Memoirs of Mabell Countess of Airlie* (1962), 96.

97 The Countess of Selborne to her eldest son, Roundell Viscount Wolmer, n.d. [1902] in MS. Eng. hist. d.444, ff. 19–20, in the Bodleian Library, Oxford.

98 Jessica Gerard, 'Lady Bountiful: Women of the Landed Classes and Rural Philanthropy' in *Victorian Studies*, Vol. 30, No. 2 (Winter 1987), 206.

99 Raleigh Trevelyan, *Grand Dukes and Diamonds. The Wernhers of Luton Hoo* (1991), 145 and 175.

100 Mary Drew, *Memoir of Laura Tennant* (unpublished MSS. in the British Library, 1887) in Add. MS.64,270, 11–12, in the Mary Gladstone papers.

101 Daphne Bennett, *Margot. A Life of the Countess of Oxford and Asquith* (1985), 62.

102 Jessica Gerard, 'Lady Bountiful', 190.

103 Susan Tweedsmuir, op. cit., 79.

104 Lady Greville, op. cit., 165–6.

105 Daphne Bennett, op. cit., 62. M. Jeanne Peterson, *Family, Love, and Work in the Lives of Victorian Gentlewomen* (1989), 138.

106 Lady Clodagh Anson, *Victorian Days* (1957), 46–7.

107 See, for example, the Log Book for Newcastle Street Boys' School, London, at the Greater London Record Office, EO/DIV.5/NEW/LB/1, entry for 28 November, 1894: 'Lady Jeune called and made enquiries about the home conditions of the Children. Many of the parents are out of employment'. Three days earlier she had visited the school 'to make arrangements about the supply of Dinners during the Winter months'.

108 Consuelo Vanderbilt Balsan, op. cit., 149–52.

CHAPTER FOUR

1 Lady Cynthia Asquith, *Remember and Be Glad* (1952), 57.

2 Lady Greville, *The Gentlewoman in Society* (1892), 129–30.

3 Lady Cynthia Asquith, *Haply I May Remember* (1950), 222.

4 *The Autobiography of Margot Asquith* (2 Vols), Vol. 1 (1936 Penguin Books

edn.), 75. The book was first published in 1920.

5 Daphne Bennett, *Margot. A Life of the Countess of Oxford and Asquith* (1985), 50–1.

6 Margaret Wyndham to her mother, Lady Leconfield, 1 November, 1911 in Petworth House Archives at West Sussex Record Office, PHA.1647. Maureen E. Montgomery, *Gilded Prostitution. Status, money, and transatlantic marriages 1870–1914* (1989), 101.

7 Emily Lutyens, *A Blessed Girl* (1989 edn.), 173.

8 James Pope-Hennessy, *Queen Mary 1867–1953* (1959), 167.

9 Birthday Book of Mary Elizabeth Lucy, entry for 23 April, 1883, consulted by kind permission of Sir Edmund Fairfax-Lucy, Bart.

10 Alice Fairfax-Lucy ed., *Mistress of Charlecote. The Memoirs of Mary Elizabeth Lucy* (1990 edn.), 163–4 and Birthday Book of Mary Elizabeth Lucy, entry for 9 January, 1884.

11 Lady Cynthia Asquith, *Remember and Be Glad*, 59.

12 Quoted in Pat Jalland, *Women, Marriage and Politics 1860–1914* (1988 edn.), 21–2.

13 Presentation Lists for Levées and Drawing-Rooms at the Public Record office, LC6.100 for 1880 and LC6.117 for 1897.

14 See, for example, *Manners and Rules of Good Society or Solecisms to be Avoided* by a Member of the Aristocracy, 32nd edn. (1910), 76–7. *The Manners of the Aristocracy* by One of Themselves (n.d. *c.* 1882), 160–1.

15 *The Manners of the Aristocracy*, 159.

16 Presentation Lists for Levées and Drawing-Rooms, LC6.106 for 1886, LC6.117 for 1897, and LC6.120 for 1900.

17 Consuelo Vanderbilt Balsan, *The Glitter and the Gold* (1973 edn.), 75.

18 Lucy Masterman ed., *Mary Gladstone. Her Diaries and Letters*, 2nd edn. (1930), 375 and 382. The Drawing-Room attended by Mary Drew was relatively small, with only 163 presentations made.

19 *The Autobiography of Margot Asquith*, Vol. 1, 121. *The Queen*, 8 May, 1897, 901. Presentation Lists for Levées and Drawing-Rooms for 1897.

20 Maureen E. Montgomery, op. cit., 150–1.

21 *Etiquette for Gentlemen. A Complete Guide to the Rules and Observances of Good Society* (1900), 10.

22 Diary of Lord Carrington at the Bodleian Library, MS.Film 1102.

23 *Etiquette for Gentlemen*, 9–10.

24 Mary Lady Trevelyan, *The Number of my Days* (Unpublished typescript at Newcastle University Library), 28.

25 Presentation Lists for Levées and Drawing-Rooms, LC6.100 for 1880 and LC6.117 for 1897.

26 See the reasons given for presentation in the 1880 Presentation Lists.

27 Erica Beale ed., Ethel Raglan, *Memories of Three Reigns* (1928), 183.

28 Lady Greville, op. cit., 114.

29 Lady Cynthia Asquith, *Remember and Be Glad*, 59.

30 Lady Greville, op. cit., 115–17.

31 Lady Augusta Fane, *Chit-Chat* (1926), 63.

32 Lady Augusta Fane, op. cit., 64.

33 Mary Lady Trevelyan, op. cit., 27–8.

34 *Lady's Realm* (March 1902), 652–3.

35 Diana Cooper, *The Rainbow Comes and Goes* (1958), 94.

36 Diana Cooper, op. cit., 96.

37 Philip Ziegler, *Diana Cooper* (1983 Penguin Books edn.), 53.

38 Philip Ziegler, op. cit., 53. Diana Cooper, op. cit., 109–11.

39 Philip Ziegler, op. cit., 43. Diana Cooper, op. cit., 95.

40 Diana Cooper, op. cit., 95.

41 Nancy Cunard, *GM. Memories of George Moore* (1956), 102–3.

42 Anne Chisholm, *Nancy Cunard* (1981 Penguin Books edn.), 52–3 and 55.

43 James Pope-Hennessy, op. cit., 202.

44 Emily Lutyens, op. cit., 186.

45 Diana Cooper, op. cit., 84.

46 Diana Cooper, op. cit., 84–5.

47 Lady Augustus Hervey to Frederick Hervey, 14 January, 1885 in 941/71/1 at Suffolk Record Office, Bury St. Edmunds.

48 Maria Hodnett to Frederick Hervey, 12 March, 1885 in 941/71/1 at Suffolk County Record Office, Bury St. Edmunds.

49 Jennifer Ellis ed., *Thatched with Gold. The Memoirs of Mabell Countess of Airlie* (1962), 40.

50 Jennifer Ellis ed., op. cit., 43 and 50.

51 Mary Drew, 'Memoir of Laura Tennant' (Typescript at the British Library), Mary Gladstone MSS. Add.MS.46,270, 12.

52 *The Autobiography of Margot Asquith*, 57 and Daphne Bennett, op. cit., 45–6.

53 Diana de Marly, *Worth. Father of Haute Couture* (1980), 5, 187 and 209.

54 Daphne Bennett, op. cit., 46.

55 Maureen E. Montgomery, op. cit., 94.
56 *The Tatler*, 25 January, 1911, 81. In its issue of 4 January, it had noted that the eligible Lord Leconfield was 'a *parti* of renown' and was something of a trial to 'a much-bedaughtered county which naturally regards Petworth with its 700 wonderful pictures, its china, embroideries, old books, carvings, etc., as a plum very well worth picking'.
57 Mrs George Cornwallis-West, *The Reminiscences of Lady Randolph Churchill* (1908), 47.
58 Quoted in Maureen E. Montgomery, op. cit., 10.
59 Belle Wilson to her mother in New York, 14 August, 1886, in F.4/74 at Wilton House. Quoted by kind permission of the Earl of Pembroke.
60 Nigel Nicolson, *Mary Curzon* (1977), 83–4.
61 Mary Lady Curzon's Dinner Invitation Book, 1895–1897 at the India Office Library, MSS.Eur.F.112/788.
62 Quoted in Gail MacColl and Carol McD. Wallace, *To Marry an English Lord. The Victorian and Edwardian Experience* (1989), 133.
63 Gail MacColl and Carol McD. Wallace, op. cit., 340.
64 Maureen E. Montgomery, op. cit., 124.
65 Maureen E. Montgomery, op. cit., 90.
66 Quoted in Gail MacColl and Carol McD. Wallace, op. cit., 317.
67 *The Tatler*, 4 January, 1911, 2.
68 Maureen E. Montgomery, op. cit., 239.
69 Madeline Bingham, *Earls and Girls. Dramas in High Society* (1980), 5.
70 Madeline Bingham, op. cit., 108–11.
71 *The Tatler*, 23 October, 1901, 178. Madeline Bingham, op. cit., 10–30.
72 The Duke of Manchester, *My Candid Recollections* (1932), 251–2. Maureen E. Montgomery, op. cit., 240.
73 The Earl of Rosslyn, *My Gamble with Life* (1928), 121.
74 The Earl of Rosslyn, op. cit., 240 and 242.
75 Randolph S. Churchill, *Lord Derby. 'King of Lancashire'* (1959), 26–7.
76 Quoted in Jessica A. Gerard, 'Family and Servants in the Country-House Community in England and Wales 1815–1914' (University of London Ph.D. thesis, 1982), 269–70. For details of the marriages of the Duke of Abercorn's children see, for example, *Burke's Peerage and Baronetage* for 1910.
77 Emily Lutyens, op. cit., 304.
78 Alice Fairfax-Lucy ed., op. cit., 131.
79 Pat Jalland, op. cit., 58.
80 Pat Jalland, op. cit., 66–7.
81 Frances Countess of Warwick, *Life's Ebb and Flow* (1929), 48.
82 Alice Fairfax-Lucy ed., op. cit., 159.
83 Frances Countess of Warwick, op. cit., 34.
84 Emily Lutyens, op. cit., 10.
85 Frances Countess of Warwick, op. cit., 205.
86 Sylvia Brooke, *Queen of the Head Hunters* (1972 edn.), 46.
87 Sylvia Brooke, op. cit., 48.
88 Quoted in Susan Mary Alsop, *Lady Sackville* (1928), 104.
89 Jennifer Ellis ed., op. cit., 52 and 61–2.
90 Susan Mary Alsop, op. cit., 104–5.
91 Quoted in Pat Jalland, op. cit., 120–1.
92 Pat Jalland, op. cit., 109.
93 Margaret Blunden, *The Countess of Warwick* (1967), 40–1.
94 Consuelo Vanderbilt Balsan, op. cit., 56–7.
95 Consuelo Vanderbilt Balsan, op. cit., 99.
96 Pat Jalland, op. cit., 168–9. Trevor Lummis and Jan Marsh, *The Woman's Domain. Women and the English Country House* (1990), 195.
97 Trevor Lummis and Jan Marsh, op. cit., 194.
98 Janet Trevelyan to Molly Trevelyan, 11 November, 1907 in Newcastle University Library, CPT.238.
99 Janet Trevelyan to Molly Trevelyan, 26 May, 1908 in CPT.238.
100 W.C.D. and C.D. Whetham, *The Family and the Nation* (1909), 139 and Maureen E. Montgomery, op. cit., 194.
101 Quoted in Pamela Horn, *Ladies of the Manor. Wives and Daughters in Country-house Society 1830–1918* (1991), 103.
102 Susan Mary Alsop, op. cit., 145–6.
103 Daphne Bennett, op. cit., 174–5.
104 Michaela Reid, *Ask Sir James* (1987), 231.
105 Kenneth Rose, *Curzon. A Most Superior Person* (1985 edn.), 370–1.
106 Calculated from *Burke's Peerage and Baronetage* for 1910.
107 Consuelo Vanderbilt Balsan, op. cit., 148–9.
108 Edward Wyndham to his mother, Lady Leconfield, 3 March, 1910 in Petworth House Archives at West Sussex Record Office, PHA.9654.
109 Christopher Simon Sykes, *Black Sheep* (1982), 213–19.
110 See, for example, her letters to her father, dated 7 June and October 1877, declining to accept the additional sums offered by her husband, in Blanche Eliott Lockhart ed., *Margaret Cowell Stepney, Her Letters*

(privately published, 1926), 16–17 and 20–1.

111 Blanche Eliott Lockhart ed., op. cit., 21–2, 263–4 and 392–9. *The Times*, 5 July, 1909.

112 Angela Lambert, *Unquiet Souls. The Indian summer of the British aristocracy* (1985 edn.), 66–7 and 79. Frances Countess of Warwick, op. cit., 205. John Vincent ed., *The Crawford Papers. The Journals of David Lindsay twenty-seventh Earl of Crawford and tenth Earl of Balcarres 1871–1940 during the years 1892 to 1940* (1984), 109, entry for 24 May, 1908.

CHAPTER FIVE

1 Quoted in Pamela Horn, *The Rise and Fall of the Victorian Servant* (1990 edn.), 17.

2 Cynthia Asquith, *Remember and Be Glad* (1952), 74–5.

3 Lady Clodagh Anson, *Victorian Days* (1957), 270–1.

4 John Pearson, *Façades. Edith, Osbert, and Sacheverell Sitwell* (1978), 45. Pamela Horn, *The Rise and Fall of the Victorian Servant* (1990 edn.), 100.

5 John Vincent ed., *The Crawford Papers. The Journals of David Lindsay twenty-seventh Earl of Crawford and tenth Earl of Balcarres 1871–1940 during the years 1892 to 1940* (1984), 39, entry for 2 June, 1897.

6 John Vincent ed., op. cit., 39. According to another account of the event, the Prime Minister ironically retorted, 'It was a dark morning and I am afraid that at the moment my mind must have been occupied by some subject of less importance.'

7 Violet Greville, 'Men-Servants in England' in *National Review* (February 1892), 812.

8 The Marchioness of Bath, *Before the Sunset Fades* (1967), 17.

9 Richard Greville Verney Lord Willoughby de Broke, *The Passing Years* (1924), 5. Census return for Blenheim Park for 1891 at the Public Record Office, RG.12.1173.

10 Jill Franklin, 'Troops of Servants: Labour and Planning in the Country House 1840–1914' in *Victorian Studies*, Vol. XIX, No. 2 (Dec., 1975), 227–8.

11 Census return for 20 Arlington Street, London for 1891 at the Public Record Office, RG.12.68, and for Hatfield House, RG.12.1112.

12 John Duke of Bedford, *A Silver-plated Spoon* (1959 edn.), 17.

13 Leslie Field, *Bendor. The Golden Duke of Westminster* (1986 edn.), 33. Gervas Huxley, *Victorian Duke. The Life of Hugh Lupus Grosvenor First Duke of Westminster* (1967), 137–8.

14 Frederick John Gorst, *Of Carriages and Kings* (1956), 127.

15 Frederick John Gorst, op. cit., 197.

16 The Marchioness of Bath, op. cit., 9 and 13.

17 Randolph S. Churchill, *Lord Derby 'King of Lancashire'. The Official Life of Edward, Seventeenth Earl of Derby 1865–1948* (1959), 104.

18 Joan Morgan and Alison Richards, *A Paradise out of a Common Field. The Pleasures and Plenty of the Victorian Garden* (1990), 149–50.

19 Joan Morgan and Alison Richards, op. cit., 150.

20 Census return for Dudley House, Park Lane, for 1881 at the Public Record Office, RG.11.94.

21 Entry in the *Post Office Trade Directory for London* for 1898, entry under Servants' Registry Offices and Homes.

22 *The Domestic Servants' Advertiser*, 8 July, 1913, 14, for both recommendations.

23 Information provided by the late Miss O. Lloyd Baker of Hardwicke Court, Gloucestershire, in correspondence with the author, 19 November, 1974.

24 Census return for Carlton Gardens for 1881 at the Public Record Office, RG.11.330.

25 Frances Countess of Warwick, *Life's Ebb and Flow* (1929), 209–10.

26 Samuel Mullins and Gareth Griffiths, *Cap and Apron. An Oral History of Domestic Service in the Shires, 1880–1950* (1986), 16.

27 Lady Maud Cecil to William Palmer, Viscount Wolmer, 18 October, 1885 in MS.Selborne adds. 1, f.55, at the Bodleian Library, Oxford.

28 Gervas Hervey, op. cit., 129–30.

29 Richard Greville Verney Lord Willoughby de Broke, op. cit., 49.

30 Edith Sitwell, *Taken Care Of* (1965), 27.

31 Pauline Dower, *Living at Wallington* (1984), 20.

32 Pauline Dower, op. cit., 16.

33 Jennifer Ellis ed., *Thatched with Gold. The Memoirs of Mabell Countess of Airlie* (1962), 36 and 54–55.

34 Nigel Nicolson, *Mary Curzon* (1977), 82.

35 Nigel Nicolson, op. cit., 90.

36 G.H. Fleming, *Victorian 'Sex Goddess': Lady Colin Campbell and the Sensational Divorce Case of 1886* (1990 edn.), 87.

Marlborough provided Lady Colin with a palazzo in Venice on condition that he paid her an annual visit, and Whistler's picture of Lady Colin, painted in the nude, hung in his bedroom. There were also photographs of her hidden in many of his cupboards. Anita Leslie, *Jennie* (1992 edn.), 138.

37 G.H. Fleming, op. cit., 93–4, 107–8, and 236.

38 Edith Sitwell, op. cit., 64.

39 Anita Leslie, op. cit., 267 and 293. For details of the valet's career see, for example, Anita Leslie, op. cit., 150 and 270.

40 Mrs D.K. Dence of Leatherhead, Surrey, in correspondence with the author, 19 October, 1974.

41 Pauline Dower, op. cit., 14. Mrs Dower also noted that the staff 'were expected to avoid meeting any of the family or guests on the stairs or in the passages or gallery'.

42 Noel Streatfeild ed., *The Day Before Yesterday* (1956), 91.

43 Charles Booth, *Life and Labour of the People in London*, 2nd Series, Industry, Vol. IV (1903), 227–8.

44 *The Times*, 19 April, 1905 and 21 July, 1909.

45 Frederick John Gorst, op. cit., 88.

46 Douglas Sutherland, *The Yellow Earl. The Life of Hugh Lowther 5th Earl of Lonsdale 1857–1944* (1965), 64.

47 Quoted in Pamela Horn, op. cit., 25.

48 Household Servants' Wages Book at Wilton House and London, 1913–20 at Wiltshire Record Office, Pembroke MSS. 2057/A5/34. At the Duke of Richmond's Goodwood in 1891 the house steward received £120 per annum; the under butler £40; the 1st footman £34 and the steward's room boy, £18. As at Wilton, the housekeeper received £60. See Jill Franklin, op. cit., 223.

49 Consuelo Vanderbilt Balsan, *The Glitter and the Gold* (1973 edn.), 60–2.

50 Consuelo Vanderbilt Balsan, op. cit., 63.

51 Lady Augusta Fane, *Chit-Chat* (1926), 51.

52 The Marchioness of Bath, op. cit., 17.

53 Frederick John Gorst, op. cit., 127.

54 Frank Dawes, *Not in Front of the Servants* (1973), 88.

55 Frederick John Gorst, op. cit., 148. Gorst was paid £100 per annum as a junior Royal footman, this title arising from the fact that his employer, the Duke of Portland, was Master of the Horse to King Edward VII. This honour allowed the Duke to use the state carriage and to have four matched Royal footmen in his household. The four were on call for Royal functions and were paid by the Crown.

56 Charles Booth, op. cit., 2nd Series, Industry, Vol. III, 61.

57 Gareth Stedman Jones, *Outcast London* (1976 Penguin Books edn.), 34–5.

58 Hilary and Mary Evans, *The Party That Lasted 100 Days. The Late Victorian Season* (1976), 152.

59 Hilary and Mary Evans, op. cit., 154.

60 Hilary and Mary Evans, op. cit., 142. *The Times*, 3 July, 1909.

61 Cicely McDonnell, 'The Advantages of Marrying a Soldier' in the *Navy and Army Illustrated*, quoted in Philip Warner, *Army Life in the '90s* (1975), 81.

62 *The Times*, 3 July, 1909.

63 Quoted in Noel St. John Williams, *Judy O'Grady and the Colonel's Lady. The Army Wife and Camp Follower since 1660* (1988), 166.

64 Frances Countess of Warwick, op. cit., 205.

65 *The Observer*, 17 March, 1991 and Ralph Nevill, *Night Life. London and Paris. Past and Present* (1926), 50–1.

66 Ralph Nevill, op. cit., 51–2.

67 Charles Eyre Pascoe, *London of To-day. An Illustrated Handbook for the Season* (1885), 307 and 322.

68 Diana de Marly, *Worth. Father of Haute Couture* (1980), 101 and 162.

69 Barbara Worsley-Gough, *Fashions in London* (1952), 74.

70 James Pope-Hennessy, *Queen Mary 1867–1953* (1959), 169.

71 *The Tatler*, 14 June, 1911, 283.

72 Jennifer Ellis ed., op. cit., 27.

73 Cynthia Asquith, op. cit., 75–6.

74 Susan Tweedsmuir, *The Edwardian Lady* (1966), 56. Charles Eyre Pascoe, op. cit., 322–3.

75 Barbara Worsley-Gough, op. cit., 71.

76 Barbara Worsley-Gough, op. cit., 73.

77 David W. Gieve, *Gieves and Hawkes, No. 1 Savile Row, London 1785–1985. The Story of a Tradition* (1985), 24, 29, and 33.

78 Charles Eyre Pascoe, op. cit., 329. T.S. Simey and M.B. Simey, *Charles Booth, Social Scientist* (1960), 116.

79 Richard Walker, *The Savile Row Story* (1988), 69 and 79.

80 Richard Walker, op. cit., 69.

81 *Select Committee of the House of Lords on the Sweating System*, Parliamentary Papers, 1888, Vol. XX, Q.3964–3965.

82 Richard Walker, op. cit., 69.

83 Richard Walker, op. cit., 82.

84 Quoted in Hilary and Mary Evans, op. cit., 139–40.

85 Gareth Stedman Jones, op. cit., 35 and 376. T.S. Simey and M.B. Simey, op. cit., 131 and 207.

86 *The Tatler*, 25 January, 1911, 86.

87 *The Tatler*, 25 January, 1911, 86.

88 David Cannadine, *The Decline and Fall of the British Aristocracy* (1990), 113. By 1905, Dudley, then Lord-Lieutenant of Ireland, was seeking to resign that position because of his financial problems. He had been twice writted by Irish tradesmen. John Vincent ed., op. cit., 68.

89 Julia Cartwright ed., *The Journals of Lady Knightley of Fawsley* (1915), 336 and Lady Knightley's diary for 1879 at Northamptonshire Record Office, K.2898, entries for 8, 13 September, 6, 10, 16 and 17 October.

90 Entry in Lady Knightley's diary, K.2904, for 7 May, 1889.

91 Entries in Lady Knightley's diary, K.2905, for 6 and 26 August, 1890. To add to their problems in December 1890, the Daventry bank with which they dealt changed hands and Sir Rainald was required to pay off the debt incurred for stocking the farms. To do this and to pay off another smaller mortgage of £6,000 the Knightleys went to London on 17 December, and Sir Rainald executed 'a fresh mortgage of £31,000 – to which my jointure & pin money have to be postponed – and again – like last year – I had to explain before a Commission that I knew all about it'. Entry in Lady Knightley's diary for 17 December, 1890.

92 John Vincent ed., op. cit., 68–9.

93 Brian Abel-Smith, *A History of the Nursing Profession* (1960), 58. Robert Dingwall, Anne Marie Rafferty and Charles Webster, *An Introduction to the Social History of Nursing* (1988), 59–60, and 79. Brian Abel-Smith, *The Hospitals 1800–1948* (1964), 194.

94 G.H. Fleming, op. cit., 41.

95 Michaela Reid, *Ask Sir James* (1987), 224–5. Philip Magnus, *King Edward The Seventh* (1964), 296–7.

96 Frances Countess of Warwick, *Afterthoughts* (1931), 39.

97 Philip Magnus, op. cit., 268–9. Frances Countess of Warwick, *Afterthoughts*, 40.

98 Lord Ormathwaite, *When I was at Court. Master of the Ceremonies to King Edward VII and King George V* (1937), 132–3.

99 See *Fremden-Liste von Bad Ems für das Jahr 1890* at Stadtarchiv Bad Ems. *Newest Guide of Ems and Environs with Official Taxes* (1883), 27–8. List of Visitors to Bad Ems, annual totals and nationalities at Stadtarchiv, Bad Ems. In the late 1850s an 'English' church was also built in the town.

100 *Newest Guide of Ems*, 24. Karl Billaudelle, *Vergnügliches Emser Kur-und Badebüchlein* (1986), 44.

101 *The Queen*, 22 May, 1897, 1035.

102 Karl Billaudelle, op. cit., 32.

103 Anthony Glyn, *Elinor Glyn* (1968 edn.), 95 and 103.

104 May Harcourt to Lady Harcourt in MS.Harcourt dep. 647 at the Bodleian Library, Oxford, ff.176–8, 7 September, 1905.

105 Lady Selborne to Lord Selborne in MS. Selborne Adds. 3, 10 June, 1914, f.158, at the Bodleian Library. See also letter of 21 June, 1914, f.167, written on the apparent eve of their departure for England.

CHAPTER SIX

1 Ralph Nevill, *The Reminiscences of Lady Dorothy Nevill* (n.d. *c.* 1906), 124.

2 Anita Leslie, *Jennie* (1992 edn.), 194.

3 Philip Magnus, *King Edward the Seventh* (1964), 246 and 274.

4 Janet Morgan, *Edwina Mountbatten. A Life of Her Own* (1992 edn.), 28.

5 Philip Magnus, op. cit., 274–5.

6 Philip Magnus, op. cit., 275.

7 The Duke of Portland, *Memories of Racing and Hunting* (1935), 172, 188, 210 and 242.

8 *The Tatler*, 1 November, 1911, 52. Richard Greville Verney Lord Willoughby de Broke, *The Passing Years* (1924), 95.

9 Richard Greville Verney Lord Willoughby de Broke, op. cit., 57.

10 Daphne Bennett, *Margot. A Life of the Countess of Oxford and Asquith* (1985), 29, 143 and 150. Mrs George Cornwallis-West, *The Reminiscences of Lady Randolph Churchill* (1908), 74.

11 *Country Life*, 14 October, 1911. A special supplement of 'Hunts of the United Kingdom' for the season 1911–1912. This listed the number of days of hunting, subscriptions, the name of the master and the honorary secretary, and other details.

12 G.E. Mingay ed., *The Victorian Countryside* (1981), Vol. 2, 462 and 484.

13 Guy Paget, *The History of the Althorp and Pytchley Hunt 1634–1920* (1937), 227.

14 G.E. Mingay ed., op. cit., 463.

15 Jonathan Garnier Ruffer, *The Big Shots. Edwardian Shooting Parties* (1984 edn.), 133. G.E. Mingay, ed., op. cit., 483.

16 John Vincent ed., *The Crawford Papers. The Journals of David Lindsay twenty-seventh Earl of Crawford and tenth Earl of Balcarres 1871–1940 during the years 1892 to 1940* (1984), 316, entry for 6–10 August, 1913.

17 Pamela Horn, *The Changing Countryside in Victorian and Edwardian England and Wales* (1984), 107.

18 *Royal Commission on Agricultural Depression*, Parliamentary Papers, 1895, Vol. XVI, Report by Assistant Commissioner Mr Wilson Fox on Suffolk, 73, and Report by Assistant Commissioner Mr R. Rew on North Devon, 25.

19 Jonathan Garnier Ruffer, op. cit., 135.

20 Mrs George Cornwallis-West, op. cit., 10.

21 Jonathan Garnier Ruffer, op. cit., 46.

22 Jonathan Garnier Ruffer, op. cit., 27 and 34. Sir Philip Magnus, op. cit., 91.

23 Jonathan Garnier Ruffer, op. cit., 86.

24 Jonathan Garnier Ruffer, op. cit., 87.

25 Frances Countess of Warwick, *Afterthoughts* (1931), 39. Keith Middlemas, *The Life and Times of Edward VII* (1972), 110. John Vincent ed., op. cit., 153, 291.

26 Frances Countess of Warwick, *Afterthoughts*, 39.

27 Jonathan Garnier Ruffer, op. cit., 48.

28 Jonathan Garnier Ruffer, op. cit., 48.

29 Lady Augustus Hervey to Frederick 4th Marquess of Bristol, 30 September, 1908, at Suffolk Record Office, Bury St. Edmunds, 941/71/2.

30 Frederick 4th Marquess of Bristol to Lady Augustus Hervey, 11 October, 1908, in 941/71/2.

31 Diary of Geoffrey Gathorne-Hardy for 1896 at Suffolk Record Office, Ipswich, HA.43.1737, entry for 6 January.

32 Quoted in Jonathan Garnier Ruffer, op. cit., 82.

33 Lady Maud Wolmer to Viscount Wolmer in Selborne MSS. at the Bodleian Library, Oxford, letter dated 7 June, 1892 in MS. Selborne Addl. 1, ff. 113–14.

34 Mrs George Cornwallis-West, op. cit., 148–9. The Marchioness of Londonderry, *Retrospect* (1938), 101. *The Tatler*, 6 September, 1911, ii. *The Tatler* considered the Duchess of Bedford 'the finest lady shot in the Kingdom'.

35 Quoted in Jonathan Garnier Ruffer, op. cit., 88.

36 Philip Magnus, op. cit., 260.

37 Frances Countess of Warwick, *Life's Ebb and Flow* (1929), 231.

38 Frances Countess of Warwick, *Life's Ebb and Flow*, 229.

39 Frances Countess of Warwick, *Life's Ebb and Flow*, 229–30.

40 Jonathan Garnier Ruffer, op. cit., 87.

41 Frances Countess of Warwick, *Life's Ebb and Flow*, 230.

42 Jonathan Garnier Ruffer, op. cit., 100. Philip Magnus, op. cit., 231.

43 Emily Lutyens, *A Blessed Girl* (1989 edn.), 287. Elizabeth Longford, *A Pilgrimage of Passion. The Life of Wilfrid Scawen Blunt* (1979), 302–6. Leslie Field, *Bendor. The Golden Duke of Westminster* (1983), 74.

44 *Royal Commission on Agricultural Depression*, Parliamentary Papers, 1897, Vol. XV, General Report, 141. Pamela Horn, op. cit., 46. F.M.L. Thompson, 'Stitching it Together Again' in *Economic History Review*, Vol. XLV, No. 2, (May 1992), 372, notes that the newer business magnates purchased land on a considerable scale during this period. Of a group of millionaires and half-millionaires he has identified, three out of five acquired landed estates during their lifetimes, and a further one-fifth 'generated landed successors in the next generation'.

45 *The Tatler*, 1 November, 1911, 52.

46 *The Tatler*, 1 November, 1911, 52.

47 The Duke of Portland, *Men Women and Things* (1937), 256–63.

48 Quoted in Madeleine Beard, *English Landed Society in the Twentieth Century* (1989), 21. David Cannadine, *The Decline and Fall of the British Aristocracy* (1990), 376.

49 Frances Countess of Warwick, *Afterthoughts*, 173.

50 Frances Countess of Warwick, *Life's Ebb and Flow*, 42–3.

51 Eileen Quelch, *Perfect Darling. The Life and Times of George Cornwallis-West* (1972), 90. George Cornwallis-West, *Edwardian Hey-days* (1930), 224–5.

52 Maggie Wyndham to her mother, Lady Leconfield, in Petworth House Archives at West Sussex Record Office, PHA.1638, 21 October, 1901.

53 Maggie Wyndham to her mother, 16 October, 1901, in PHA.1638.

54 Richard Harding Davis, 'Three English Race Meetings' in *Harper's New Monthly Magazine*, Vol. 87 (July, 1893), 262–5.

55 Richard Harding Davis, op. cit., 260–1.

56 George Cornwallis-West, op. cit., 149.

57 The Earl of Rosslyn, *My Gamble with Life* (1928), 64, 70, 82, 97, 159, 221 and 274. On one occasion in 1893 he bet about £15,000 on one of his own horses; he stood to gain £60,000 if it won, but it did not.

58 *The Autobiography of Lord Alfred Douglas* (1929), 3.

59 H. Montgomery Hyde, *Lord Alfred Douglas* (1984), 131–2.

60 Philip Magnus, op. cit., 253–4.

61 Keith Middlemas, op. cit., 98.

62 Christopher Sykes, *Four Studies in Loyalty* (1946), 22–3 and 29.

63 Christopher Sykes, op. cit., 34–7.

64 Diary of Sir Edward Hamilton at the British Library, Add. MSS.48,651, entry for 11 August, 1889. Philip Magnus, op. cit., 223. John Vincent ed., op. cit., 127, entry for 16 May, 1909.

65 Philip Magnus, op. cit., 222–3.

66 *The Times*, 2 June, 1891, 11; 4 June, 1891, 7; 10 June, 1891, 9. Philip Magnus, op. cit., 224.

67 *The Times*, 10 June, 1891, 9. See also *The Times*, 3 June, 1891, for evidence from the Prince of Wales. Later Berkeley Levett became ADC to the Duke of Connaught. The Earl of Rosslyn, op. cit., 38.

68 Gail MacColl and Carol McD. Wallace, *To Marry an English Lord* (1989), 241–3.

69 Diary of Sir Edward Hamilton at the British Library, Add. MSS. 48,656, entries for 24 June and 3 July, 1891, for example.

70 *The Times*, 10 June, 1891, 9.

71 Keith Middlemas, op. cit., 86.

72 George Cornwallis-West, op. cit., 139–40.

73 *The Tatler*, 7 March, 1906, 11 and 31 January, 1906, 182.

74 Maggie Wyndham to her mother, 5 November, 1912 in Petworth House Archives, PHA.1648 at West Sussex Record Office.

75 Jonathan Garnier Ruffer, op. cit., 48. Pamela Horn, op. cit., 45.

76 Ralph Nevill, *London Clubs. Their History and Treasures* (1911), 156–7. *The Realm*, 4 January, 1895, 302–3. The Albemarle was the first mixed club in London, and it was followed a few years later by the first exclusively female club, the Alexandra, with a membership limited to 860. Owing to its high social standing it was difficult to be elected to it. In the mid-1890s only about half-a-dozen clubs in London catered for women.

77 Ralph Nevill, op. cit., 218. Christopher Sykes, op. cit., 27–8. Sir Wemyss Reid, 'In London Club-land' in *Living London*, ed. George R. Sims, Vol. 1 (3 vols) (1902), 77.

78 Ralph Nevill, op. cit., 104.

79 Admiral Maxse to his daughter, Violet (later Lady Milner), in Violet Milner MSS, Box 18, U.1599.c.60–63 at the Bodleian Library, Oxford, 4 November [1897].

80 Diary of Sir Edward Hamilton for 1887 at the British Library, Add. MSS.48,645, entry for 21 February.

81 Sir Wemyss Reid, op. cit., 74.

82 Sir Wemyss Reid, op. cit., 80.

83 Philip Ziegler and Desmond Seward ed., *Brooks's. A Social History* (1991), 117. Ralph Nevill, op. cit., 157.

84 George Cornwallis-West, op. cit., 146. The Earl of Rosslyn, op. cit., 109. On occasion stakes of £500 were wagered on billiard matches by the Earl.

85 Douglas Sutherland, *The Yellow Earl. The Life of Hugh Lowther 5th Earl of Lonsdale 1857–1944* (1965), 75–7.

86 David Cannadine, 'Another "Last Victorian": P.G. Wodehouse and His World' in *South Atlantic Quarterly*, Vol. 77, No. 4 (1978), 482–3.

87 Philip Ziegler and Desmond Seward ed., op. cit., 175.

88 See 1891 Census Returns at the Public Record Office, R.G.12.86 for the Marlborough and White's Clubs and R.G.12.68 for Brooks's Club. At the Devonshire Club, similarly, with a resident staff of 46, between a third and a half were under 20; at the Army and Navy, with a resident staff of 74, the under-twenties were over a quarter of the total.

89 Lady Augustus Hervey to Frederick Hervey at Suffolk Record Office, Bury St. Edmunds, in 941/71/1/, 4 January, 1885.

90 Major-General Sir Louis C. Jackson, *History of the United Service Club* (1937), 82.

91 Major-General Sir Louis C. Jackson, op. cit., 98.

92 Douglas Sutherland, op. cit., 83.

93 Douglas Sutherland, op. cit., 110.

94 Madeline Bingham, *Earls and Girls. Dramas in High Society* (1980), 115–16.

95 Madeline Bingham, op. cit., 122.

96 Criminal Law Amendment Act 1885, 48 & 49 Vict., Ch. 69, Clause 11. Most of the Act was concerned with the outlawing of juvenile female prostitution.

97 H. Montgomery Hyde, *The Cleveland Street Scandal* (1976), 43–4.

98 E.F. Benson, *As We Were* (1930), 90–3.

Who Was Who, 1916–1928 (1947), entry under Lady Henry Somerset. In 1895 Lady Henry founded an industrial farm colony for inebriate women at Duxhurst, Surrey. This was the first such institution opened in England; she also had a home for training workhouse children, and was an enthusiastic worker for the temperance cause.

99 H. Montgomery Hyde, op. cit., 44.

100 Christopher Simon Sykes, *Black Sheep* (1982), 251.

101 H. Montgomery Hyde, op. cit., 28–30.

102 Christopher Simon Sykes, op. cit., 253. There were even rumours connecting Prince Eddy, the Prince of Wales's elder son, with the Cleveland Street brothel. 'To add insult to injury, the other patrons apparently referred to him as Victoria.' John Van der Kiste, *Edward VII's Children* (1989), 50.

103 H. Montgomery Hyde, op. cit., 52–3.

104 H. Montgomery Hyde, op. cit., 79.

105 H. Montgomery Hyde, op. cit., 95–6 and 98–9.

106 H. Montgomery Hyde, op. cit., 90–6.

107 H. Montgomery Hyde, op. cit., 246–7.

108 Rupert Hart-Davis ed., *Selected Letters of Oscar Wilde* (1989 edn.), 107. H. Montgomery Hyde, *Lord Alfred Douglas* (1984), 27–8.

109 Richard Ellmann, *Oscar Wilde* (1987), 393–4.

110 Richard Ellmann, op. cit., 394.

111 Richard Ellmann, op. cit., 395.

112 H. Montgomery Hyde, *Lord Alfred Douglas*, 79–81. Richard Ellmann, op. cit., 416–17 and 424–5.

113 *The Times*, 25 May, 1895, 17, and 27 May, 1895, 4.

114 Richard Ellmann, op. cit., 431.

115 Quoted in Christopher Simon Sykes, op. cit., 261.

CHAPTER SEVEN

1 F.M.L. Thompson, 'English Landed Society in the Twentieth Century. I. Property: Collapse and Survival' in *Transactions of the Royal Historical Society*, 5th Series, Vol. 40 (1990), 4.

2 Philip Magnus, *King Edward the Seventh* (1964), 348.

3 W. Ormsby Gore, MP to Lord Willoughby de Broke, postmarked 20 December, 1913, in Willoughby de Broke Papers at the House of Lords Record Office, WB/2/109.

4 Frances Countess of Warwick, *Afterthoughts* (1931), 24.

5 Frances Countess of Warwick, *Afterthoughts*, 24–5.

6 John Vincent ed., *The Crawford Papers. The Journals of David Lindsay twenty-seventh Earl of Crawford and tenth Earl of Balcarres 1871–1940 during the years 1892 to 1940* (1984), 72, entry for 3 March, 1904.

7 John Vincent ed., op. cit., 62, entry for 22 June, 1900.

8 In 1899, for example, the Assistant Under-Secretary at the War Office, G. Fleetwood-Wilson referred to the resentment felt in governmental circles against the 'dirty, stock exchange jew lot'. Raleigh Trevelyan, *Grand Dukes and Diamonds. The Wernhers of Luton Hoo* (1991), 121. Similarly, in July 1900, Lord Carrington complained of the way 'London Society toadies [the] S. African German Jews. . . . They are subsidising half London and the women take their beastly money as greedily as the men.' Lord Carrington's Diary for 1900 MS. Film 1104, 3 July, 1900. E.C. Black, *The Social Politics of Anglo-Jewry 1880–1920* (1988), 335.

9 Richard Greville Verney Lord Willoughby de Broke, *The Passing Years* (1924), 180–1. David Cannadine, *The Decline and Fall of the British Aristocracy* (1990), 185–6.

10 Sir Henry H. Howorth to Lord Willoughby de Broke, 11 August, 1911, in Willoughby de Broke Papers, WB/3/12.

11 2nd Viscount Colville to Lord Willoughby de Broke, 25 February, 1914, in Willoughby de Broke Papers, WB/8/87.

12 Margot Asquith to the 2nd Earl of Selborne in MS Selborne 74, f.79 in the Bodleian Library, Oxford.

13 *The Autobiography of Margot Asquith*, Vol. 1 (2 vols) (Penguin Books edn., 1936), 119.

14 Daphne Bennett, *Margot. A Life of the Countess of Oxford and Asquith* (1985), 225–6.

15 Mary Lady Trevelyan, *The Number of My Days* (Unpublished autobiography, n.d. c. 1964) at Newcastle University Library, 56.

16 Pamela Horn, *Ladies of the Manor. Wives and Daughters in Country-House Society 1830–1918* (1991), 170.

17 Frances Countess of Warwick, *Afterthoughts*, 46–7.

18 John Vincent ed., op. cit., 273, entry for 22 April, 1912.

19 Frances Countess of Warwick, *Afterthoughts*, 48–9 and 103–4.

20 Frances Countess of Warwick, *Afterthoughts*, 103–4.

21 David Cannadine, op. cit., 350.

22 Alan Sykes, 'The Radical Right and the Crisis of Conservatism before the First World War' in *Historical Journal*, Vol. XXVI, No. 3 (1983), 667. Gregory D. Philips, *The Diehards. Aristocratic Society and Politics in Edwardian England* (1979), 8–9.

23 F.M.L. Thompson, 'English Landed Society in the Twentieth Century. I. Property: Collapse and Survival', 5. In 1911, over a fifth of the councillors and aldermen of the forty-seven English county councils were listed in the exclusive pages of *Walford's County Families* for that year. Pamela Horn, *The Changing Countryside in Victorian and Edwardian England and Wales* (1984), 187.

24 J.P.D. Dunbabin, 'Expectations of the New County Councils, and their Realization' in *Historical Journal*, Vol. 8, No. 3 (1965), 354 and 370–1.

25 Pamela Horn, *The Changing Countryside*, 188. Gregory D. Phillips, op. cit., 70.

26 Gregory D. Phillips, op. cit., 74–5.

27 J.P.D. Dunbabin, op. cit., 369.

28 Pamela Horn, *Ladies of the Manor*, 176.

29 Mrs George Cornwallis-West, *The Reminiscences of Lady Randolph Churchill* (1908), 99.

30 Martin Pugh, *The Tories and the People 1880–1935* (1985), 13, 112–13 and 127.

31 Pamela Horn, *Ladies of the Manor*, 176–7.

32 Pat Jalland, *Women, Marriage and Politics 1860–1914* (1988 edn.), 243.

33 Mary Lady Trevelyan, op. cit., 76.

34 John Vincent ed., op. cit., 231, entry for 14 October, 1911.

35 James Pope-Hennessy, *Queen Mary 1867–1953* (1959), 468. Elizabeth Longford, *A Pilgrimage of Passion. The Life of Wilfred Scawen Blunt* (1979), 399.

36 James Pope-Hennessy, op. cit., 468.

37 *Proceedings on the Trial of the Controverted Election: East Dorset*, Parliamentary Papers, 1910, Vol. LXXIII, 2.

38 *Proceedings on the Trial of the Controverted Election*, 4, 5 and 10. Pamela Horn, *The Changing Countryside*, 192.

39 *Proceedings on the Trial of the Controverted Election*, 13.

40 W.H. Folk to Frederick Hervey in Hervey MSS. at Suffolk Record Office, Bury St. Edmunds, 941/71/10, 29 January, 1906.

41 H.C. Laurence to Frederick Hervey in Her-vey MSS. 941/71/9, 25 September, 1905.

42 Henry Donne to Frederick Hervey in Hervey MSS. 941/71/9, 3 October, 1905.

43 John Vincent ed., op. cit., 139, entry for 5 December, 1909.

44 R.J. Olney, 'The Politics of Land' in G.E. Mingay ed., *The Victorian Countryside* (1981), 67.

45 Walter Long, *Memories* (1923), 80 and 85.

46 Pat Jalland, op. cit., 247–8.

47 May Harcourt to Lady Harcourt, 26 November, 1909 in MS.Harcourt dep. 648, f.32, at the Bodleian Library.

48 H.J. Hanham, 'The Sale of Honours in late Victorian England' in *Victorian Studies*, Vol. III, No. 3 (March 1960), 277, 283–5.

49 H.J. Hanham, op. cit., 288–9. Eric Alexander 3rd Viscount Chilston, *Chief Whip. The Political Life and Times of Aretas Akers-Douglas 1st Viscount Chilston* (1961), 197–200. Akers-Douglas was Conservative Chief Whip from 1885 to 1895 and as early as June 1889 he wrote to Lord Salisbury about a certain Conservative candidate for Cardiganshire who had 'repeatedly pressed his claims for a Baronetcy promised him', allegedly by Lord Iddesleigh. David Cannadine, op. cit., 303–4.

50 Lady St. Helier, *Memories of Fifty Years* (1909), 210 and 243.

51 Peter Gordon ed., *The Red Earl. The Papers of the Fifth Earl Spencer 1835–1910*, Vol. II (Northamptonshire Record Society, Vol. XXXIV, 1986), 14.

52 Peter Gordon ed., op. cit., 13–14.

53 Elizabeth Longford, op. cit., 267–9. David Cannadine, op. cit., 513.

54 Diaries of Sir Edward Hamilton at the British Library, entry for 6 February, 1887, Add. MSS.48,645 and for 10 May, 1887, Add. MSS.48,646.

55 Robert Blake, 'Victorian Brooks's' in Philip Ziegler and Desmond Seward ed., *Brooks's. A Social History* (1991), 63.

56 Robert Blake, op. cit., 67.

57 Roy Jenkins, 'Edwardian Brooks's' in Philip Ziegler and Desmond Seward ed., op. cit., 77.

58 Quoted in Gregory D. Phillips, op. cit., 116.

59 F.M.L. Thompson, *English Landed Society in the Nineteenth Century* (1963), 325. F.M.L. Thompson, 'English Landed Society in the Twentieth Century. II. New Poor and New Rich' in *Transactions of the Royal Historical Society*, 6th Series, Vol. I (1991), 3.

60 Madeleine Beard, *English Landed Society in the Twentieth Century* (1989), 10–11.

61 Gregory D. Phillips, op. cit., 88. Gervas Huxley, *Victorian Duke. The Life of Hugh Lupus Grosvenor First Duke of Westminster* (1967), 147.

62 Gregory D. Phillips, op. cit., 190.

63 The Hon. Vicary Gibbs and H. Arthur Doubleday eds., *The Complete Peerage* (Vol. 3) (1913), Appendix B, 592–6.

64 Lady Randolph Churchill, *Small Talks on Big Subjects* (1916), 84.

65 Diary of Geoffrey Gathorne-Hardy for 1899 at Suffolk Record Office, Ipswich, HA.43.1737, 24 December, and for 1900, HA.43.1737, 8 January.

66 Diary of Geoffrey Gathorne-Hardy for 1900, 9 January.

67 Geoffrey Gathorne-Hardy to his father, 2 June, 1900, written from a hospital bed in South Africa in HA.43/1737.

68 Margaret Blunden, *The Countess of Warwick* (1967), 143–4. Frances Countess of Warwick, *Life's Ebb and Flow* (1929), 180.

69 Margaret Blunden, op. cit., 145.

70 Lady Cranborne to Lady Edward Cecil, 17 November, 1899 in Violet Milner papers, U.1599.C.77/6 at the Bodleian Library, Oxford.

71 Susan Tweedsmuir, *The Edwardian Lady* (1966), 19.

72 Lady Cranborne to Lady Edward Cecil, 24 May, 1900, in Violet Milner papers, U.1599.C.77/14.

73 Susan Tweedsmuir, op. cit., 18–19. Lady Randolph Churchill, *Small Talks*, 85.

74 Lady Cranborne to Lady Edward Cecil, 10 May, 1900, in Violet Milner papers, U.1599.C.77/14.

75 The Viscountess Milner, *My Picture Gallery 1886–1901* (1951), 183. Jennifer Ellis ed., *Thatched with Gold. The Memoirs of Mabell Countess of Airlie* (1962), 88.

76 Lady Scott to the Hon. Edward Cadogan, 6 April, 1900, SA/SS/11 in Cadogan Papers at the House of Lords Record Office. Also letters from her maid, Nana, to the Hon. Edward Cadogan, 6 December [1899] and 24 March [1900] in SA/NA/1 and 5 in Cadogan Papers. The elopement had caused much distress to her parents as well as her husband, and her father, Earl Cadogan, had even offered to resign his position as Lord-Lieutenant of Ireland, but this had been rejected by Lord Salisbury.

77 Lady Scott to her mother, Lady Cadogan, 9 May, 1900, SA/SS/15 and 10 and 28 June, 1900, SA/SS/18 and 19. Thomas Pakenham, *The Boer War* (1982), 382.

78 The Viscountess Milner, op. cit., 184.

79 Frances Countess of Warwick, *Life's Ebb and Flow*, 181.

80 Gregory D. Phillips, op. cit., 118–19.

81 Richard Greville Verney Lord Willoughby de Broke, op. cit., 244.

82 Quoted in Gregory D. Phillips, op. cit., 128–9. See also Lord Willoughby de Broke, 'A Plea for an Unreformed House of Lords' in *The National Review*, Vol. 49 (July 1907), 776.

83 Richard Greville Verney Lord Willoughby de Broke, op. cit., 246–7.

84 Cynthia Asquith, *Remember and Be Glad* (1952), 126–7.

85 Sir James Fergusson, *The Curragh Incident* (1964), 17–18.

86 David Cannadine, op. cit., 48–9. Chris Cook, *A Short History of the Liberal Party 1900–88*, 3rd edn. (1989), 47–48. Gregory D. Phillips, op. cit., 125.

87 John Vincent ed., op. cit., 136, entry for 4 October, 1909.

88 John Grigg, *Lloyd George. The People's Champion 1902–1911* (1978), 222–3.

89 John Grigg, op. cit., 225.

90 *Parliamentary Debates. The House of Lords*, Fifth Series, Vol. IV, 30 November, 1909, col. 1342.

91 Duke of Abercorn to Lord Ampthill, 26 June, 1911 in Willoughby de Broke Papers, WB.2/18. For general background see, for example, Chris Cook, op. cit., 50–4. Philip Magnus, op. cit., 430–1, 437, 443 and 445.

92 Sir Powlett Milbank Bt. to Lord Willoughby de Broke in Willoughby de Broke Papers, 22 July, 1911, WB.2/30.

93 The Marquess of Hertford to Lord Willoughby de Broke, 23 July, 1911, in Willoughby de Broke Papers, WB.2/32. Roy Jenkins, *Mr Balfour's Poodle* (1954), 150–3.

94 Copy of a letter from the Duke of Somerset to Lord Lansdowne sent by the Duchess of Somerset to Lord Willoughby de Broke, 30 July, 1911, in Willoughby de Broke Papers, WB.2/59.

95 *Parliamentary Debates. The House of Lords.* Fifth Series, Vol. IX, 9 August, 1911, col. 961–2. Ampthill went on to say that he and his friends could not 'stand by and see this crime perpetrated, this outrage continued, without offering resistance even though our resistance be entirely hopeless'.

96 Roy Jenkins, op. cit., 172. Chris Cook, op. cit., 55.

97   Lady Halsbury to Lord Willoughby de Broke, 11 August, 1911, in Willoughby de Broke Papers, WB.3/3. Roy Jenkins, op. cit., 184.

98   Roy Jenkins, op. cit., 184.

99   The Duke of Somerset to Lord Willoughby de Broke, 7 October, 1911 in Willoughby de Broke Papers, WB.3/74.

100 Quoted in Roy Jenkins, op. cit., 184.

101 A copy of the letter is in the Willoughby de Broke Papers, WB.6/9. For details of the Union Defence League see Walter Long, op. cit., 193–8. A.T.Q. Stewart, *The Ulster Crisis* (1967), 73.

102 A.T.Q. Stewart, op. cit., 93–5. Gregory D. Phillips, 'The "Diehards" and the Myth of the "Backwoodsmen"' in *Journal of British Studies*, Vol. XVI No. 2 (Spring 1977), 117.

103 David Cannadine, op. cit., 527. A.T.Q. Stewart, op. cit., 203–4.

104 A.T.Q. Stewart, op. cit., 217.

105 Walter Long, op. cit., 201–3. A.T.Q. Stewart, op. cit., 134.

106 A.T.Q. Stewart, op. cit., 136. Documents marked 'Very Secret' in Milner papers, MS.Milner dep. 157, ff. 3–5 at the Bodleian Library, Oxford. According to Lord Crawford, Lord Iveagh had been subscribing about £1,000 a month to the Union Defence League, prior to January, 1913. John Vincent ed., op. cit., 300, entry for 8 January, 1913.

107 Lord Willoughby de Broke to Lieutenant-General Sir George Richardson, Commander Ulster Volunteer Force, 31 March, 1914 in Willoughby de Broke Papers, WB.10/3.

108 Captain Frank Hall, Military Secretary, to Lord Willoughby de Broke, 23 March, 1914 in Willoughby de Broke Papers, WB.10/4.

109 Martin Pugh, op. cit., 165.

110 A.T.Q. Stewart, op. cit., 162, 170 and 175. According to Stewart, an operation for the coercion of Ulster had been planned but it was mismanaged; hence the need for the Government's retreat.

111 Robert Rhodes James, *Anthony Eden* (1986), 27 and 30.

112 The 7th Earl Stanhope to Lord Willoughby de Broke, 23 March, 1914 in Willoughby de Broke Papers, WB.10/5.

113 Michael and Eleanor Brock ed., *H.H. Asquith Letters to Venetia Stanley* (1982), 57. This was written on 22 March, 1914.

114 John Vincent ed., 329, entry for 19 March, 1914. Daphne Bennett, op. cit., 221.

115 Roy Jenkins, op. cit., 190. Gregory D. Phillips, 'Lord Willoughby de Broke and the Politics of Radical Toryism, 1909–1914' in *Journal of British Studies*, Vol. XX, No. 1 (1980), 223–4.

116 The Duke of Northumberland to Lord Willoughby de Broke, 7 February, 1914 in Willoughby de Broke Papers, WB.8/35. Gregory D. Phillips, 'The "Diehards" and the Myth of the "Backwoodsmen"', 117.

117 Lord Selborne to J. Comyn Platt, 19 September, 1912 in MS.Selborne 77, f.22, at the Bodleian Library, Oxford.

118 Gregory D. Phillips, *The Diehards*, 200.

119 Elizabeth Countess of Fingall, *Seventy Years Young. Memories Told to Pamela Hinkson* (1937), 352–3.

120 [Ethel A.P. Grenfell Baroness Desborough] *Pages from a Family Journal 1888–1915* (privately printed, 1916), 439. Walter Long, op. cit., 201.

121 Gregory D. Phillips, *The Diehards*, 155.

122 Gregory D. Phillips, *The Diehards*, 88–9.

123 F.M.L. Thompson, *English Landed Society*, 332.

124 The Duke of Portland, *Men Women and Things* (1937), 3.

125 John Vincent ed., op. cit., 532, entry for 31 December, 1931.

126 Stephen Glover, 'The old rich: a survey of the landed classes' in *The Spectator*, 1 January, 1977, 15–16.

Index